Astrid Mørland

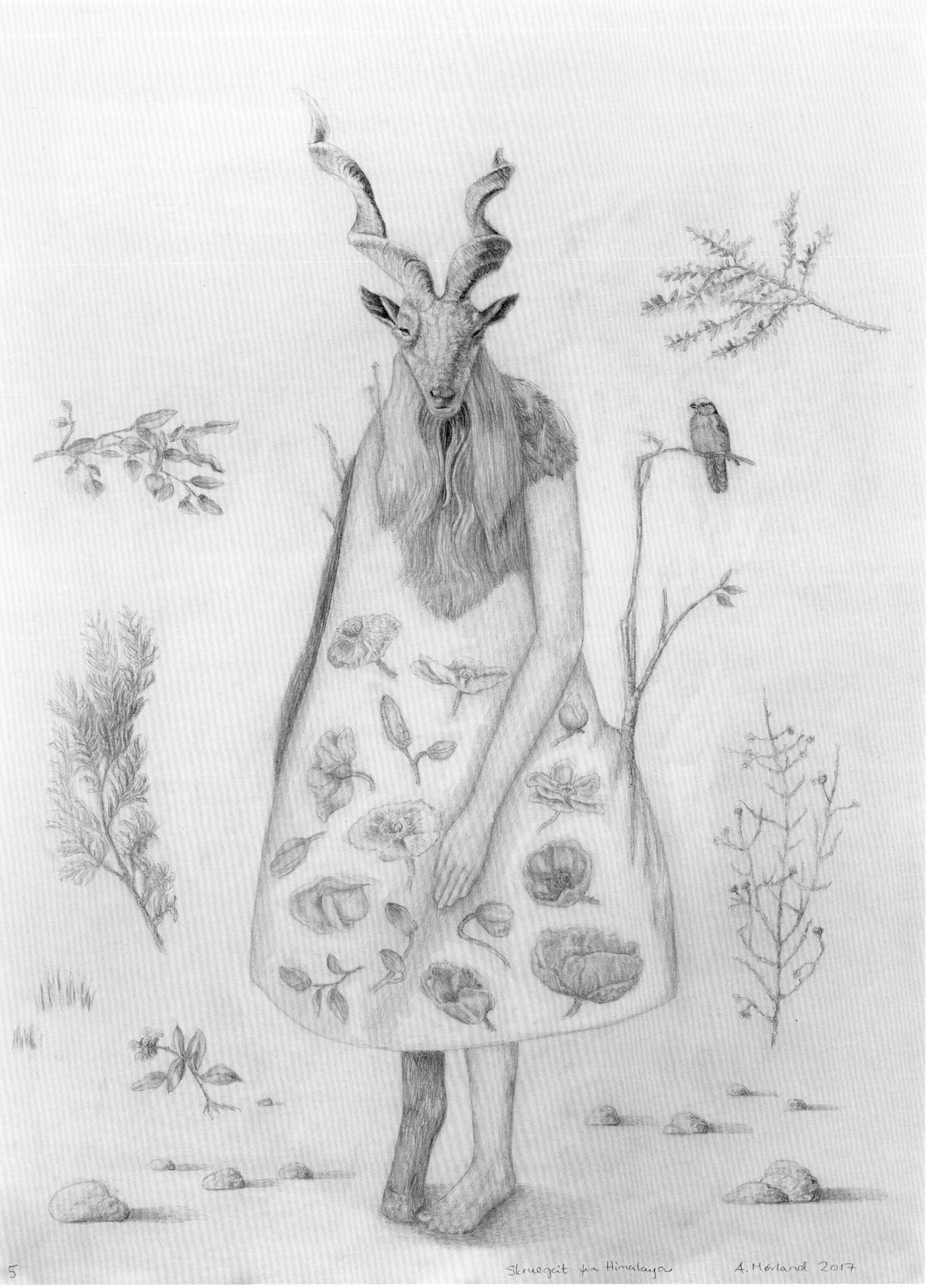

Skruegeit fra Himalaya
A. Mørland 2017

ASTRID MØRLAND
Wearing Apparel

edited by Tone Lyngstad Nyaas

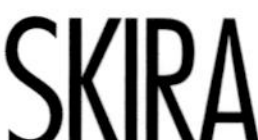

This monograph was published on occasion of the exhibition *Astrid Mørland: Wearing Apparel*, curated by Tone Lyngstad Nyaas and held at the Haugar Art Museum from 20 February to 9 May 2021

Cover
The Last Guardian 2 (detail), 2019
Pencil on paper, 86 x 62 cm

Page 2
Buck with a Floral Dress,
Screw Goat from the Himalayas, 2017
Pencil on paper, 70 x 51 cm

Art Director
Marcello Francone

Design
Luigi Fiore

Editorial Coordination
Emma Cavazzini

Copy Editor
Doriana Comerlati

Layout
Antonio Carminati

Translations
Stig Oppedal

Photo Credits
All photos are by Tomas Moss, except:
Pål Gunnæs: p. 145
Bjørn Harstad: pp. 39, 50, 51, 52, 55, 56, 65, 66, 67, 77, 79, 93, 121, 123
Astrid Mørland: pp. 22, 23, 73, 100, 118, 120, 125, 143
Frode Ringen: pp. 130, 131
Hanne Tyrmi: p. 134
Thomas Widerberg: pp. 40, 60

First published in Italy in 2021 by
Skira editore S.p.A.
Palazzo Casati Stampa
via Torino 61
20123 Milano
Italy
www.skira.net

Printed and bound in Italy. First edition

ISBN: 978-88-572-4474-7

Distributed in the world by Thames and Hudson Ltd., 181A High Holborn, London WC1V 7QX, United Kingdom.

Acknowledgements
Javier Aguilar Giner
Vanja Sodefjed Kjærnes
Kjetil Galleberg
Tomas Moss

Special thanks for their support and collaboration to

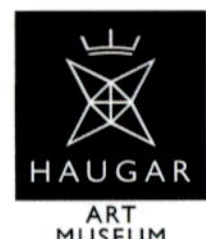

N
B Norske billedkunstnere
K

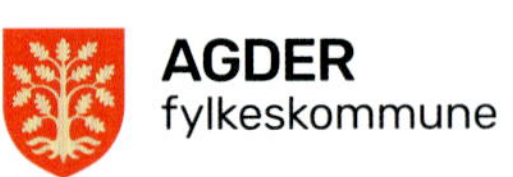

Contents

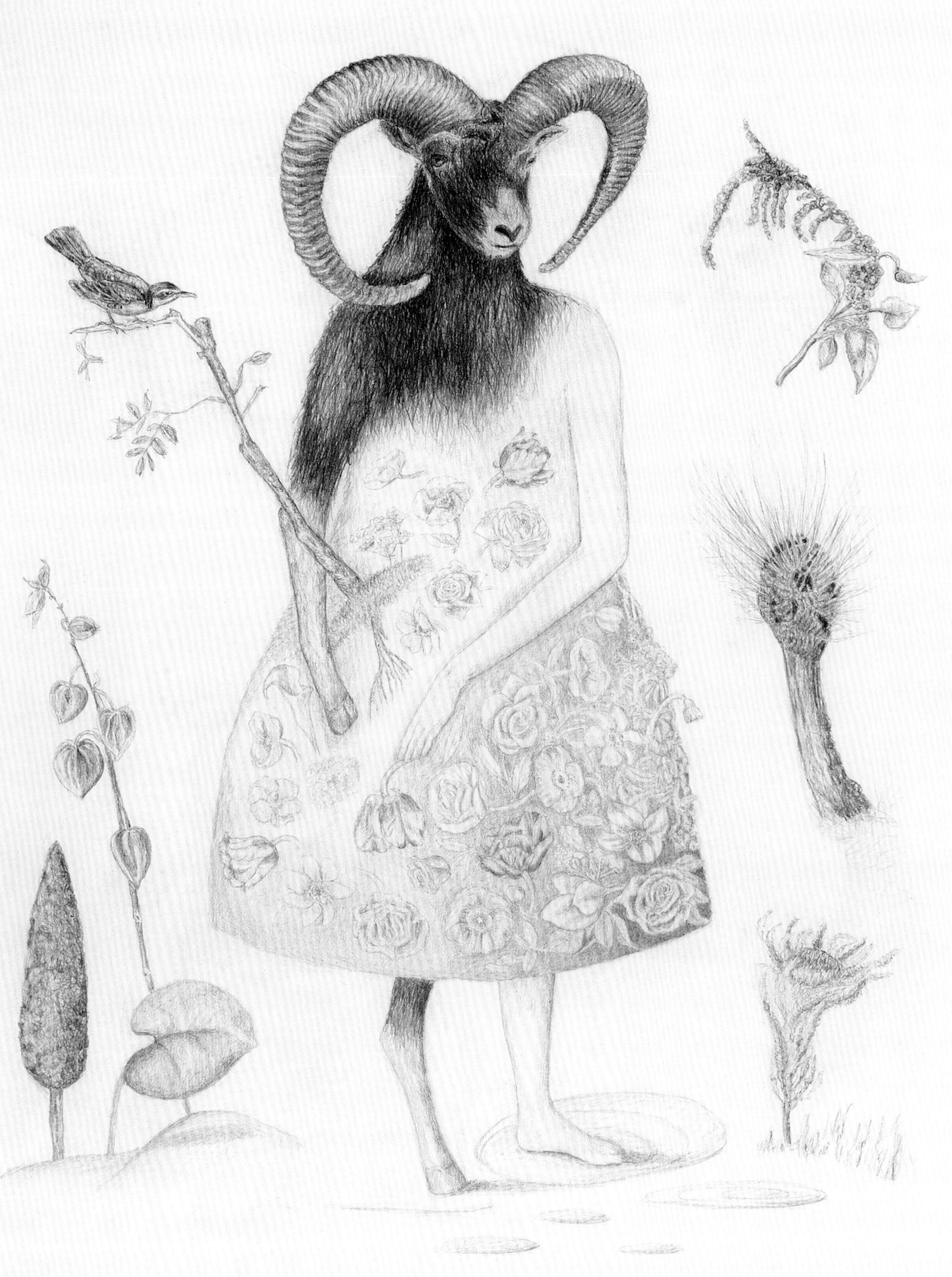
Mufflonsau fra Sardinia Korsika
A. Morland 2017

In Search of Lost Connections

Anna Lange Malmanger

Astrid Mørland is a versatile, curious, and contemplative artist. With keen insight she explores critical themes, such as humanity's existential conditions and the delicate relationship between man and nature. For many years she has worked with paintings, drawings, textiles, and installations, and her figurative universe is often characterised by a surrealist idiom and recurring motifs. Particularly central to her art is the form of the dress, which assumes a profound symbolism. This motif often appears in Mørland's paintings and drawings and is further explored in her textile pieces and her three-dimensional works made of stones, pine cones, mussels, and other natural materials. Recently, the artist has also created richly detailed embroideries of animals and insects on dresses, a subtle reminder of the major environmental challenges we are facing today.

On the whole, Mørland's art frequently features animals, or else human figures with animal traits. Such figures are imbued with a positive meaning in her works, akin to the surrealist representation of animals as symbolising, for instance, the free, untamed, and true side of humanity. This symbolism thereby also refers to an inner dimension and a deeper consciousness, something that clearly informs her enigmatic pictures. In Mørland's later works, these animal figures acquire a more concrete meaning, as they more specifically comment on the lack of a balance between man, animal, and nature. In this respect, animals become an ideal for us, since they are able to co-exist with nature.

*

The starting point for this essay is Astrid Mørland's two series of drawings, *Buck with a Floral Dress* (2017) and *The Last Guardian* (2019). Similar motifs are also on display in the painting series *Buck and Orchid* (2019). These works focus on the unity of animal and man, more specifically a standing buck clad in a dress and having partially human limbs. The buck-human hybrid seems almost poetic, nostalgically evoking the lost harmony and community that once existed. Combining a technical virtuosity with symbol-laden figures and a sensitive expression, Mørland visualises this fateful development as well as the fact that humans and animals are inextricably part of the same world.

The series *Buck with a Floral Dress* features twelve drawings of endangered horned bucks hailing from different parts of the planet. The dresses they have on are amply adorned with miscellaneous flowers, while the bucks themselves are endowed with a human arm and leg. Each composition finely depicts a standing, dress-wearing buck surrounded by carefully designed trees and vegetation. A small, tender bird sits on a branch, which in nearly all the pictures springs forth from the floral dress. Birds are commonly associated with freedom and our soul and inner life, and as such a bird's free nature and unfettered movement may symbolise a search for a deeper connection. This sense is strengthened by the close dialogue between the buck and the bird.

By gathering a great variety of nature around the dress-clad bucks, Mørland's drawings may bring to mind botanical and zoological wall charts that

*Buck with a Floral Dress,
Mufflonsheep from Sardinia,
Corsica*, 2017
Pencil on paper, 70 x 51 cm

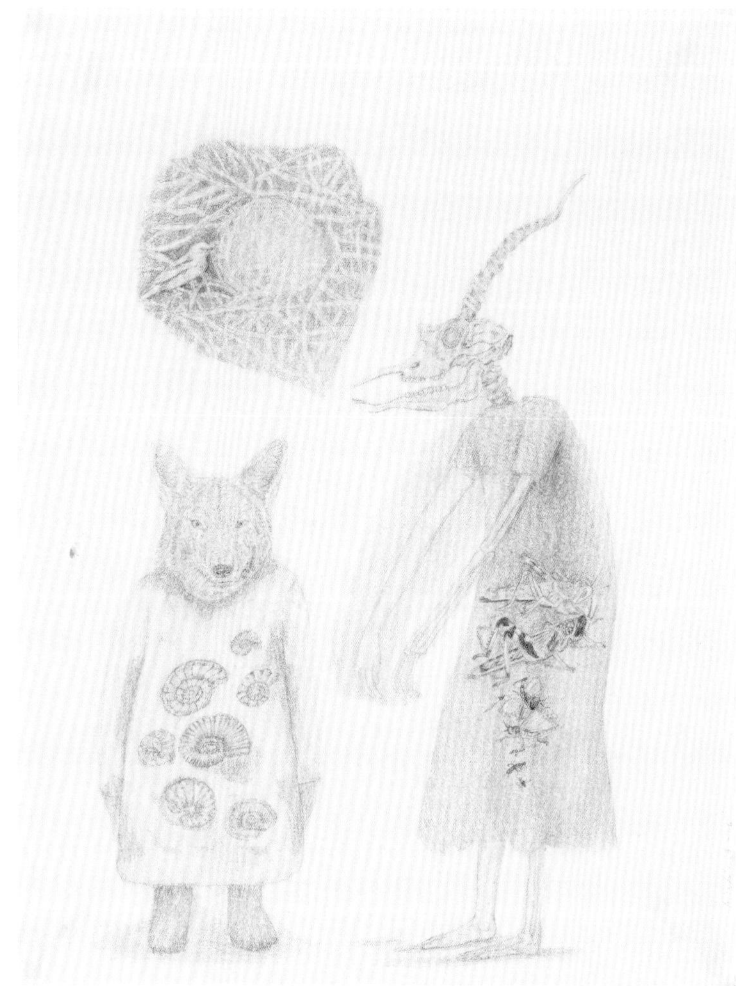

meticulously represent and register various plants and animals. In this manner, the artist seems to direct our attention to the study of nature, thereby suggesting our fundamental need to categorise, understand, and control this nature, something that in the long run has increased the schism that today typifies the relationship between humans and animals, and in a wider sense between humans and nature.

An earlier series of eight drawings from 2016, titled *In a Hundred Years Everything Will Be Forgotten*, shows a prototype of the dress-clad buck motif. Each drawing depicts two different animals clad in a dress adorned with representations of plants, insects, and reptiles. These pairs are engaged in a dialogue of sorts, and overlooking them is a bird. In this fashion, the series may be seen as a dialectical process between various endangered species. Mørland's realistic renderings of the animal furs and hides, as well as the birds' plumage, bring to light the fauna's rich and diverse texture. On the whole, many of Mørland's recent drawings showcase her exquisite technique, testifying to her efforts to accurately render animals who are in danger of becoming extinct. By virtue of her outfitting them with dresses that provide small glimpses into nature, the figures acquire both an absurd appearance and a complex meaning.

The Last Guardian from 2019 develops elements from *In a Hundred Years Everything Will Be Forgotten*. Above all, this series of three drawings elaborates on *Buck with a Floral Dress* in regard to both theme and composition. Here as well, the bucks are attired in dresses and once again feature both human and animal parts, as in a dreamlike image of a higher synthesis. Moreover,

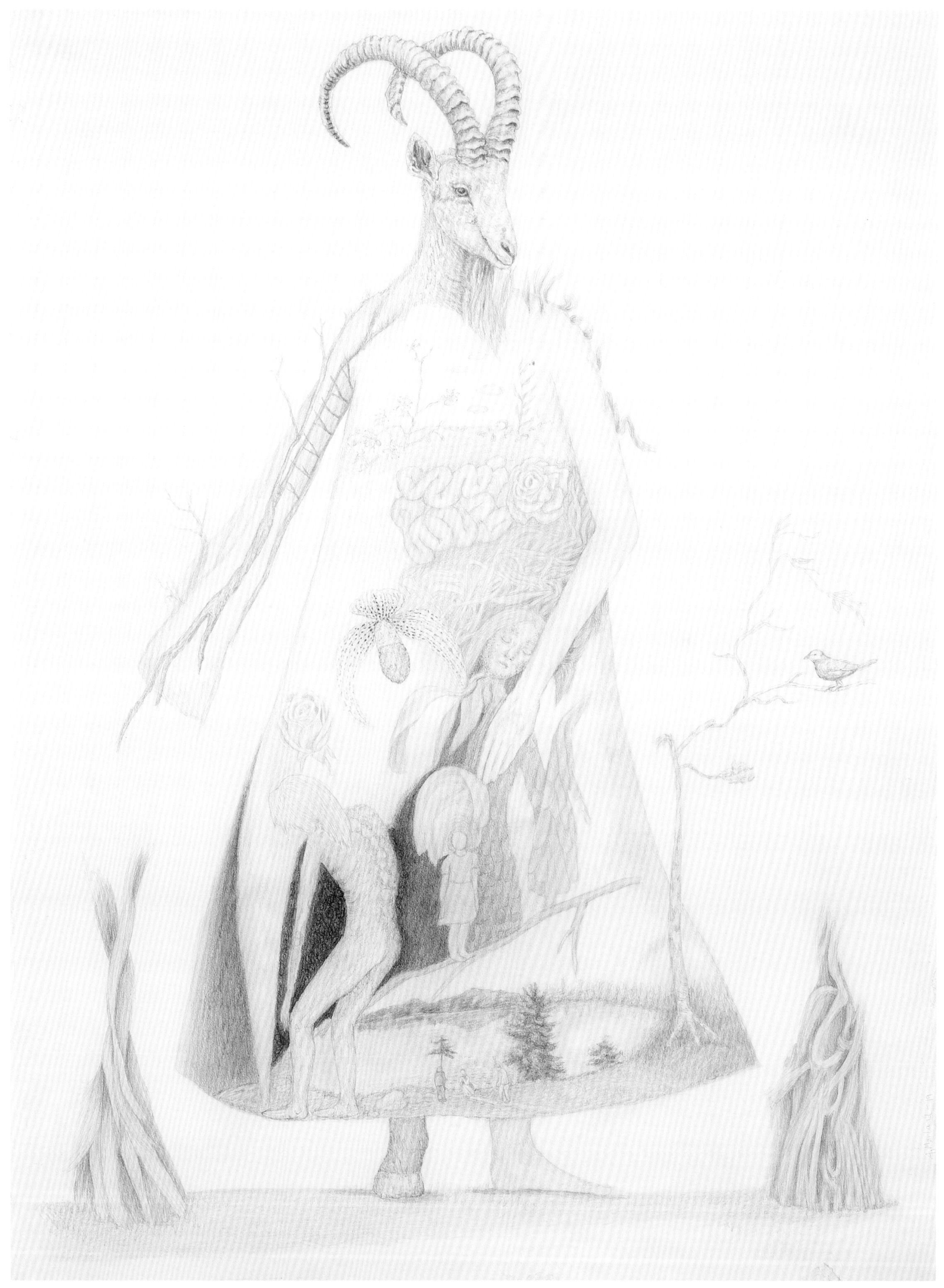

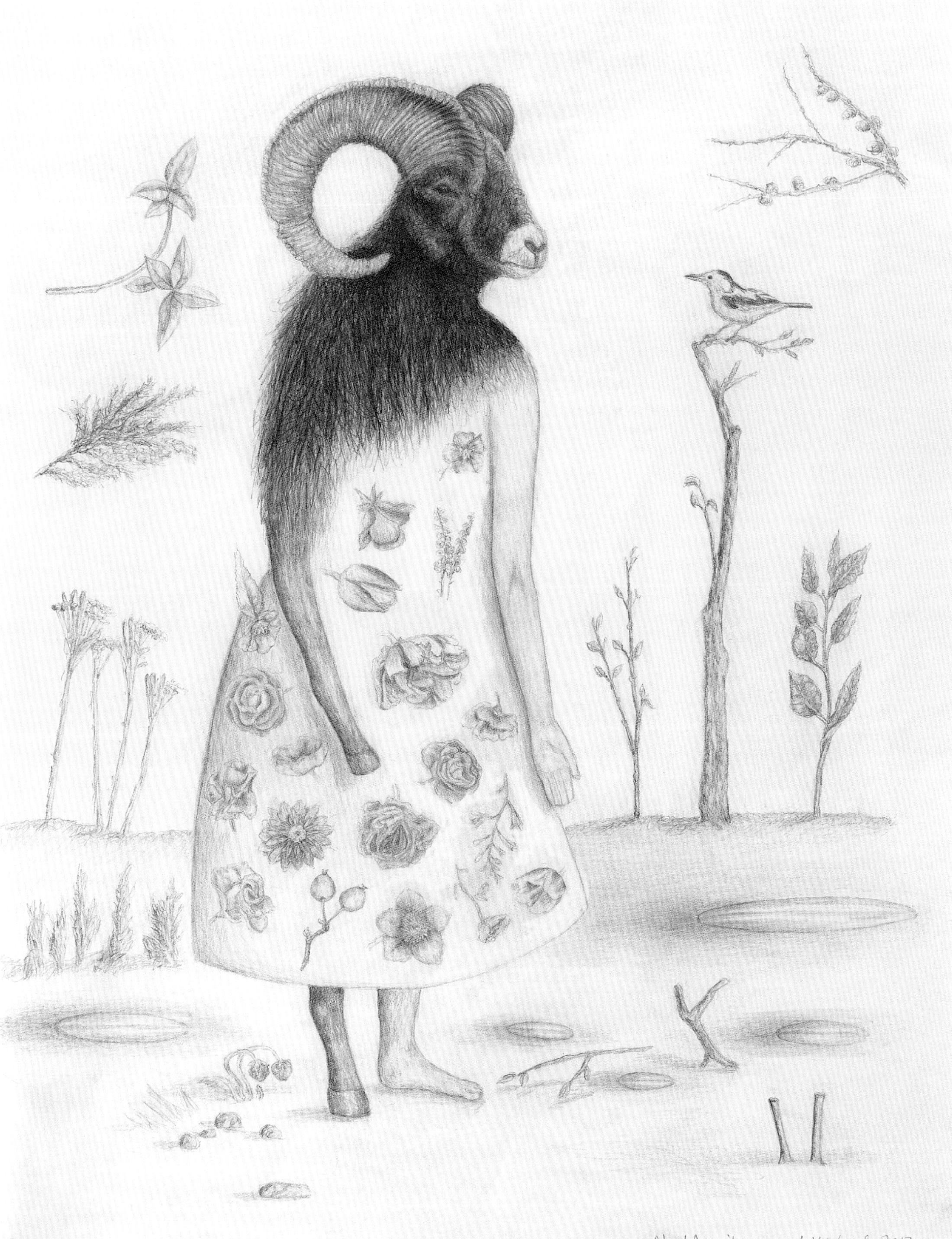

2.

Tykkhornsau fra Nord Amerika   A. Mørland 2017

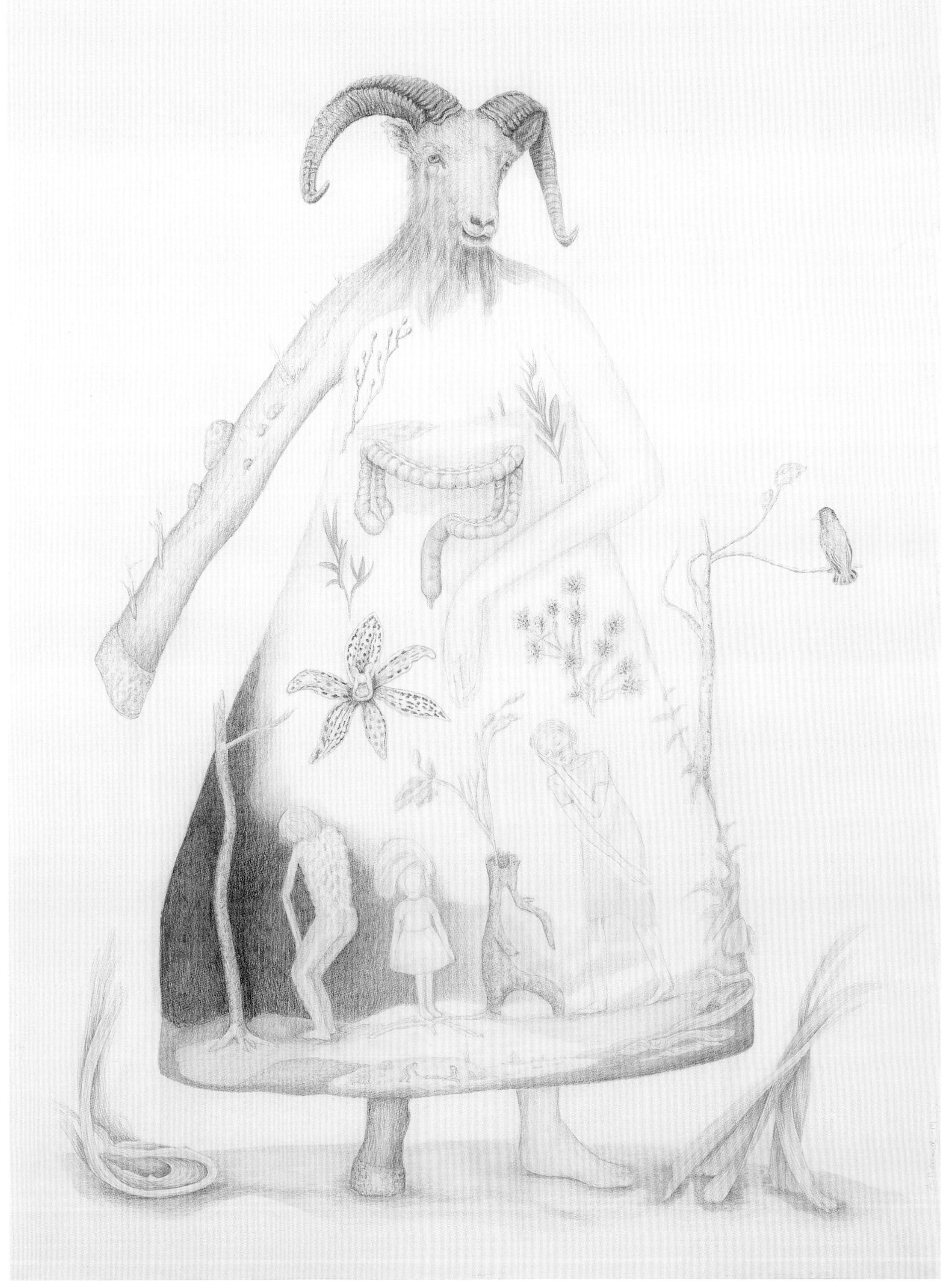

the realistic depictions of nature are once again combined with a surrealist imagery.

In these drawings, however, the buck's extended animal "arm" becomes more integrated as part of nature, in that it somewhat morphs into trees, twigs, and stones. This metamorphosis suggests the animal's symbiotic relationship with nature, as a contrast to humanity's more destructive one. For Astrid Mørland, the buck can be seen as a symbol of the urgent environmental challenges of our time. At risk of disappearing forever from several areas on earth, the bucks stand forth here as representative guardians of nature. Their powerful horns and tree-like arms express strength and invest the dress-clad bucks with authority. Likewise, the human arms emphasise this custodial role by virtue of them protectively touching the isolated figures and shapes of the dress universe.

The Last Guardian, too, reveals a small bird perching on a protruding branch. By contrast, however, the plants we previously saw depicted around the bucks have instead been incorporated in the dress, which now displays an enigmatic world of landscapes, flowers, intestines, and human figures in sorrow and pain. A sense of melancholy permeates these scenes, further underscoring the feeling of anguish and despair. What does nevertheless provide hope is the serene deportment and presence of the buck, which stands there as a stoic guardian of a better tomorrow.

*

The frequently recurring dress motif in Mørland's artistic universe takes on many meanings, alluding to qualities such as the feminine, the life-giving, the vulnerable, the trusting, and the protective. Since a dress covers the body, it also conceals the wearer's nakedness even as it affords some protection. Thus, the motif concerns the tension between an outer and inner dimension, between a façade and an underlying depth. This is suggested by, among other things, the depicted intestines, an obvious reference to our physical and existential vulnerability. Just as the body depends on all the inner organs to work together as a fine-tuned machine, we too are part of a wider context where all the components need to act in concert and carry out their respective tasks in order to maintain a vital balance. By clothing the anthropomorphic animal in a dress encompassing vegetation, figures, and intestines, Mørland hints at the complex relationship between humans and nature, but also at existing in a complicated world.

We encounter the dress-wearing buck once again in the series of paintings entitled *Buck and Orchid* (2019), where the skeleton of a little girl circles around the buck, evoking death, sorrow, and loneliness. In one of the five paintings in the series, the skeleton hovers in the purple picture plane, while in another one she is depicted sitting against a warm, yellow background. In yet another painting she stands close by the buck, appearing to seek comfort and aid from the animal. In all of these paintings as well, the monumental

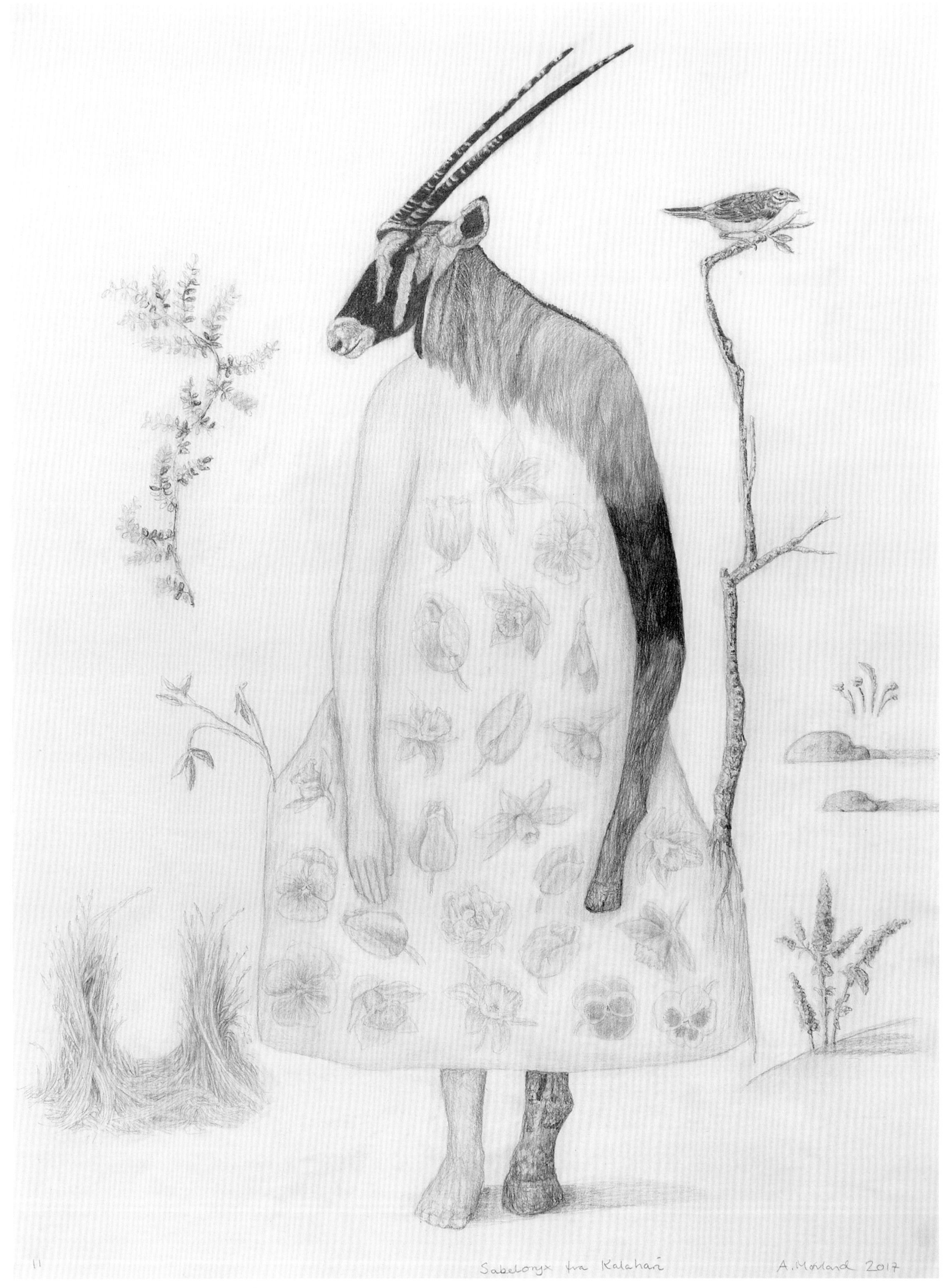
11
Sabeloryx fra Kalahari
A. Morland 2017

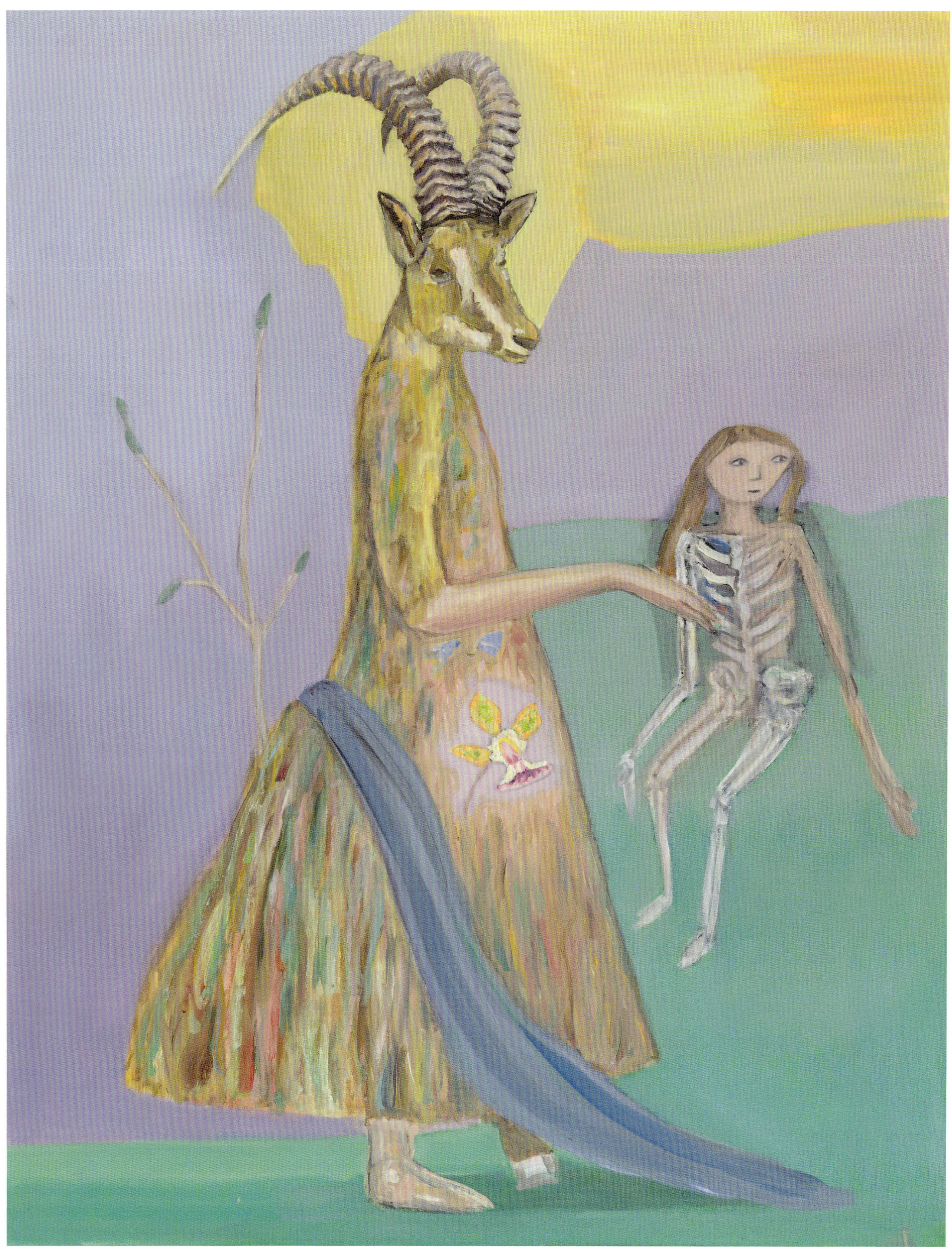

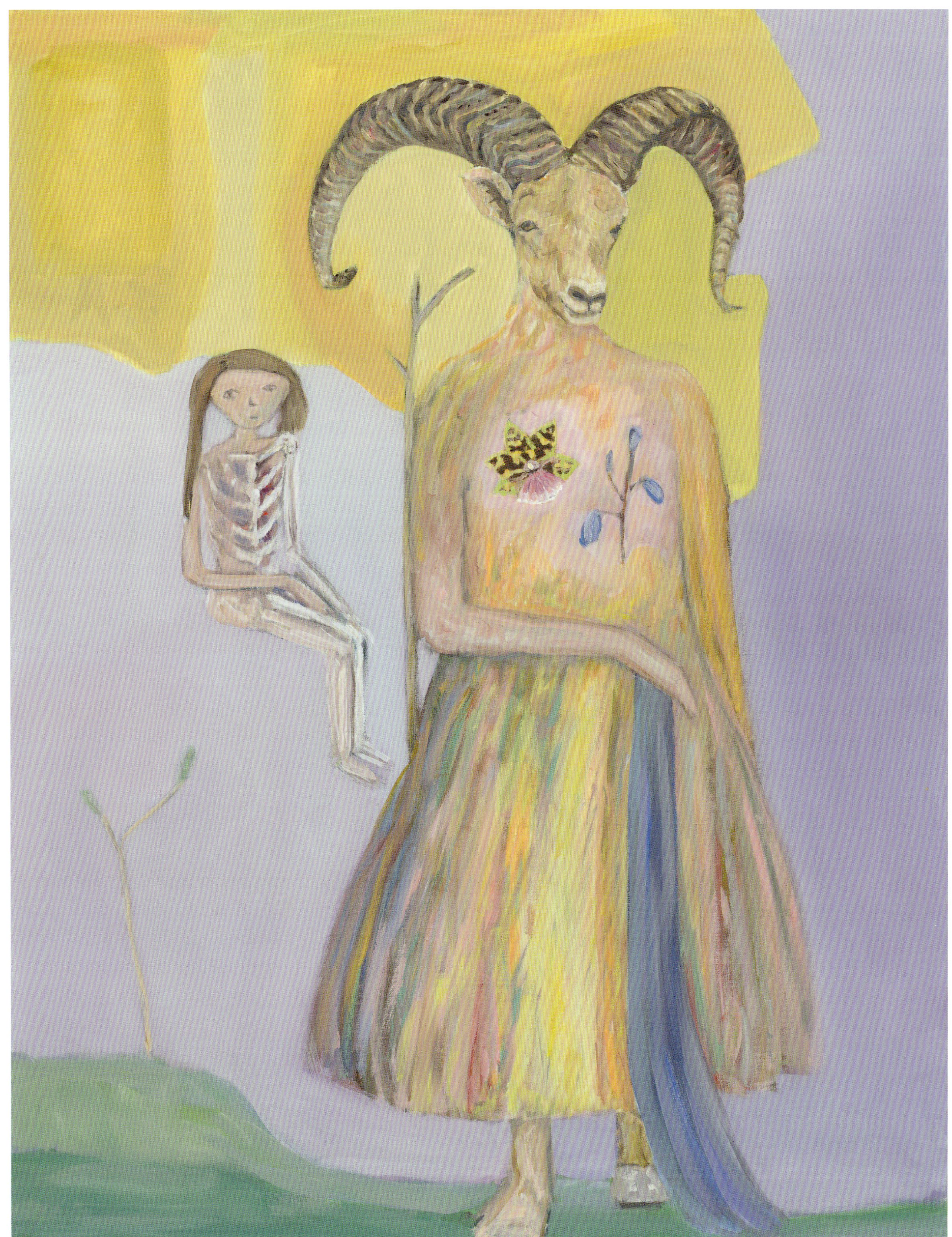

buck dominates the composition and takes on the guise of a well-intentioned guardian. A yellow colour field surrounds the buck's head as a sort of large, luminous halo, giving the hybrid animal an almost sublime and sacral role: the buck stands there as a dignified, melancholic figure gazing out towards us, with a look in its eyes that perhaps seems both sad and accusatory.

In contrast to the broad fields of colour in the background, the dress is composed of sketchier brushstrokes in a variety of hues and adorned with orchids, an ancient and delicate flower renowned for its beauty and perfection. The delicate orchid seems an apt symbol of the vulnerability of nature in our day and age – but also of the fragility of human existence. All five paintings feature a blue river flowing from the dress and down to the ground, with the life-giving water seeming to suggest optimism about the future, as does the buck's protective arm, which in one of the pictures touches the girl's vulnerable skeleton in a way that restores a connection of sorts between nature and man. This is accentuated by how the frail figure is now grounded in the green field of colour, an extension of the earth the buck is standing on.

In recent years, Mørland has also created carefully detailed embroideries of insects and birds for dresses. Similar to the various *Buck* series, these embroideries reflect her increasing concern with the great environmental challenges of our times. With her exquisite and time-consuming handicraft, she seeks to patiently preserve the fragile creatures that are at risk of disappearing – creatures that are so fundamental to the very survival of humankind. As such, the laborious act of creation is a contemplative process, where the artist seeks to give permanent form to something that risks becoming lost forever.

*

A common thread runs through Astrid Mørland's oeuvre. Throughout her many years as an artist, she has stayed true to a figurative expression, exploring a dreamlike pictorial universe rich in symbols and pregnant meaning. Her paintings often represent an alienated reality where mournful figures and fractured shapes create their own connections and tensions in an attempt to reach a deeper understanding. Using a range of expressions, Mørland continues to ponder on the human condition in her inquisitive art, posing questions about our existence in a world where death, vulnerability, and loneliness serve as the framework of our lives. The various aforementioned series of dress-clad bucks also revolve around such themes, and in particular focus on the lost balance between man and nature. Evoking a fragile universe, Mørland's art invites us to *reflect*.

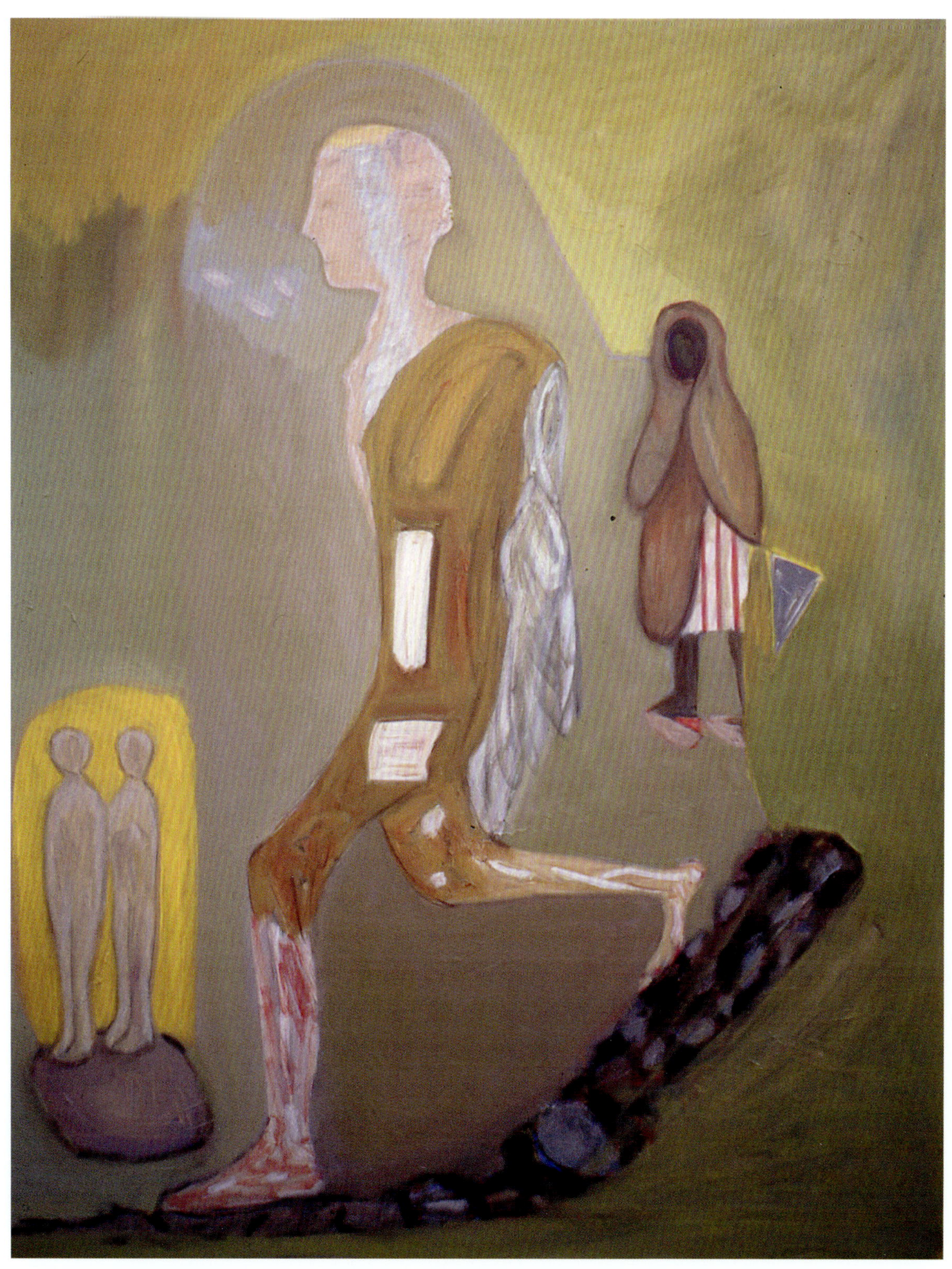

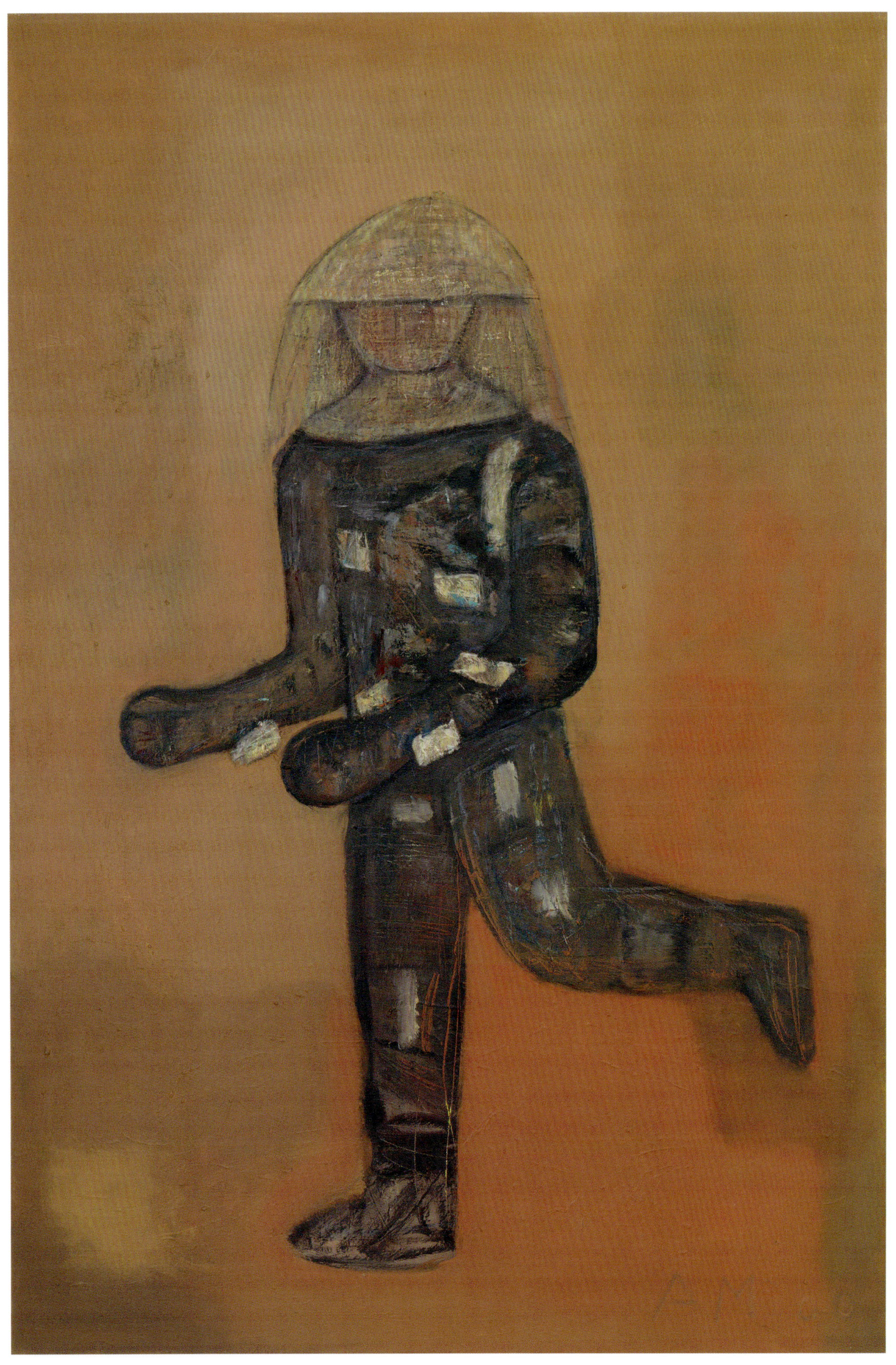

Life Runner 2, 2000
Oil on canvas, 150 x 110 cm

Life Runner, 1999
Pencil on paper, 84 x 54 cm

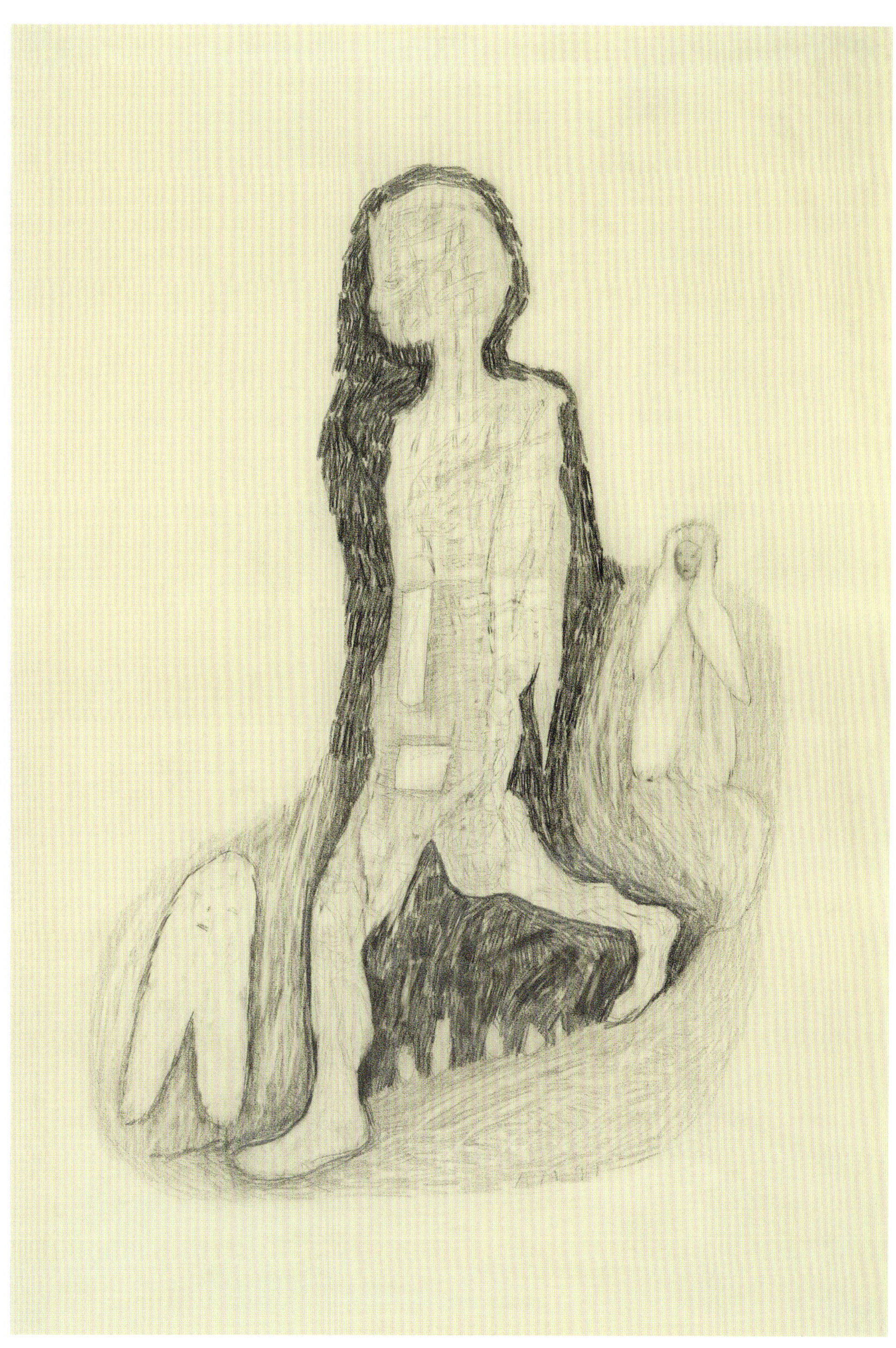

Synne Lea

The rain stops. Just as slowly as it began.
It changes its mind and comes back. Begins again.
Can't let go, can't stop. Like love.

I am alone now. I have to laugh myself.
The night is a thornbush that dreams climb around in.

Puberty, 2007
Mixed media object, 60 x 40 cm

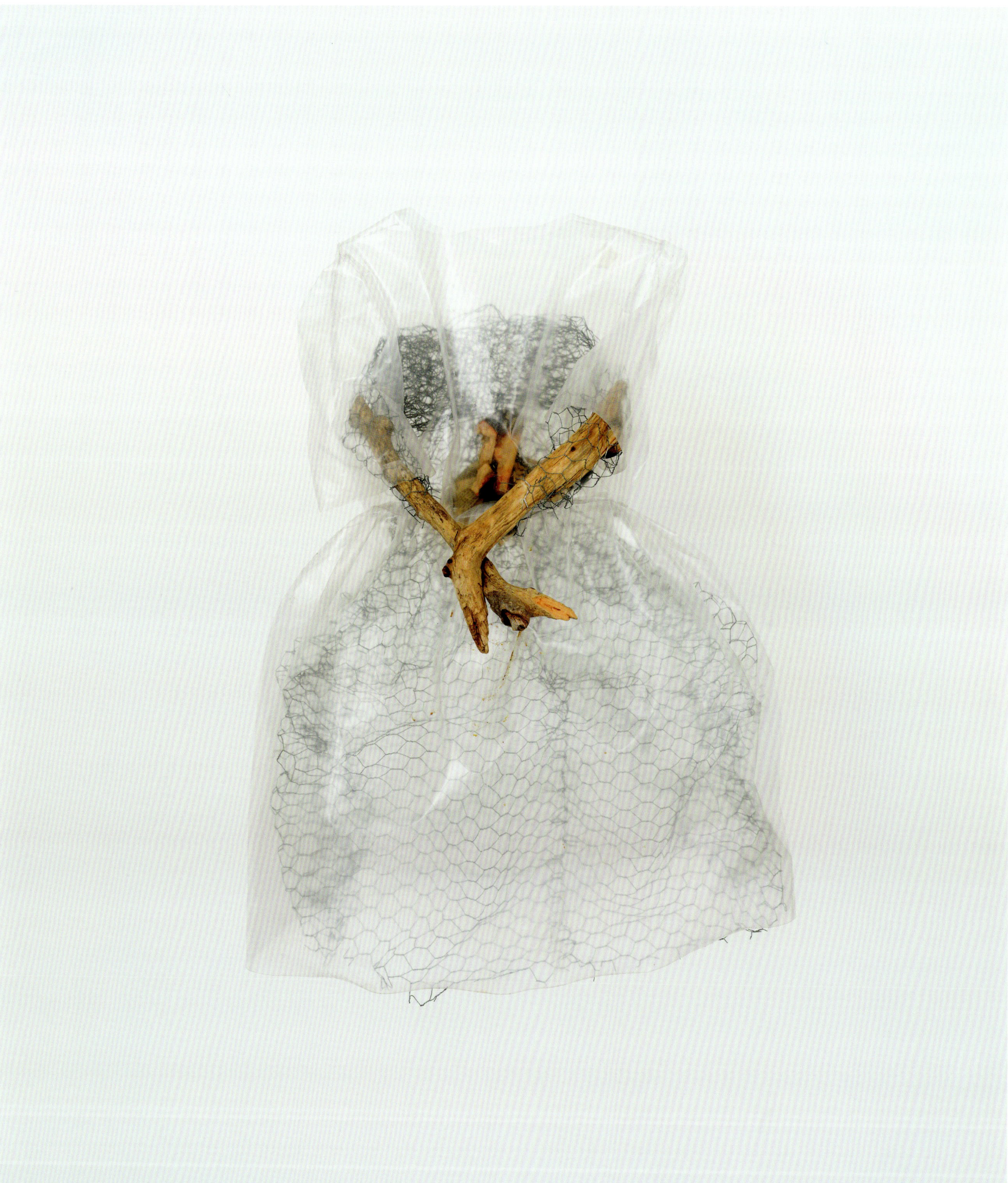

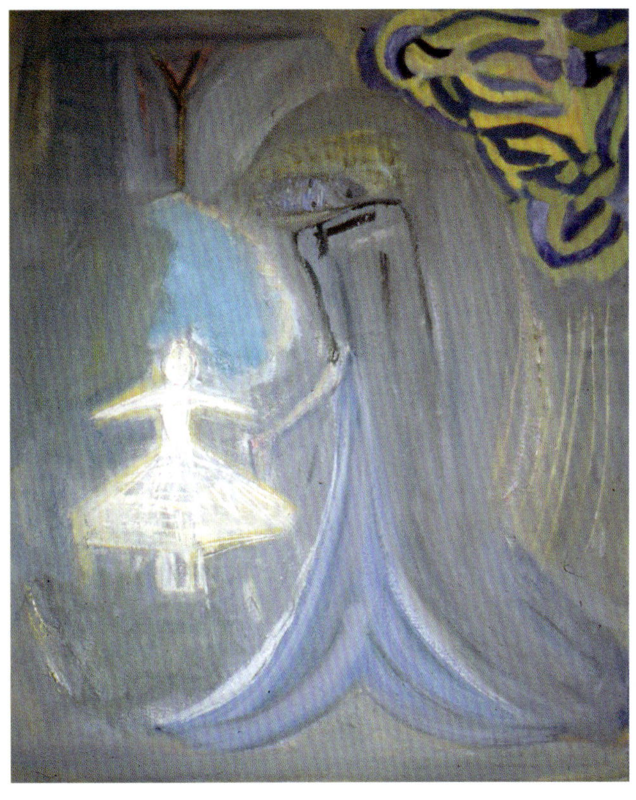

White Ballerina, 2007
Oil on canvas, 72 x 60 cm

I take the wee
nights, the blue smudges, before
the days divide the darkness between them.

I know a bed that sleeps over at my place.

Reunion, 1999
Oil on canvas, 160 x 118 cm

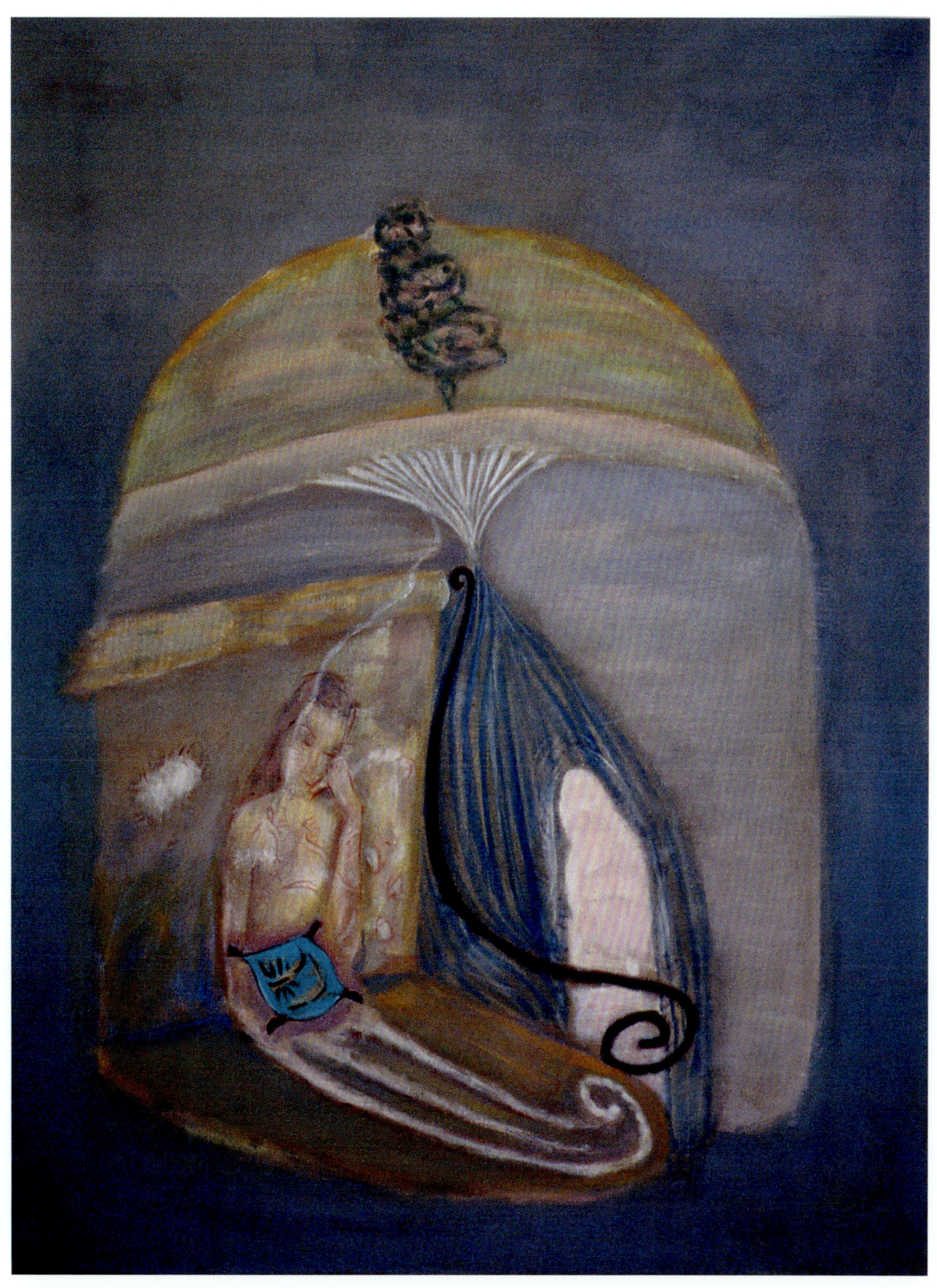

She used to ask me about the way home.
You are home, I replied.
Then she told me the way home.

Tell me about something you lost, I asked.
I once had a child, she answered.

On the Other Side, 2007
Oil on canvas, 95 x 120 cm

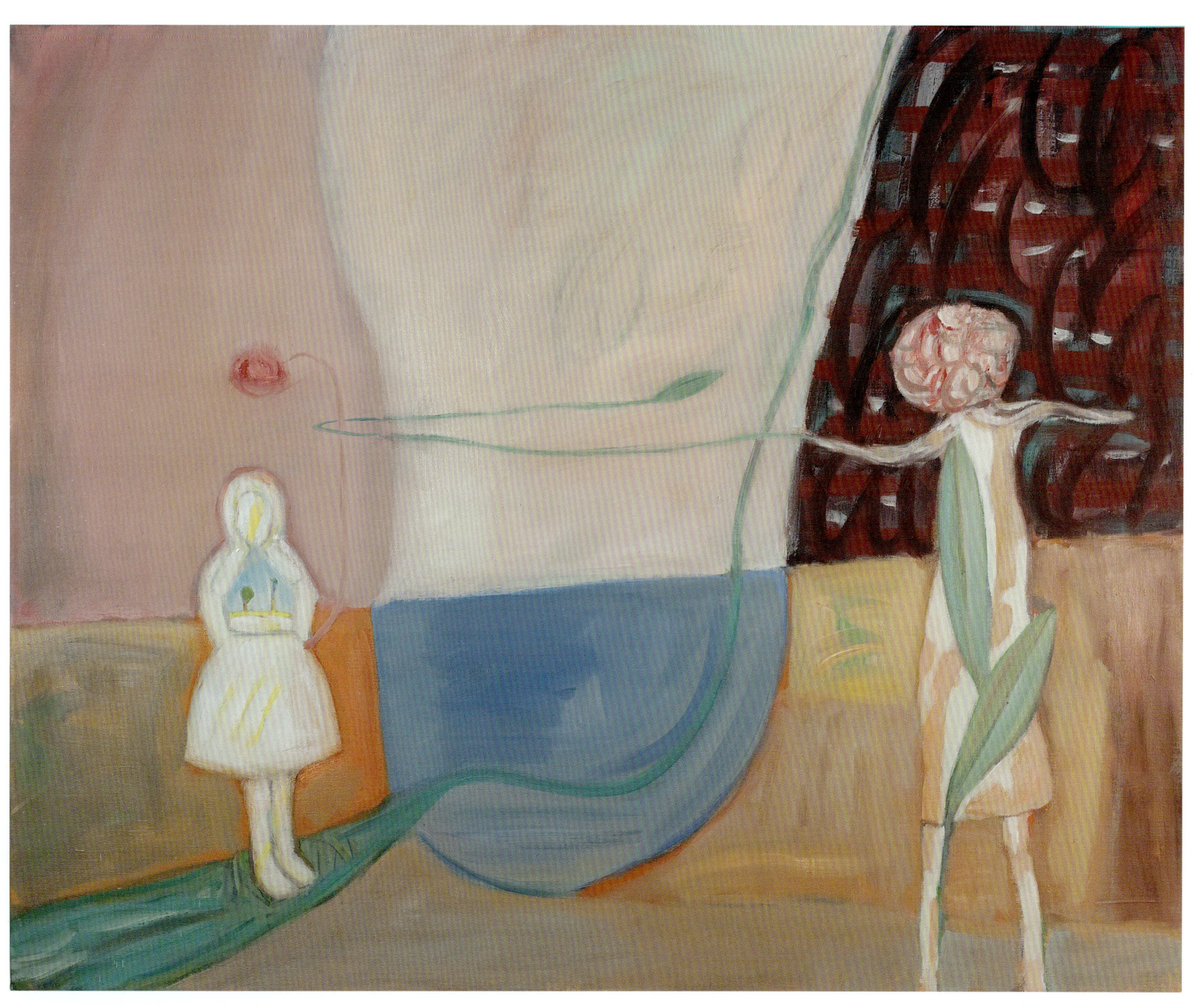

Sometimes I pack my belongings.

They say the night sleeps, and if you are lucky
and see the exact moment
the night sleeps most heavily, you can slip past it.

The nights are prison guards, they stand between
their kids and the children out on the streets.

There is a separate postal service
for dreams. They carry all they can

on their backs. The rest they swallow
and haul in their stomachs across the border.

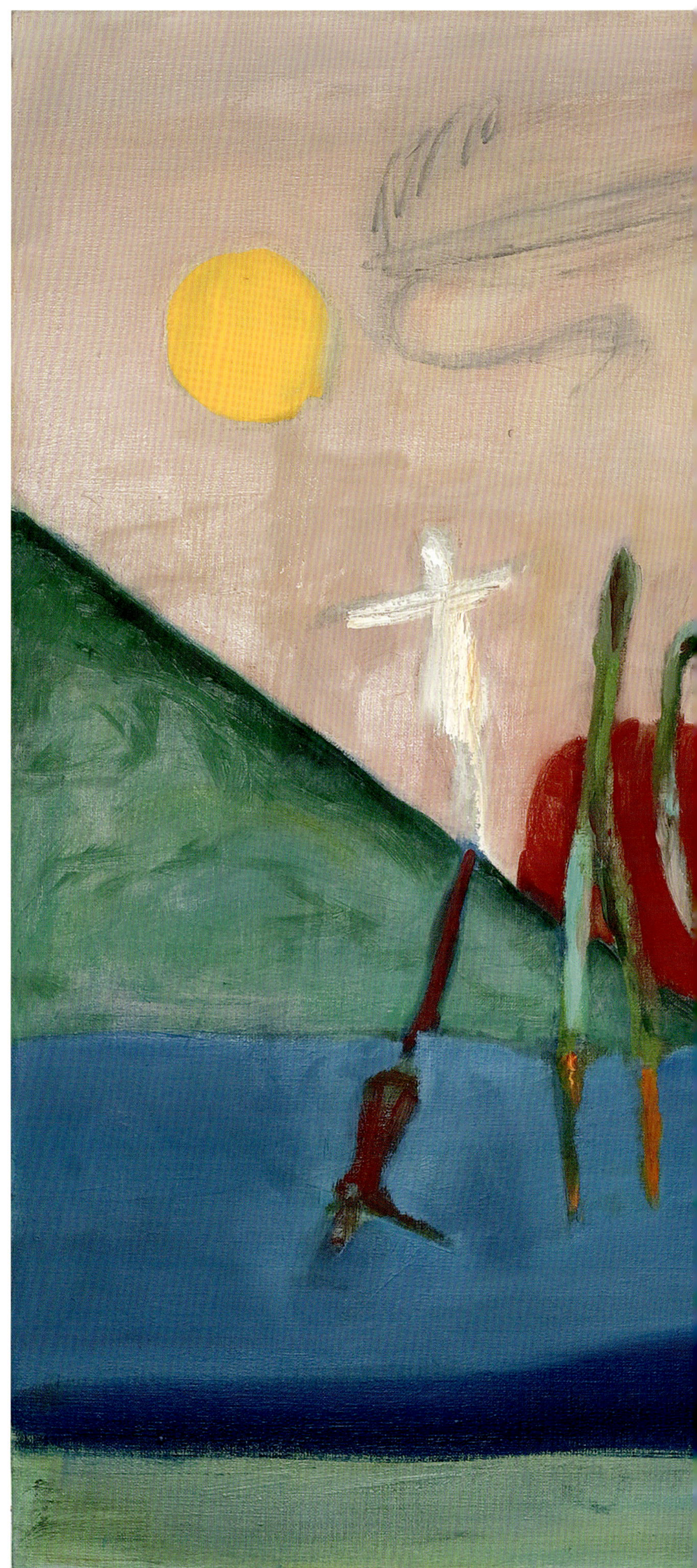

The Solar Cycle, 2007
Oil on canvas, 90 x 110 cm

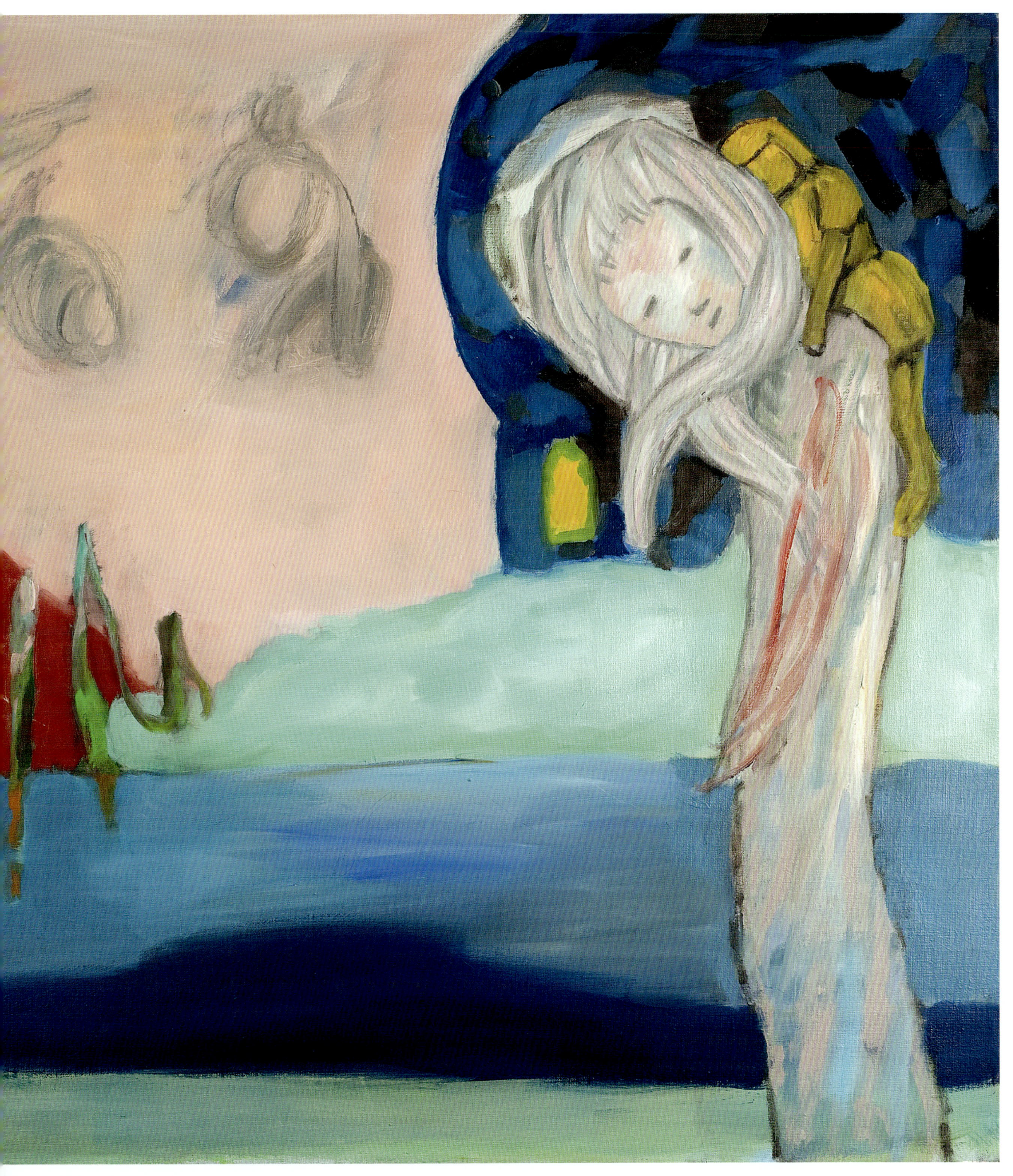

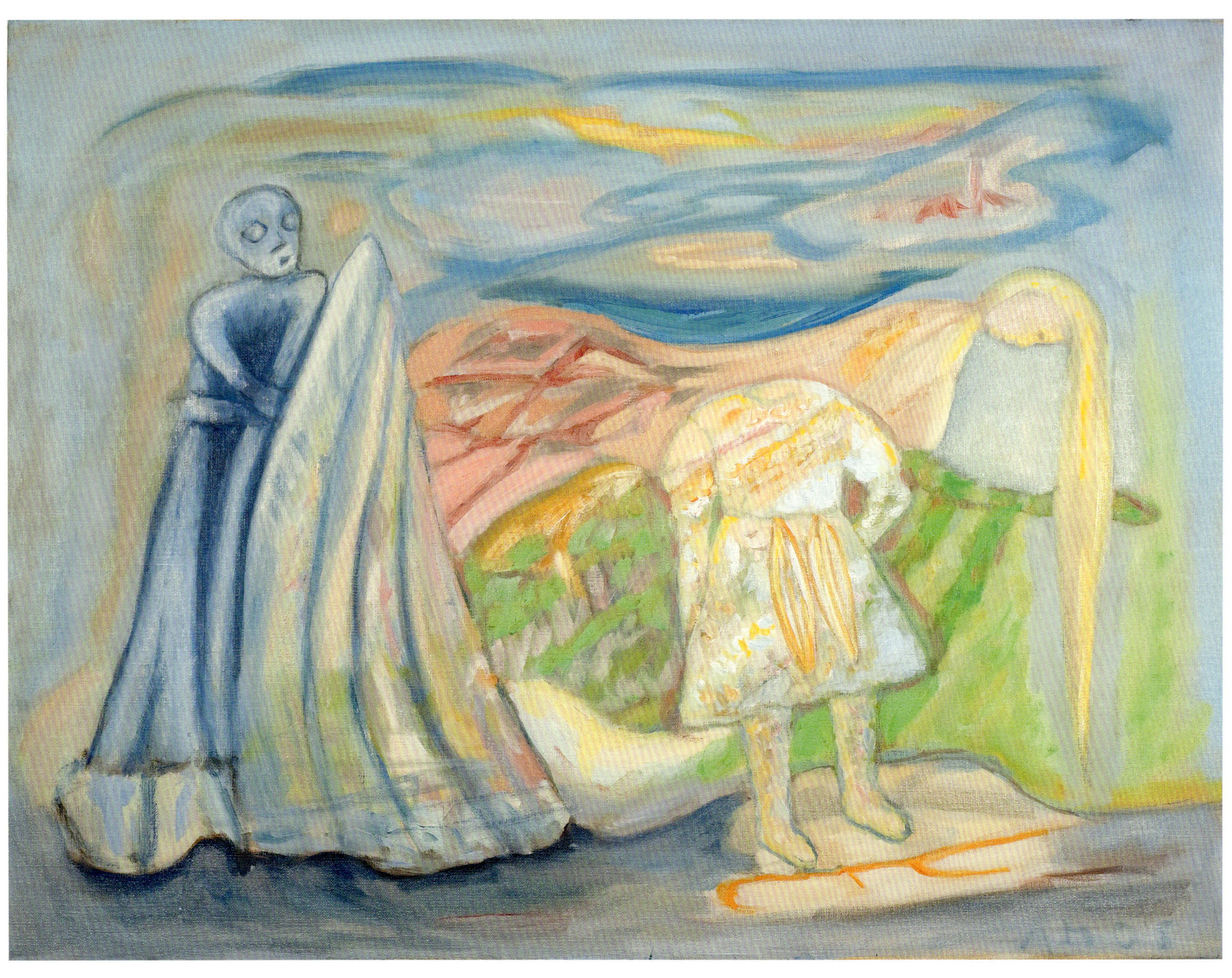

Tonight I dreamt that the forest had been chopped down.
It fell, a loud thump, it looked as though it fell from the sky,
as though the sky suddenly let go, and without being
held by the air and light the forest fell, the ground shook.
More and more trees kept falling till only a single flower
remained.

Everything else had been trampled and ruined.
Only this flower still stood.

I did everything I could to protect it, make it thrive,
make it live.
I took care of it, watered it, gave it shelter from the wind
and frost, I sang.

But then it died as well.
The entire forest was flat. Completely empty.
It was like that for a long while.

Then along came a child and an old person. They sat there,
right next to the dead flower. They slept there, walked
around a bit, but never far away. They did nothing more
than that.

Then the forest started to bloom, to grow, to want.
The way the spring does. Nakedly, flatly, fully, suddenly.

Spring, 2008
Oil on canvas, 65 x 90 cm

I'm not trying to prevent deforestation.
I'm planting a tree.

The child went down to the creek in the twilight,
all the way to the mouth of the creek.
She waited for the deer, the deer came when the light
had the same colour as blue clay.

It wasn't afraid of her.
She wasn't afraid of it.
The trees saw everything that happened.

When the child disappeared, the water turned around
and flowed upwards.
It rained for the first time.
Just as it had when the child was born.

Ever since it has continued to rain for the first time.
Every evening the water comes through the creek,
turns around and flows upwards.

Illuminated, 2007
Oil on canvas, 130 x 130 cm

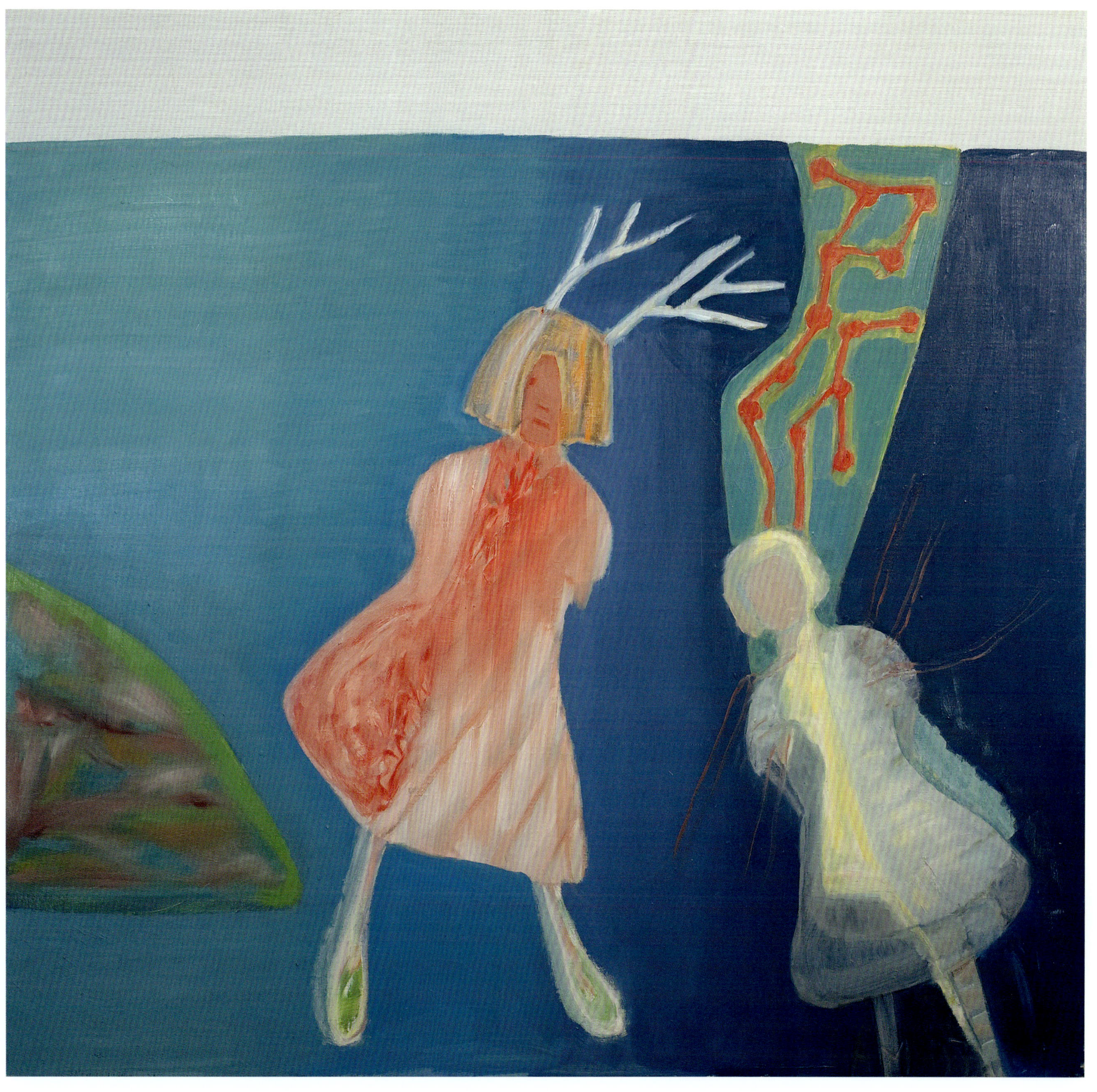

The day will never come that I will forget you.

Ask someone who lives on an island.
They won't answer that there are many ways
to live under water.

I ask you. Because you know what it's like to live
on an island.

We are still animals, you reply, we don't have
to think in order to remember.

Buck with a Floral Dress,
A Female Himalayan Tahr, 2017
Pencil on paper, 70 x 51 cm

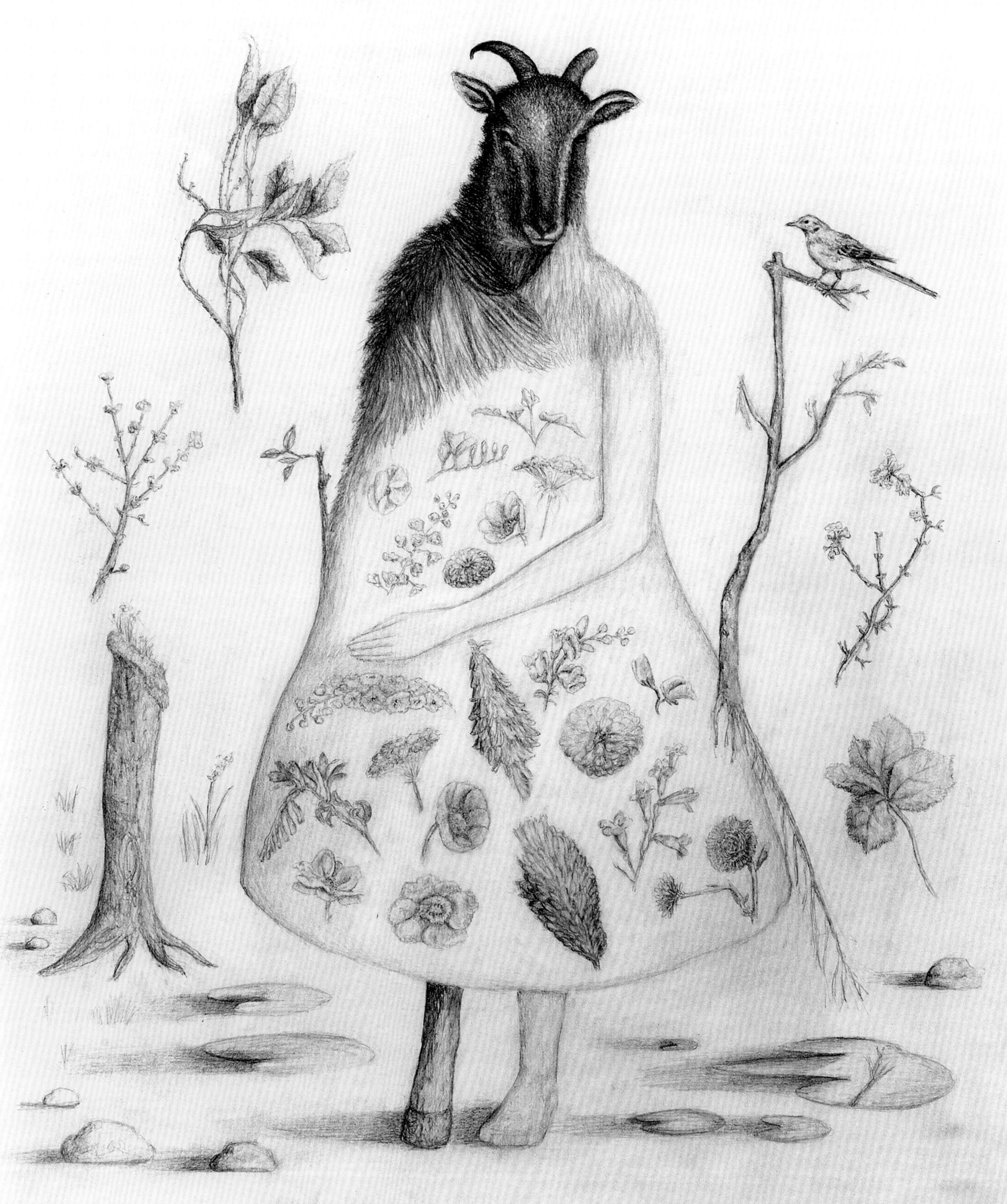

4
Tahr-geit fra Arabia, India, Himalaya
A. Mørland 2017

I hadn't forgotten how beautiful it was.
I recognised the raw smell of deer when I came.
They must have been many,
a thick herd. The grass rose in spurts.

They sift the sand where we used to go down to swim.
As we had looked for laughter, they search for our
footprints, the glittering smudges
we left behind when we got out of the water.
They collect waves the same way we collected berries
to freeze for the winter.
When they dig in the soil, they find treetops.
They imagine the lungs that the branches
must once have protected, spanning so widely.

They must have stood above the humans,
they think, just look: a more peaceful society,
slimmer bodies, longer lives.

*In a Hundred Years Everything
Will Be Forgotten 2*, 2016
Pencil on paper, 40 x 32 cm

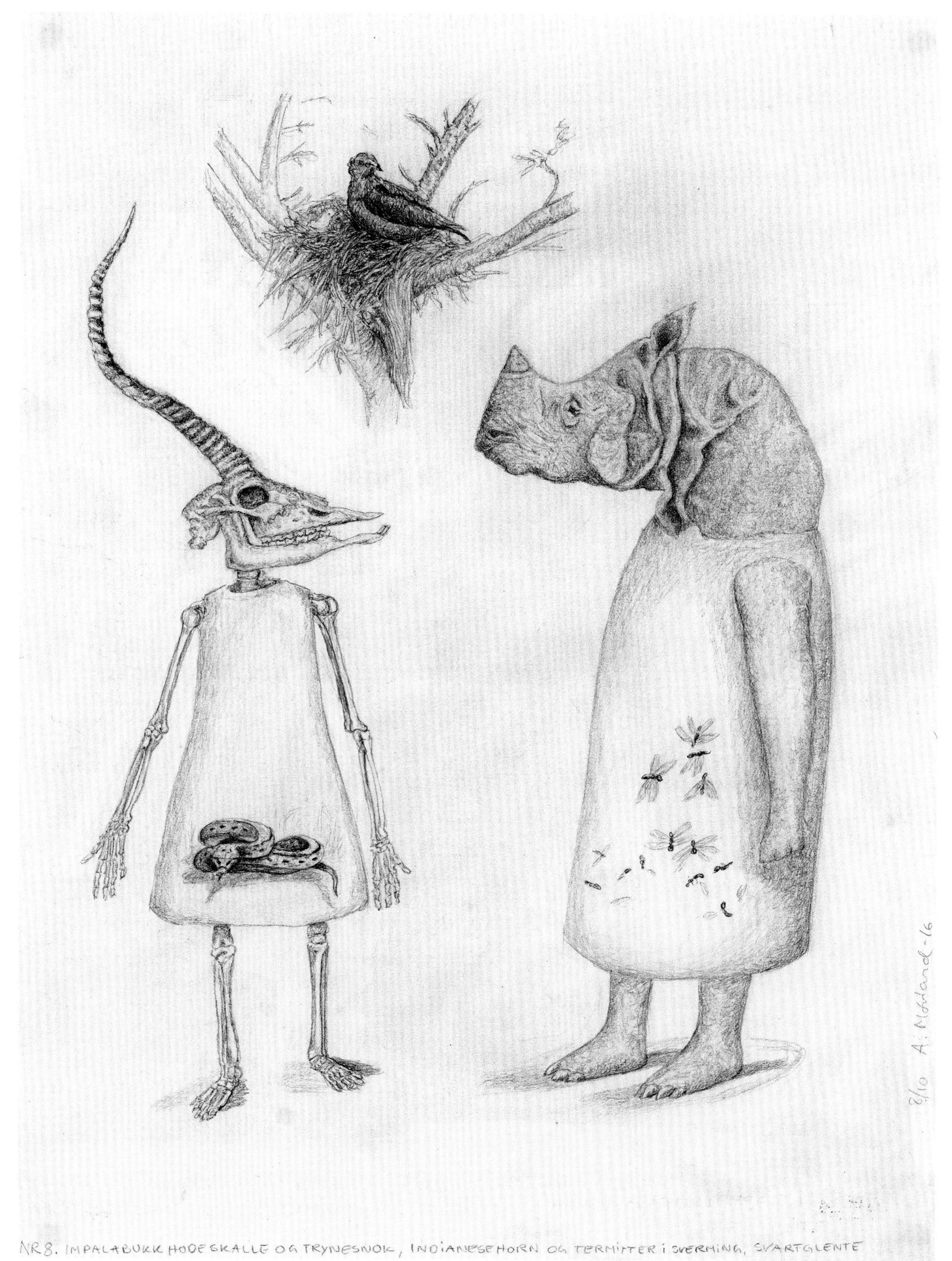

NR 8. IMPALABUKK HODESKALLE OG TRYNESNOK, INDIANESEHORN OG TERMITTER I SVERMING, SVARTGLENTE

They dream of standing next to such gigantic,
serene creatures.
Of seeing them trekking calmly across the plains.
Of walking with human-like feet.
Of seeing the sun be the sun, the sea be the sea.

They create a sky of your canvases, lie down beneath it,
and see picture behind picture, behind picture.
That is how the talk starts

with the one they have just begun to love, the one they
suddenly recall so exactly that they always have loved.
They talk of all they know, all they've never forgotten,
dreams about the world, the one we, mistakenly,
called ours, the one we, mistakenly.

While they talk, they gently change it, adding, subtracting.
I don't believe they think they are providing comfort.
In that way they resemble us.

*In a Hundred Years Everything
Will Be Forgotten 3*, 2016
Pencil on paper, 40 x 32 cm

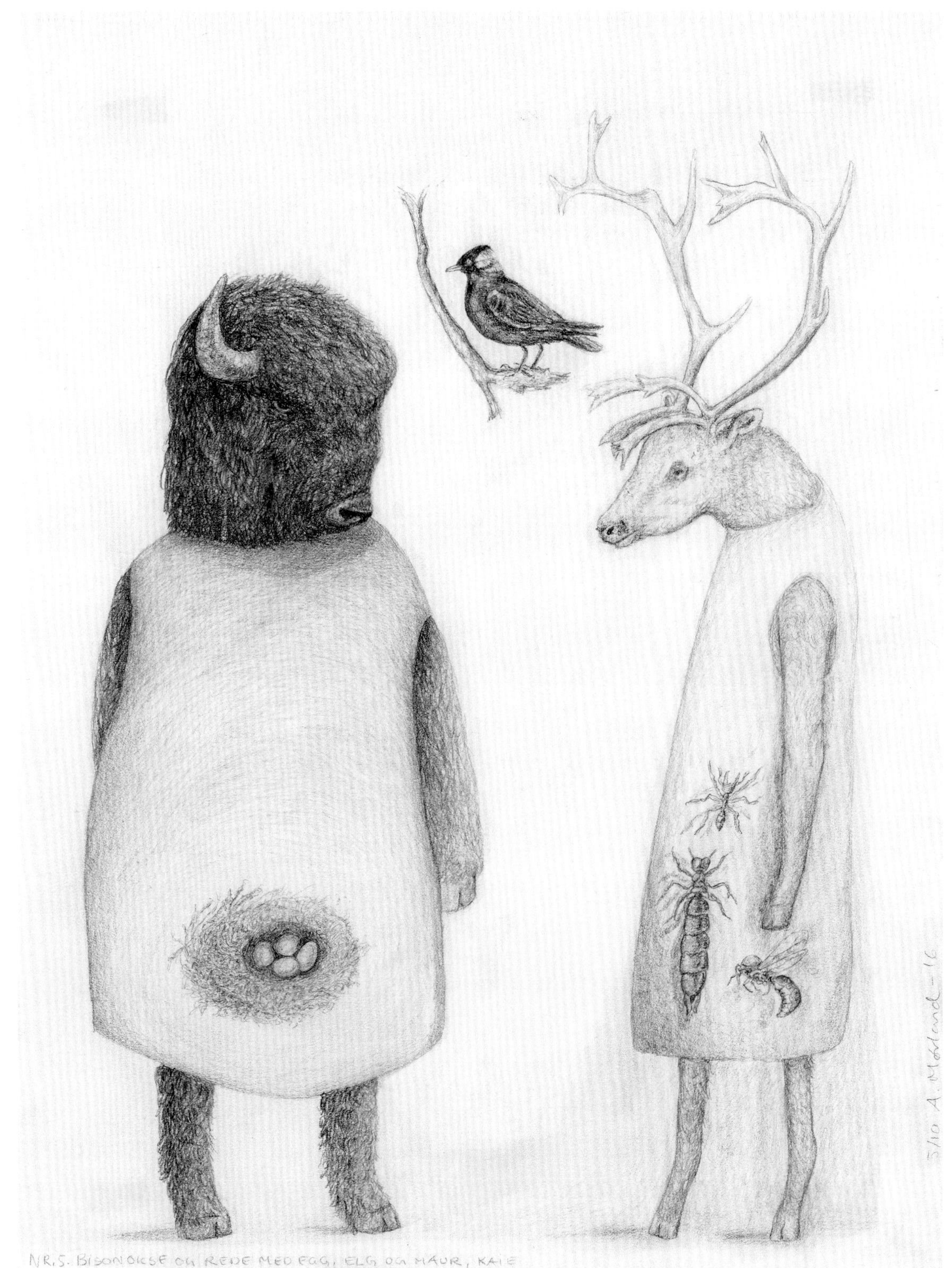

NR. 5. BISONOKSE OG REDE MED EGG, ELG OG MAUR, KAIE
5/10 A. Mørland –16

Imagine how nice it would be to live there, together.
I don't want to die, one of them says.
The other one replies.

We are still animals, we don't have to think in order
to remember. A child. We begin with a child.

Then the rain comes.
And it's raining for the first time.
The blue clay, the creek.
The child. The raw smell of love.

That morning you wake early.
The night after you don't sleep.
The light is on for a hundred years.
No one has turned it off yet.

Branch of Clouds, 2005
Oil on canvas, 130 x 130 cm

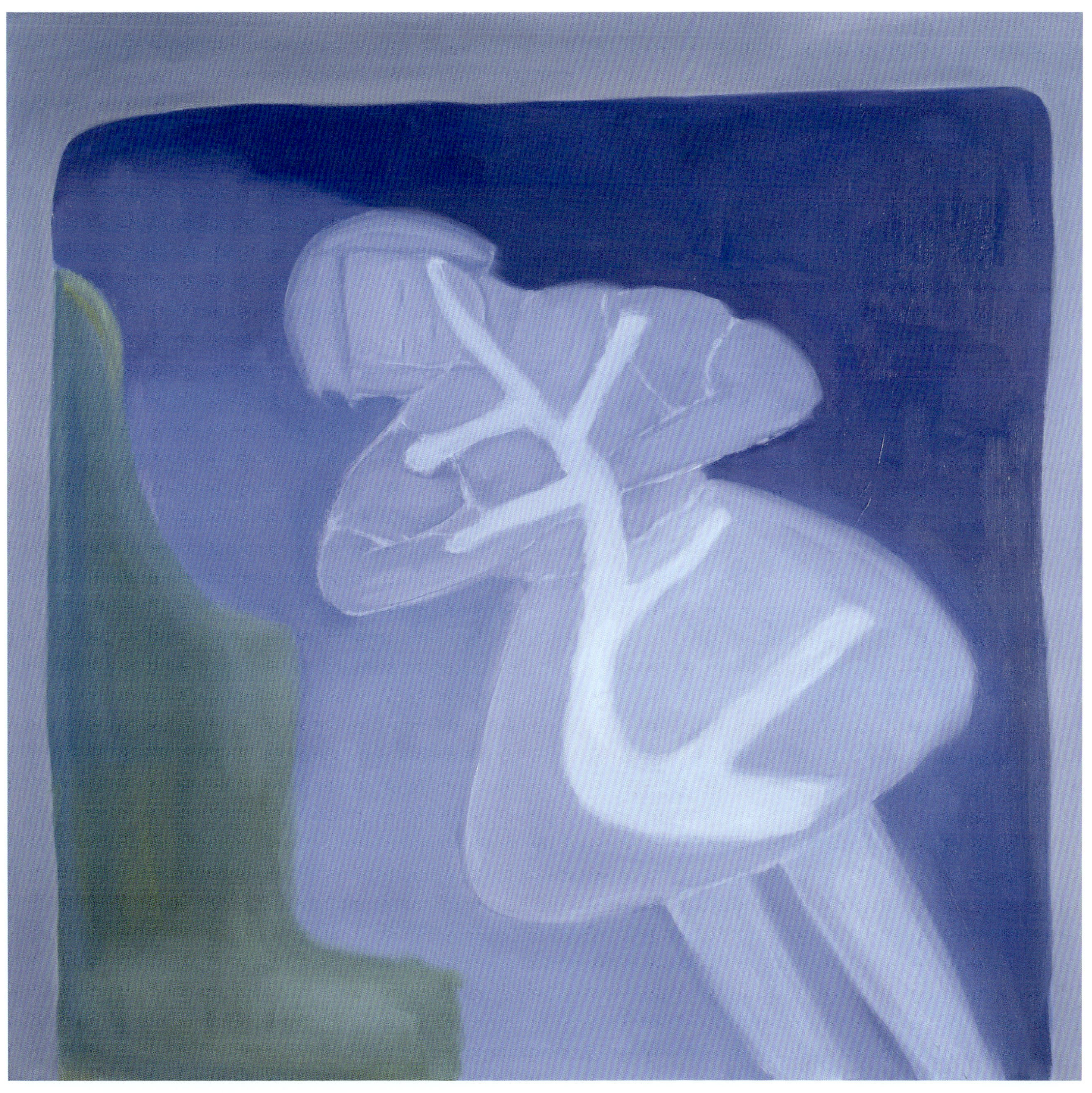

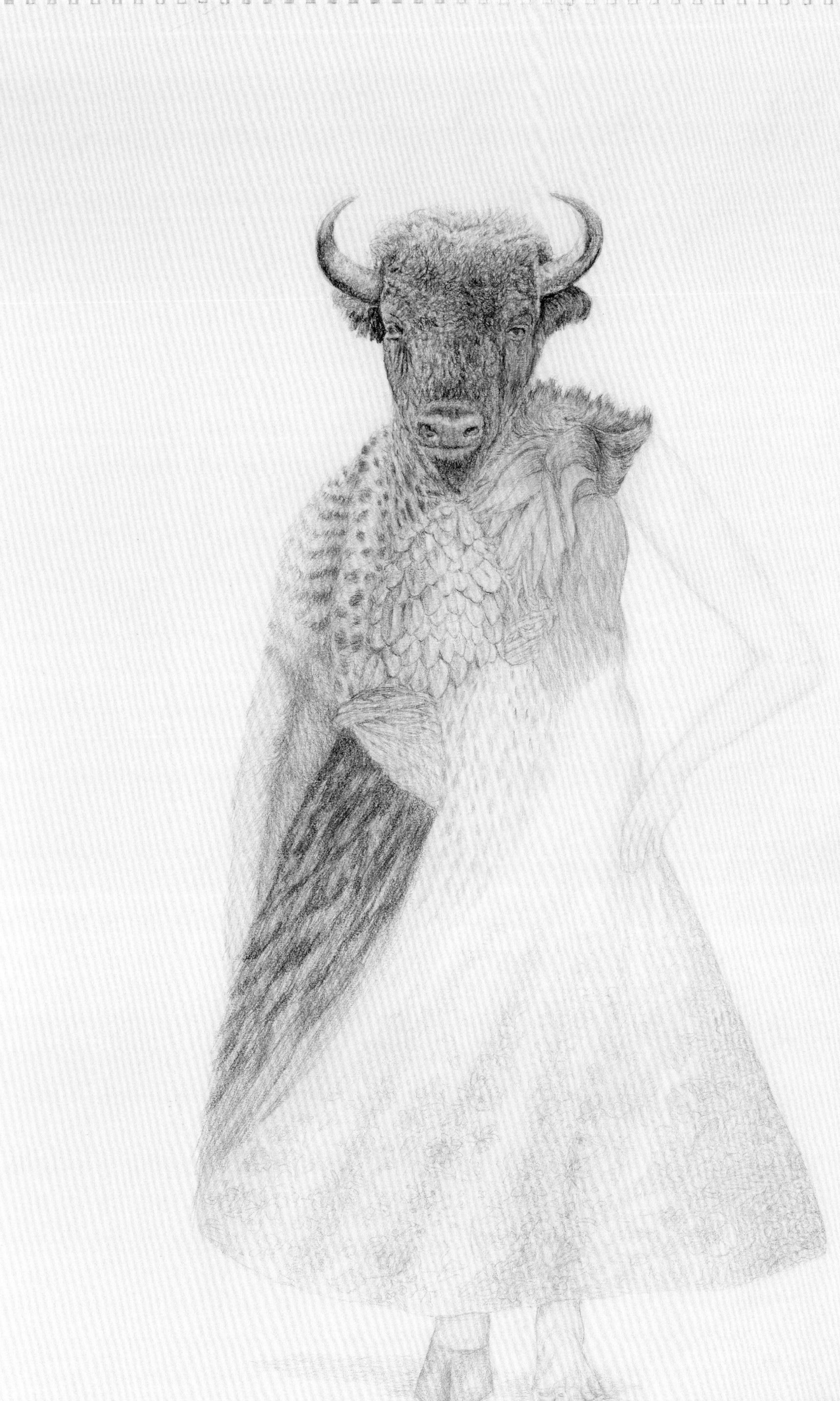

The Viewpoint: The Soul, the Dream, and a Space of Wonder

Tone Lyngstad Nyaas

Astrid Mørland (b. 1950) trained to be an artist at the Kunstgewerbeschule in Basel, Switzerland, and the National Academy of Fine Arts in Oslo. Throughout her subsequent career, she has explored art that alludes to Surrealism's associative technique and its interest in dreams and their mystical connections and juxtapositions. The fragmented body is a recurring motif in her various paintings, drawings, and installations, where the relationship between interior and exterior is suspended and where the imagery reflects themes such as ephemerality, vulnerability, and alienation. Her many interpretations of girls' dresses contrast the innocence of such clothing with an expressive, charged style of art that signals a rebellion against the conventional ideals of girlhood. Recently, Mørland has explored climate-related issues and focused on the global loss of biodiversity, a theme that is apparent in her interest in bees and in fabulous creatures that are a cross between female figures and endangered animals.

Mørland's oeuvre includes obvious references to Surrealism's interest in the subconscious, which in turn had been influenced by Sigmund Freud's psychoanalysis and dream interpretations, which provided new insight into understanding the irrational. In order to reach into the landscape of the subconscious, Surrealist artists employed an associative method in the form of automated writing and drawing, where visual connections and metamorphoses laid the groundwork for a new visual idiom. Switching one object for another, but retaining the object's recognisable form, is a recurring feature of Surrealist iconography that also permeates Mørland's visual repertoire. The same can be said of her use of human-animal hybrids, in the guise of mythic creatures, as well as the use of metamorphoses that is reflected in her visual grammar. Arguably, the enigmatic and the irrational represent the main stem of Surrealism, with automated drawing and writing and the magic of juxtaposition, in the form of collage, condensation, and displacement, representing some of the offshoots. On one of these divergent branches sit the fabled creatures that in various mythologies and legends were a symbol of humanity's subconscious dreams and of transcending physical and psychological forces. Greek mythology anthropomorphised animals, which were given human traits. These mythical creatures frequently served as metaphors that conveyed truths about corruption and the abuse of power. The Minotaur, for example – the monster with a bull's head and a human male body, the offspring of a bull and the queen of Crete – was hidden away in a labyrinth that the architect Daedalus built and that later came to symbolise the repression of a shameful family secret. The innermost halls of the maze were where they kept the hideous offspring, which was fed with young people sent from the territories Crete had conquered.[1] The Minotaur achieved a great significance in the Surrealist movement as a metaphor for the irrational, but as I will elaborate on later in the text, it also assumed a new political and symbolic meaning.

In Mørland's pictorially rich repertoire, animals figure prominently in the guise of dreamlike creatures, even as she replaces traditional structures of

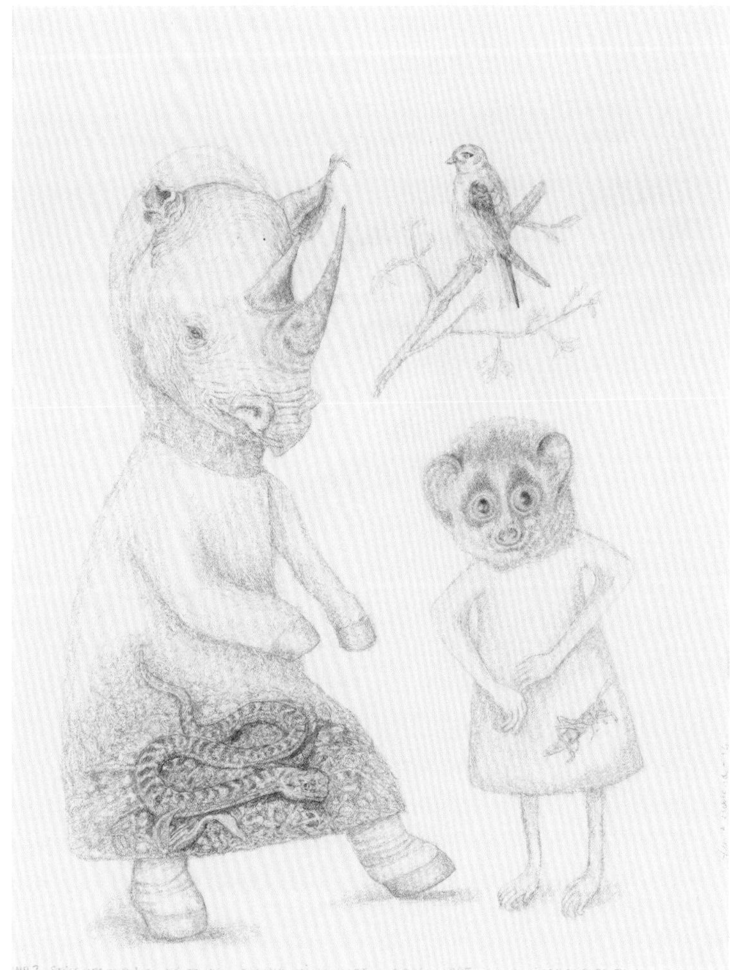

In a Hundred Years Everything
Will Be Forgotten 4, 2016
Pencil on paper, 40 x 32 cm

meaning with themes pertaining to society's repression of the massive and ongoing extinction of animal species and their habitats. For over the past fifty years, humanity's conquest of nature has exterminated two-thirds of the world's animals, something that is highly traumatic for individuals and society to take in as a reality. The ensuing collective repression of this trauma is reflected in Mørland's human-animal hybrids, which no longer symbolise the dark, uncontrollable forces of the human psyche, but rather a climate-induced sorrow and the consequences of a capitalist system that massively impacts animals, plants, and insects. Hybrid creatures thereby acquire a new relevance in contemporary discourse, even as they, akin to the mythical creatures of Surrealist art, are keenly enigmatic figures whose mystical representation of natural life cannot be reduced to a purely political content.

Surrealism's arrangements of elements from highly diverse spheres of life was elevated to an aesthetic strategy already in the 1920s. Human-animal hybrids represented an essential part of the vocabulary of this new language and are clearly present in René Magritte's painting *The Collective Invention* (1934), where we see a helpless, stranded creature that is the reverse of a traditional mermaid, with the upper body (from the abdomen up) being a fish and the rest being a woman. André Breton provided an ideological framework for the aesthetic strategy of condensation and displacement in his *Manifeste du surréalisme* (1924), which is clearly related to how the Surrealist movement developed into a progressive counter-culture opposed to the emergence of National Socialism in Germany, Franco's dictatorship in Spain, and

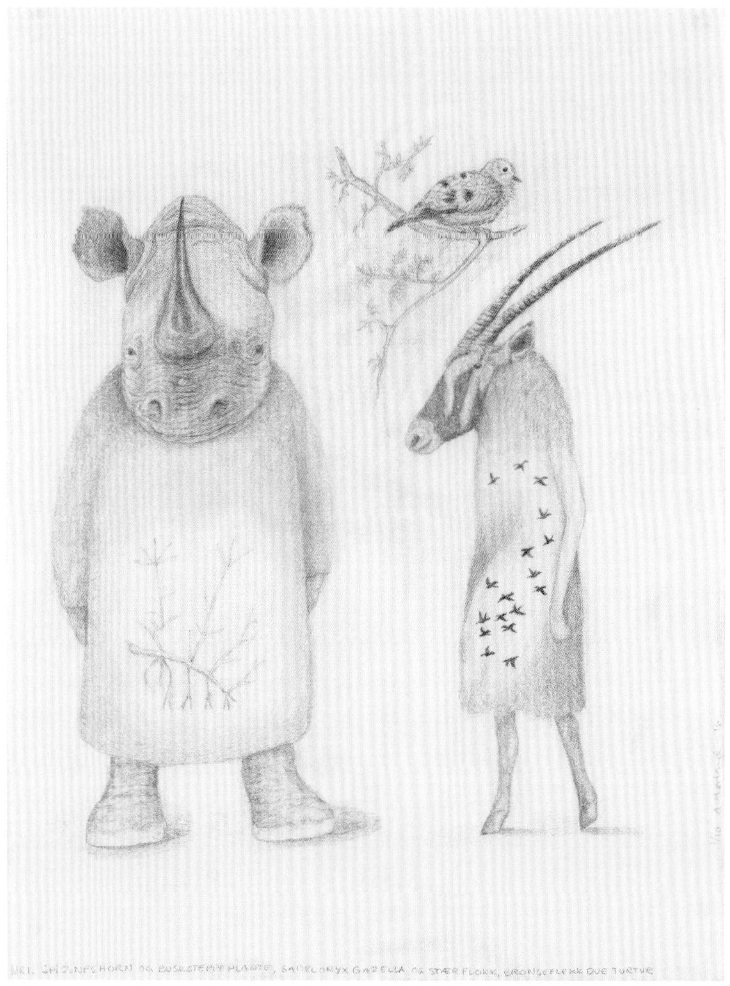

the increasingly Stalinist regime of the Soviet Union. The Surrealists fought
for an anti-Eurocentric worldview, promoted anti-racist attitudes, and showed
an increasing interest in art from indigenous populations, pre-Christian cultures, and ancient myths and legends. They rebelled against the war industry
and were critical of technological development and the increasing industri-
alisation of nature.[2] Their protest was also aimed at the conventional social
structures that had yielded to the destructive results of military force. By
expressing poetic imagery from the subconsciousness's wellspring, the Surrealists reclaimed a vulnerable existential position and individual freedom.
Breton viewed the transcendentality of dreams as an inexhaustible reservoir
of uncensored impulses and ideas that had the power to revolutionise society. These ideals were articulated in a language that was inspired by Sigmund
Freud and psychoanalysis, which celebrated the subconscious, cultivated the
Oedipus myth, and delved beneath the surface of society's rational order.[3]
Various techniques, such as the juxtaposition of surprising constellations,
were developed to liberate suppressed impulses, as exemplified by the poet
the Comte de Lautréamont's famous statement that the ideal was to create
something as beautiful as the random encounter between a sewing machine
and an umbrella on a dissection table. In Mørland's works, viewers do indeed
encounter surprising juxtapositions and a bending of the normal expectations
associated with the object's presence. These works often hide a second, enigmatic existence that only reveals itself upon closer inspection. According
to Salvador Dalí's texts, this ontology from the labyrinths of the mind is a

set of pictures that can refer to the same objective clarity, permanence, and conviction as the outer world, the phenomenological reality.[4] This degree of verisimilitude comes strongly to the fore in Mørland's objects, where what may from afar seem like a pink tulle dress is in fact dripping wax, or where an ornamental pattern turns out rather to be crawling insects.

This encounter between the innocent, the conventional, and the unnerving can be traced back to the inspiration from Meret Oppenheim's art, which Mørland became acquainted with while studying in Basel. A seminal example of the meeting between objects from highly dissimilar spheres of life can be found in Oppenheim's *Le Déjeuner en fourrure* (*The Luncheon in Fur*, 1936), where a teacup and its accessories have been lined with the fur of a Chinese gazelle. Even though the cup and the fur belong to different spheres, they are transformed in relation to bodily desire. The cup is given life, while the fur's delicate softness is a reminder of the seductive allure of wearing the fur of an exotic animal. The invitation to drink from the cup, on the other hand, inspires only nausea and disgust. This duality between attraction and repulsion creates a structure of compressed, contradictory meaning. André Breton immediately encouraged Oppenheim to participate in an exhibition of Surrealist sculpture at the Galerie Charles Ratton, which resulted in the Museum of Modern Art in New York acquiring the piece. Remaining an icon of the Surrealist era, Oppenheim's fur cup is one of the most quoted and reprinted works from the period.

Much of Freud's terminology has become a fixture of modern culture and altered humanity's self-image and attitude towards dreams, repression, desire, the death drive, and sexuality. This change in outlook on the human psyche is comparable with how *On the Origin of Species* by Charles Darwin, the founder of modern evolutionary biology, came to revolutionise our perceptions of humankind's place in nature. The principal idea advanced in *The Interpretation of Dreams* from 1899 is that dreams variously express wish fulfilments and repressions, and that the internal censorship of dreams that seeks to protect us from their unsettling content will sometimes show cracks. And Freud's analyses of the processes that shape our dreams may in fact be germane to Mørland's hybrid, mystical creatures. One such process is "overdetermination", whereby a person in a dream may be the sum total of many different persons that the individual experiences in their life. According to this logic, the identity these images lays bare is fluid in space and time, since a figure can assume various roles and morph from one position to another. In the subject's striving to maintain a self-image with a fairly permanent constitution, dreams challenge these limitations with a voice that speaks from another dimension than the rational I – what Freud calls *eine andere Schauplatz*, "another scene". Viewers find themselves in a similar position in regard to Mørland's art, where people, animals, and plants merge together in hybrids that hark back to a primeval, mythical era. In these works, the various hybrids are not merely the sum total of other creatures that morph together and dissolve the one-dimensional

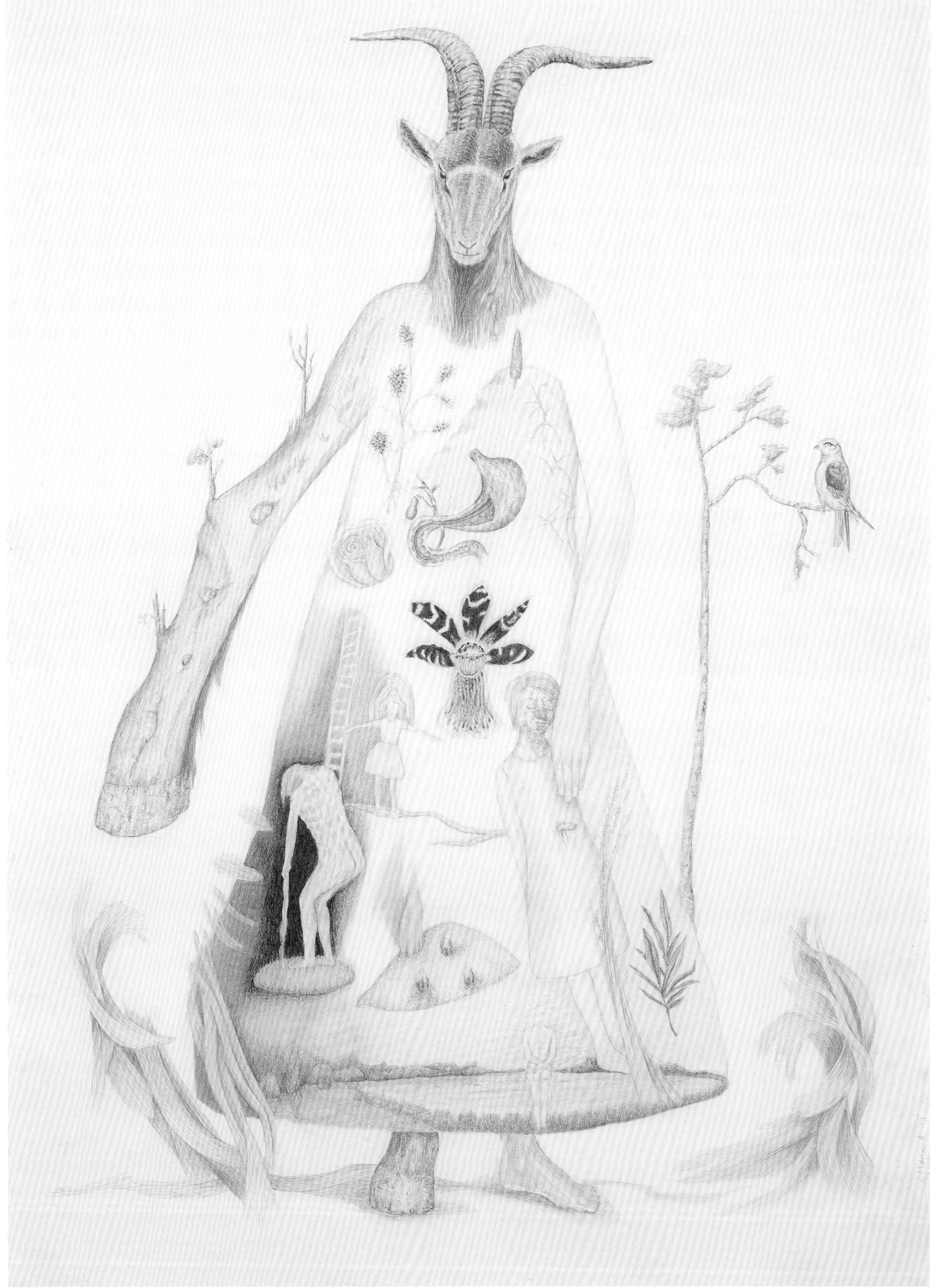

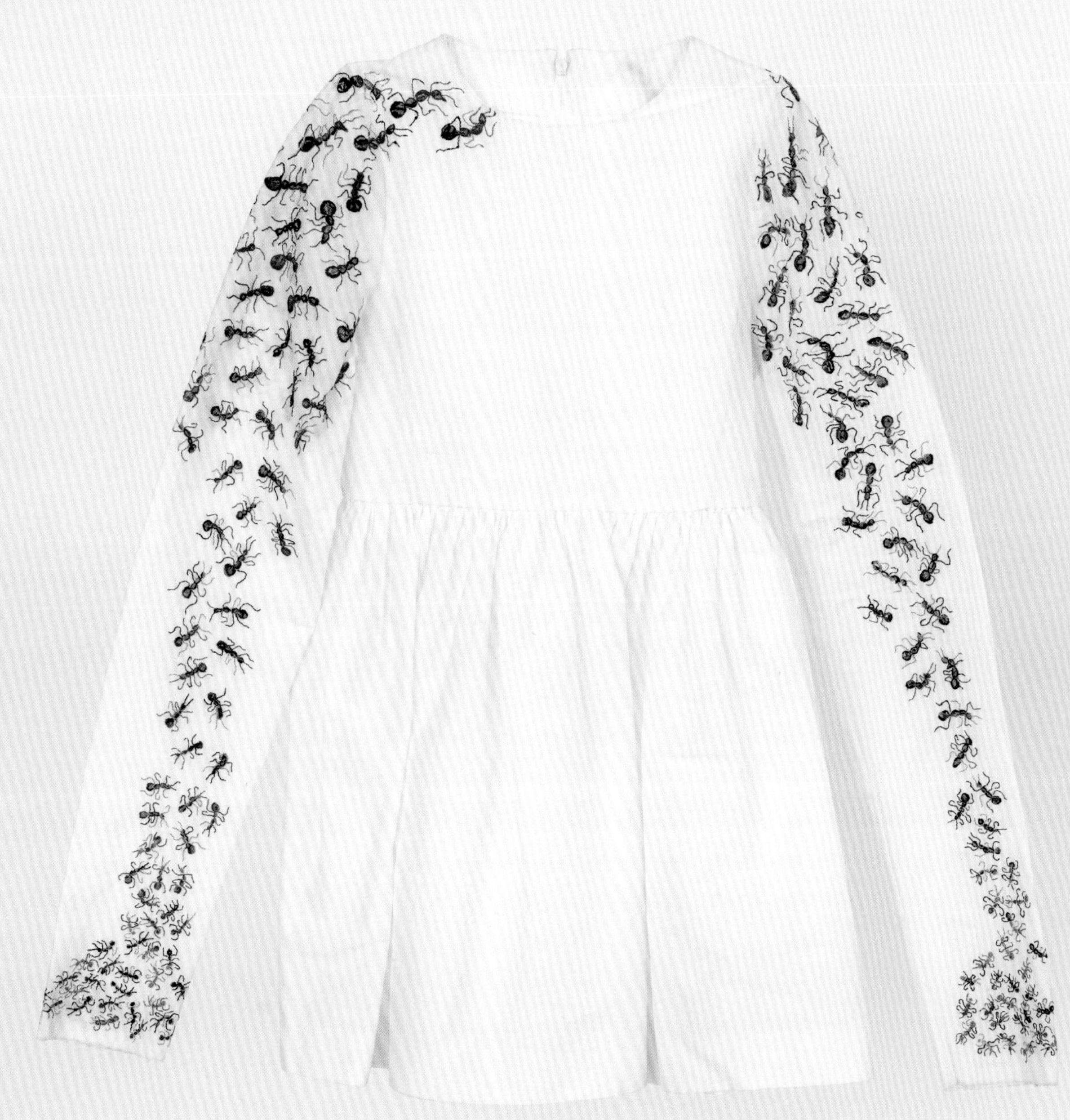

picture, but rather create displacements that transcend space and time. This reminder is intensified by how nature is treated not as a set of reified objects outside of human existence but as an essential part of humanity's psychological structures. This inseparable symbiosis manifests itself metaphorically in Mørland's art, where bodies either branch off into the elements of nature or are incorporated into the landscape as its natural extension. In *The Last Guardian*, the buck's head refers to an extinct species, with the buck standing watch over the last remnant of biodiversity as recorded in detailed depictions of plants and flowers that together resemble an herbarium. This meticulous account also alludes to the body's inner organs, where the scientific gaze's categorisation and acquisition of knowledge of natural phenomena is transfigured into a subjective landscape. Paradoxically enough, it is precisely this rational control that is abolished in these hybrid figures, which challenge us to mirror ourselves in animals and plants as an essential part of our own subconscious or pre-conscious nature. Considering how species are becoming extinct ever more rapidly, these themes in Mørland's art raise a vital question. How does the mass extinction and destruction of animal habitats affect our own mental health and introspection? Are we capable of relating to animals with humility and respect as an essential part of ourselves, and of viewing ourselves as belonging to the ecological world that underlies our very existence? Mørland calls attention to the society-wide repression that smoulders beneath the surface of a rational, instrumental social order that places capitalism at its centre as an ideology, for an increasing exploitation of nature. Her shamanistic, inexplicable hybrid figures allude to a loss of not only animal species, of not only biodiversity, but also of a part of ourselves. And if dreams can be characterised as the habitat of repression, Mørland's pictures depict a state where humanity is united with its fellow animals in a common hope of salvation. This concept manifests itself in the dress's frieze, where we see people, trees, plants, and animals continuing to mutate and coalesce.

Freud ascribed a great therapeutic value to dreams, calling them "the royal road to the subconscious". Dreams frequently reflect memories from the immediate past and from snatches of the day's events, which are typically mixed in with the latent drives of the human psyche, as our self-control breaks down and taboo emotions such as forbidden desire, angst, and guilt appear in surreal disguises. Mørland illuminates this aspect of dreaming, and in certain works her technique resembles what Freud calls "condensation", which in dreams is a process that mixes together contradictory emotions such as anxiety and admiration, or repulsion and attraction.[5] In *Ant Dress with Long Sleeves* and the series of drawings titled *Skin & Orchid* (1–5), viewers see constellations that pulsate along the contrasts between the seductive and the repulsive. The conventional perception of beauty and innocence manifests itself in richly detailed depictions of orchids, while skin diseases are in the process of dissolving and eroding the faces. *Ant Dress with Long Sleeves* features a condensation

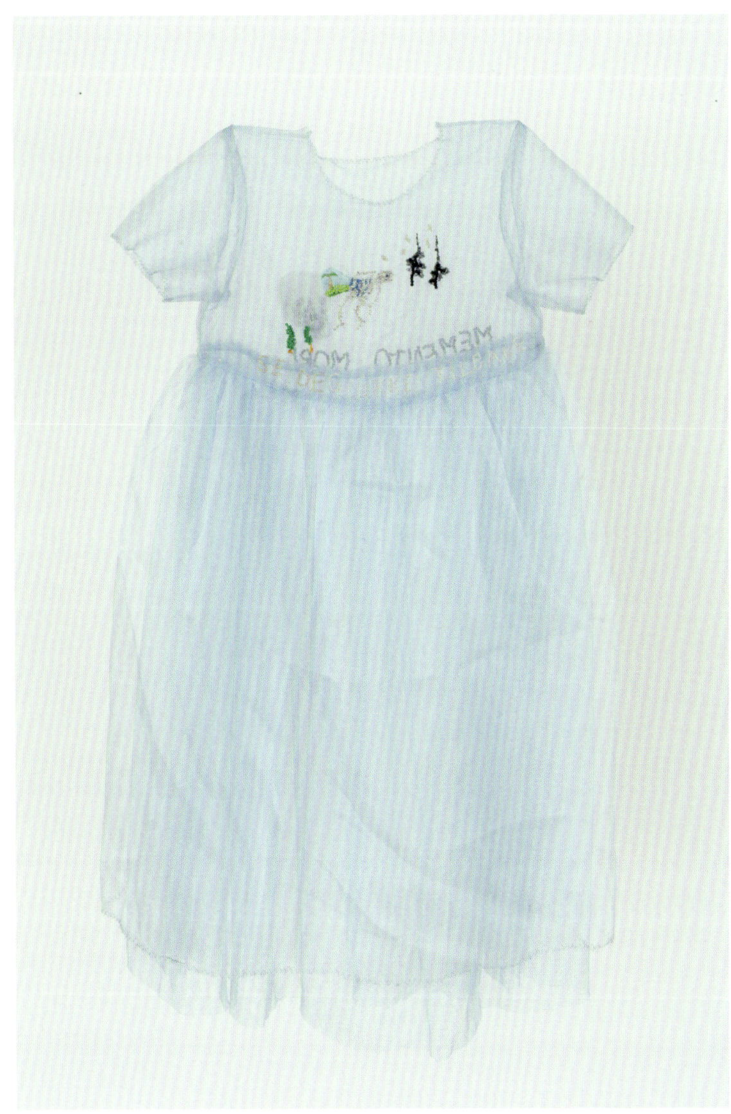

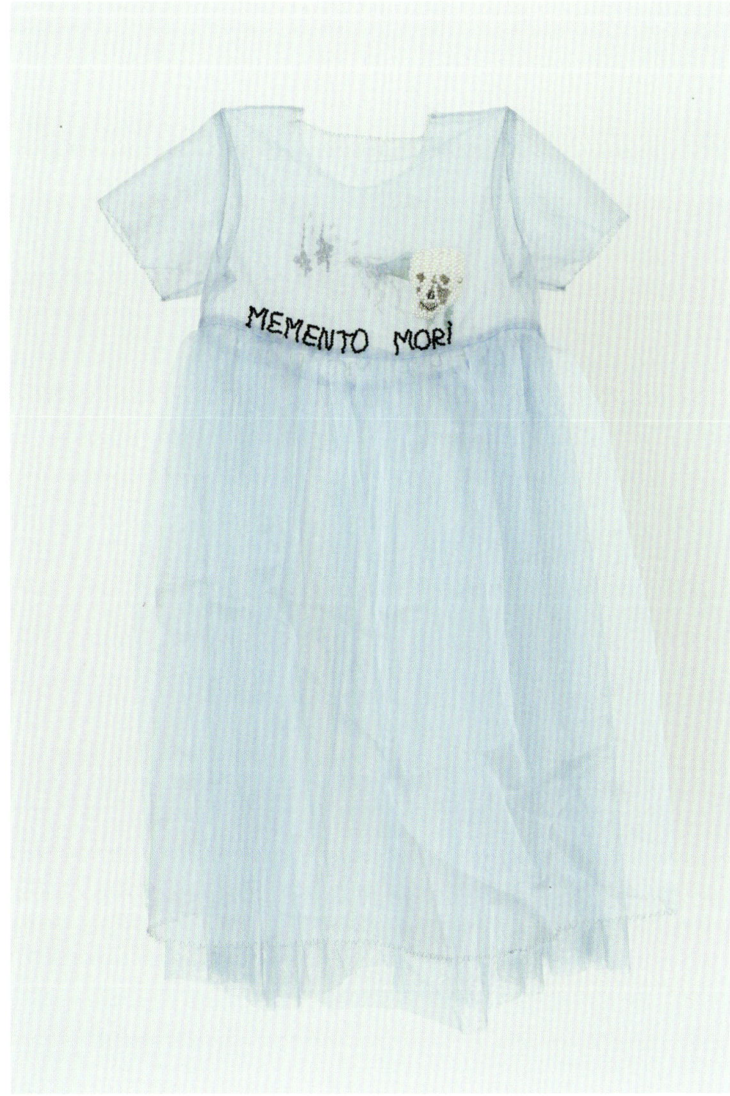

where two diverging emotions are compressed into a single object, as a flimsy, transparent dress is invaded by black ants crawling up the unusually long sleeves. The ants have come dangerously close to the neck and chest areas, something that is accentuated by perspectivist displacements, where the ants are gradually magnified as they crawl up the upper sleeves and shoulder area. This conjures up an anxious, hallucinatory perspective, if not a phobia, where the beautiful and the ornamental meet the irrationality of fear. The contrast between the chalk-white cotton fabric and the ants that threaten chaos and a loss of control is also expressed by the insects being depicted as fingers and tiny hands joining together at the lower end of the sleeves.

The concept of displacement is another central technique that Surrealist artists employed and that is also reflected in Mørland's oeuvre. It is a type of transferral or shift, as when the fear of a given creature, such as an animal or a person, is reassigned to something else. Fetishism pertains to a similar process where the desire for a person is transferred to a thing associated with this person. René Magritte's paintings typically feature displacements, for example in works where faces are hidden by foreign objects such as an apple, pumpkin, or sex organ. Faces that are veiled by textiles, such as in *The Lovers* (1928), can be traced back to a traumatic childhood experience when his mother committed suicide when he was fourteen. The sight of his dead mother with her night-

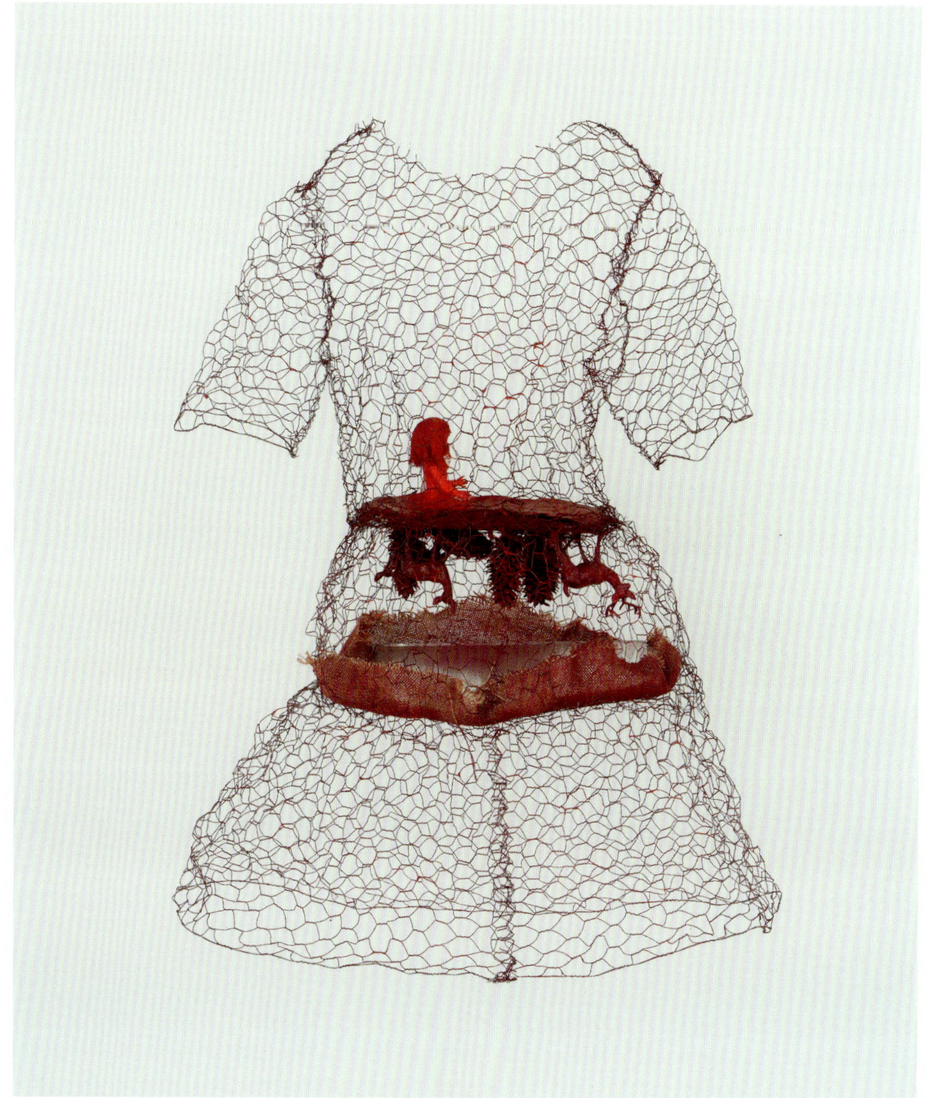

Memento mori (front and back), 2019
Mixed media object, 60 x 40 cm

Red Wildwood, 2007
Mixed media object, 60 x 40 cm

gown wrapped around her head as her body was recovered from the River Sambre would inform countless of his works, both directly and indirectly. Like-wise, Mørland's loss of her three-year-old daughter Linn in a drowning accident has had an impact on her own art. Certain works refer directly to this accident, while others deal indirectly with the loss and sorrow. This reminiscence is stylised and abstracted, even as it is integrated into other astonishing narra-tives that invite engagement, empathy, and identification. The artist thereby generalises a painful experience that in itself provides deeper insights into human suffering, in a society where emotions are untroubling, sanitised com-modities that promote apathy rather than empathy and pathos.[6] *Red Dress, Black Roses* features a condensation of conflicting elements that generate a sense of wonder that does not result in a clear-cut answer. An expressionless woman is depicted in line with the feminine ideals expressed in the dresses of the 1950s, while her face suffers from a skin disease. The blackness of the depicted roses, which traditionally symbolise beauty and ephemerality, have imbued them with an additional undercurrent of melancholia. The viewer's gaze is led to the right and into an abyss, while on the left an island may be seen where a tree is growing, providing hope.

Many of Mørland's sculptures use girls' dresses as a form, such as *Grey Fly Dress*, where the transparent, delicate girls' dress that signals innocence

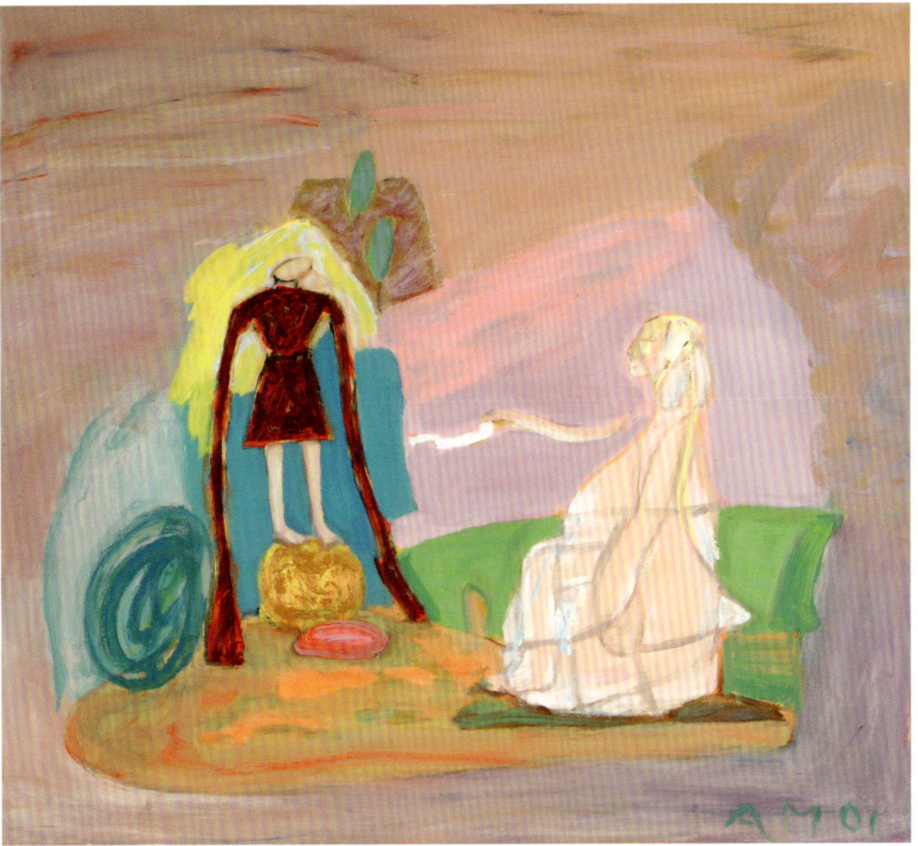

has two dead, oversized flies embroidered on the front, in the areas of the chest and abdomen. The textile sculptures are characterised by their illusionist effects, which cause a sense of disorientation upon a closer look: from a distance, the wax may seem like silk, the mussels like chainmail, the moss like velvet, and the dead flies like brooches. Certain objects have been outfitted with a natural material that evokes camouflage, the need for protection, or assimilation. Transforming the objects' substance destabilises their normal "ontological status", thus promoting new meanings and associations. Dreams and visions are visualised through "the magic of juxtaposition", entirely in line with the therapeutic techniques of psychoanalysis, which aimed at raising the subconscious to the surface.[7]

Inside out: the fragmented body and the poetics of transience

A consistent theme in Mørland's works is the interplay between the inner and the outer spheres, and between whole and fragmented bodies. In *Spring Summer, Mother Daughter*, for example, red-and-white egg shapes mounted on a young female figure conspicuously evoke female organs of fertility. The shapes have been exteriorised as a decorative supplement to the dress's surrealist design. Such a suspension of the boundaries between the outer and inner body is visualised by the inner organs moving around on the outside of the body or the body's interior being exposed. In the painting *On a Stone of Gold*, a girl is placed on a height; as in *Mother Sleeves*, the dress's extended sleeves express an attempt to grasp something unreachable, a situation that provokes an aching desire. A white figure sits in front of the girl: she is partly out of sight, but branches extend from her body to bridge the separation. In *Gesture*, by contrast, the figure engages in a joyous, dancing movement.

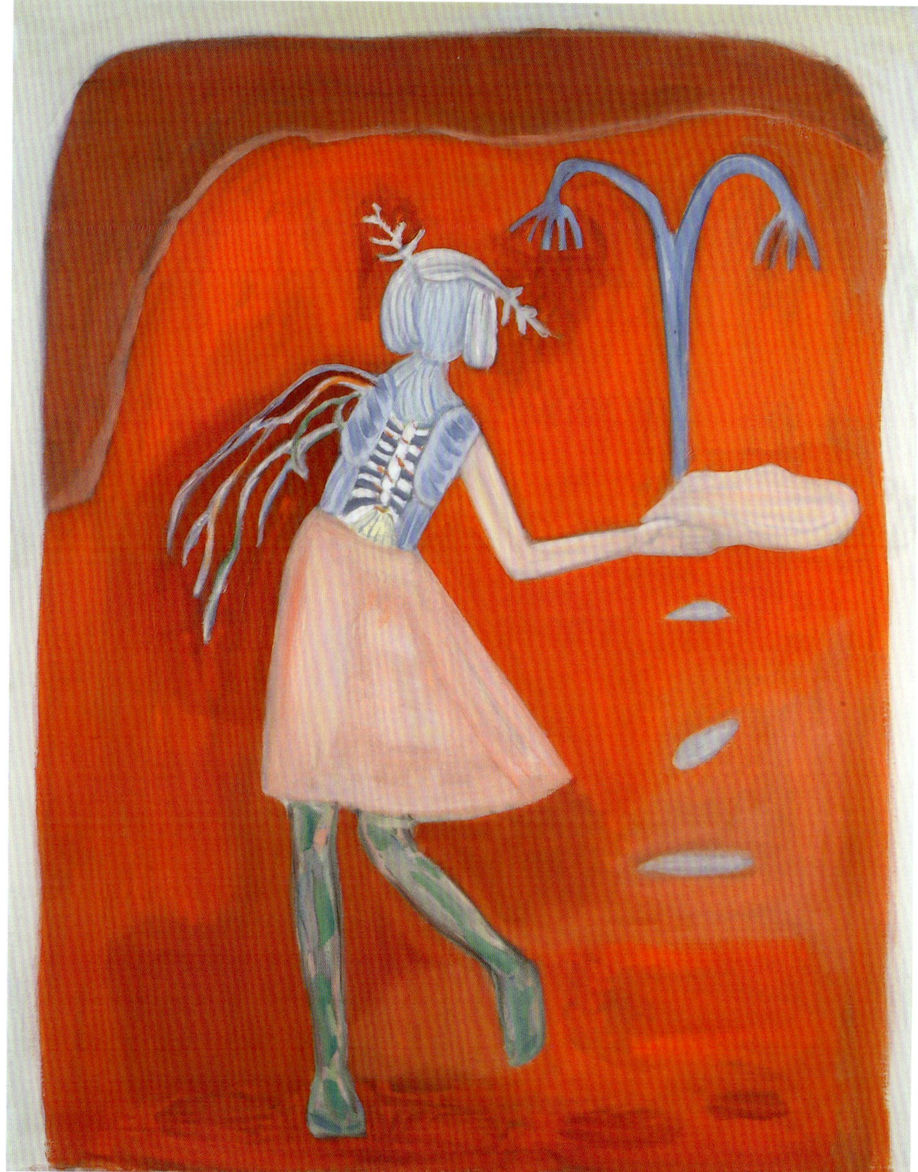

She holds up two shapes that resemble a hybrid between fallopian tubes and roots, carrying them forth like a sacrifice in a way that evokes the tradition of votive gifts. Such religious donations of inner organs, or rather representations of inner organs, were a well-known practice in the ancient world, one that is still maintained in the Catholic Church today. In the vicinity of the healing god Asclepius's sanctuary in Greece, several ceramic objects representing body parts and inner organs have been found, placed there by devotees in antiquity showing their gratitude for becoming pregnant or being cured of a disease.[8] This association with votive gifts is particularly prominent in *Porcelain Arms*, which features a subdued palette that affords the painting a transparent, blurry appearance. The hip area serves as a plinth for the torso, which itself seems to be made of bark. In front of the torso hang five arms that evoke sculptural fragments; these sacrificial gifts make up a chain, but they also incorporate the form of a dress. Theorists such as Hal Foster and Rosalind E. Krauss view such fragmented bodies in connection with the theory of abjection launched in the mid-1990s by psychoanalyst and author Julia Kristeva.[9] Works by Kiki Smith that deal with the fragmented body and bodily fluids were among those interpreted through the prism of Kristeva's texts.[10] It is interesting to relate

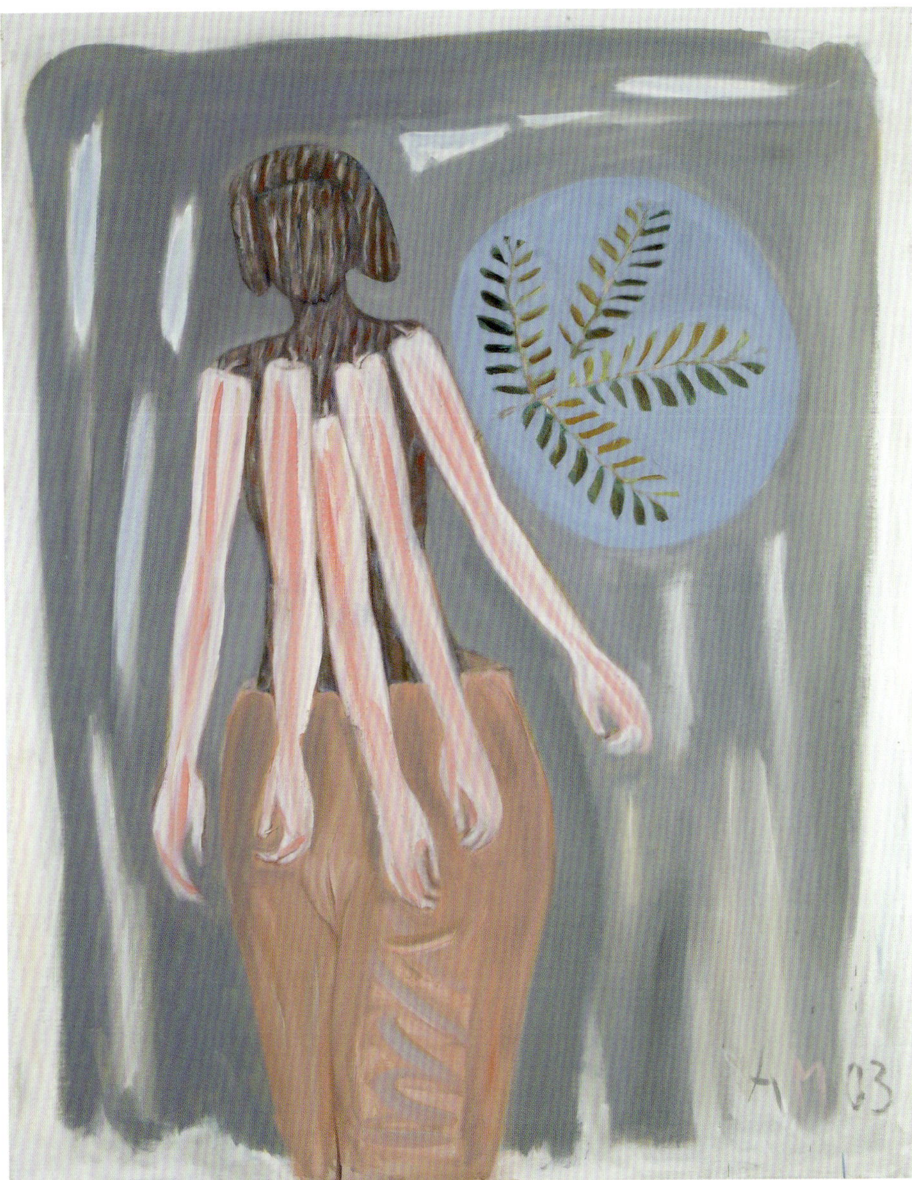

Mørland's *Porcelain Arms* to how Kiki Smith incorporated the votive tradition in her own installations of metal and plaster casts of hands and arms, whose fragmentation highlights society's alienation of the body's biological processes and impermanence, an alienation that is culturally conditioned.

The ambivalence between the attractive and the repulsive can serve as a general key to Mørland's three-dimensional works, where decorative objects prove to be foreboding signs of repressed conflicts. These contradictory forces are visualised through a poetic approach and distinctive complexity in regard to idea, form, and materials. The motif of the child's dress in Mørland's works may give rise to associations with Paula Santiago's sculptures, which often portrayed children as symbolising ingenuousness and vulnerability. Santiago works with children's clothes, typically in gossamer-light paper that she embroiders with her own hair.[11] The contrast between the innocent, vulnerable, and repulsive also employs a type of illusionism that is akin to Mørland's art. In Mørland's *Inside Out*, the materiality may from afar look like silk, though viewers who take a closer look will discover dripping wax that evokes skin and blood. The interior has bled out into the exterior, disrupting the pattern's innocent form. Turning the inside out is a type of condensation that is to be

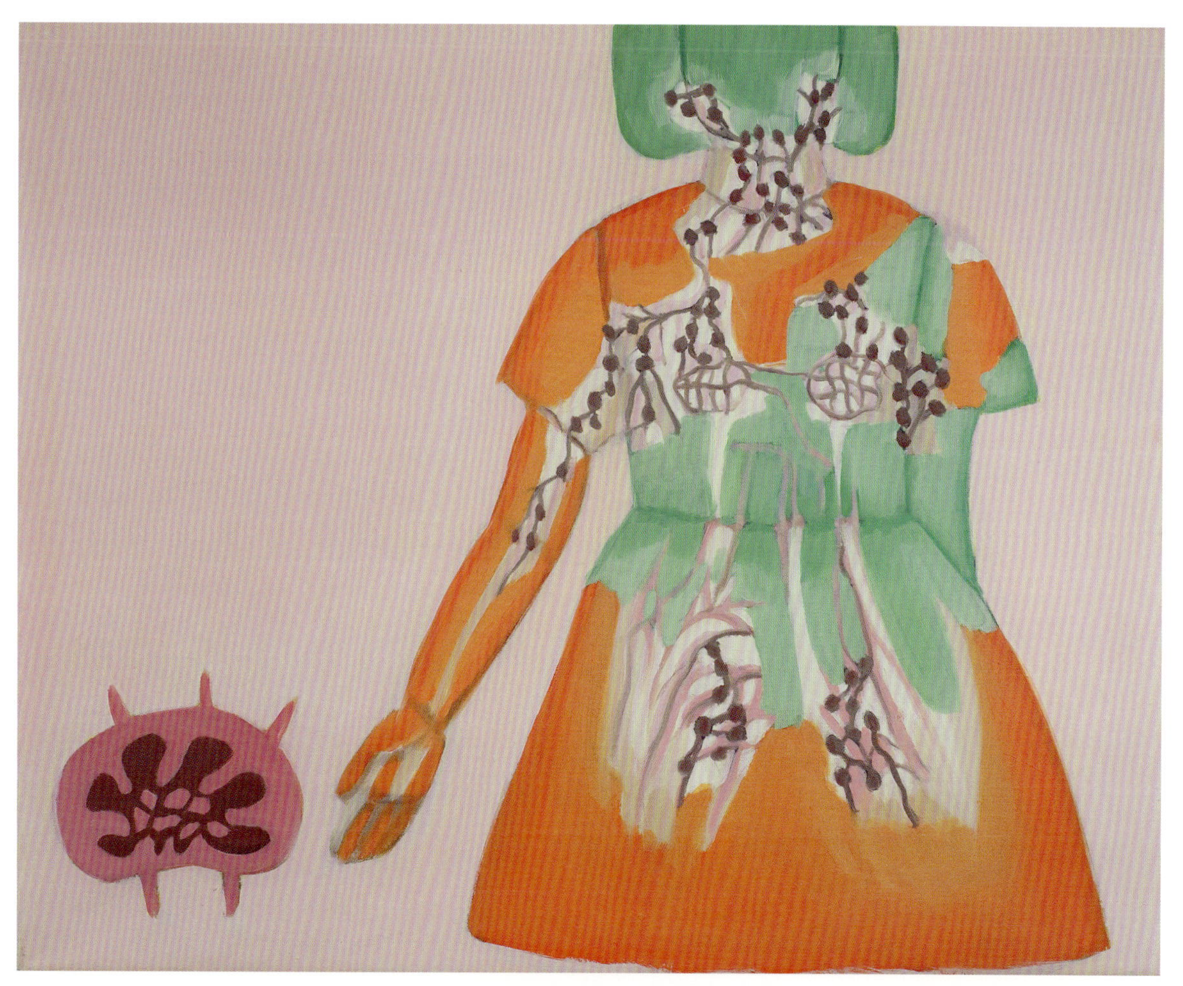

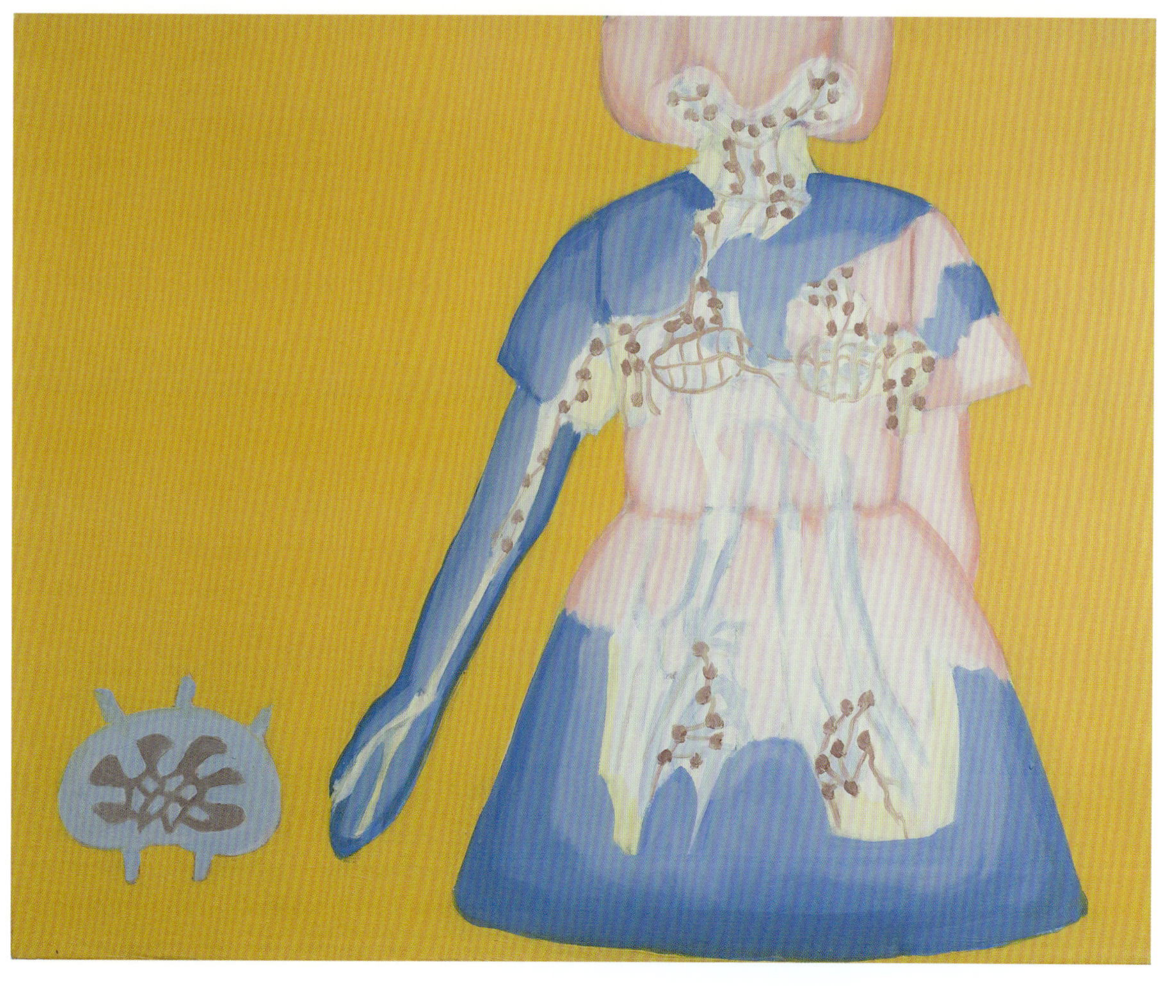

found in many of Mørland's works, such as in the series of paintings titled *Here Is My Dress*, where the matrix is repeated in a manner that alludes to the body's interior as tendons, skeletons, and molecular structures. Elements that belong to the clinical rationality of scientific research have been drawn into an irrational universe. A recurring theme in Mørland's career is her willingness to discuss taboo-laden areas of society and appreciate vulnerability. Such vulnerability is frequently misunderstood as weakness, which in turn is associated with alienation or seclusion. Contempt of weakness, or human vulnerability, is one of the greatest challenges in a fiercely competitive social structure that many of the world's systems have internalised as their primary political ideology. Human vulnerability ties in with the vulnerability of nature and the wider ramifications of species extinction, revealing how human existence is inextricably linked to nature. In a society where everything is open to exploitation and can be traded away, vulnerability is given little attention. But it continues to flow violently under the radar of society, manifesting itself in art as an essential part of the human condition.

The girl, the dress, and the latent rebellion

Mørland moved from Flekkefjord to New York in the 1950s and has reworked her memories from this stay, not least through the dresses, which hark back to the showy, bright-red tulle dress – known as *Amerika-kjolen*, "the American dress" – that created such a buzz when it was sent to Norway from American relatives. In all its pinkness, the dress alludes to a middle-class ideal of girlhood that makes the viewer think of an oversized doll's dress. This objectivisation and idealised approach is subject to a renegotiation and intervention through the dress's pattern being added surprising materials such as shells, moss, and wax. The glamorous is especially reflected in the object *Cute Dress with Dolls*, where the middle-class ideal of girlhood reflects a gaze that wants to view the little girl through the outline of an overgrown doll. This object-gaze is returned in the encounter with the dress's material of trickling wax.[12] The 1970s-era painting *Doll*, which depicted a broken doll, heralded the beginning of this theme of returning the conventional, desiring gendered gaze. For when Astrid Mørland employs the innocent, 1950s-style dress as the basic form for playing around with a mix of shifting substances, she queries the relationship between handed-down conventions regarding gender and personal freedom. In essence, the dress paintings seek to lay bare an inner mental landscape, for when something is turned inside out, the protective element exposes its trembling vulnerability. Such transfiguration was a common method in Surrealist art, as for example seen in Dalí's liquified, dripping clocks or Meret Oppenheim's fur-lined tea service. This metamorphosis of the object's functionality and materiality is occupied by inner, subjective mental images, in the way dreams shift and transcend reality by destabilising their given ontology. *Black Christmas* features a transparent dress in red and green tulle, encompassing a number

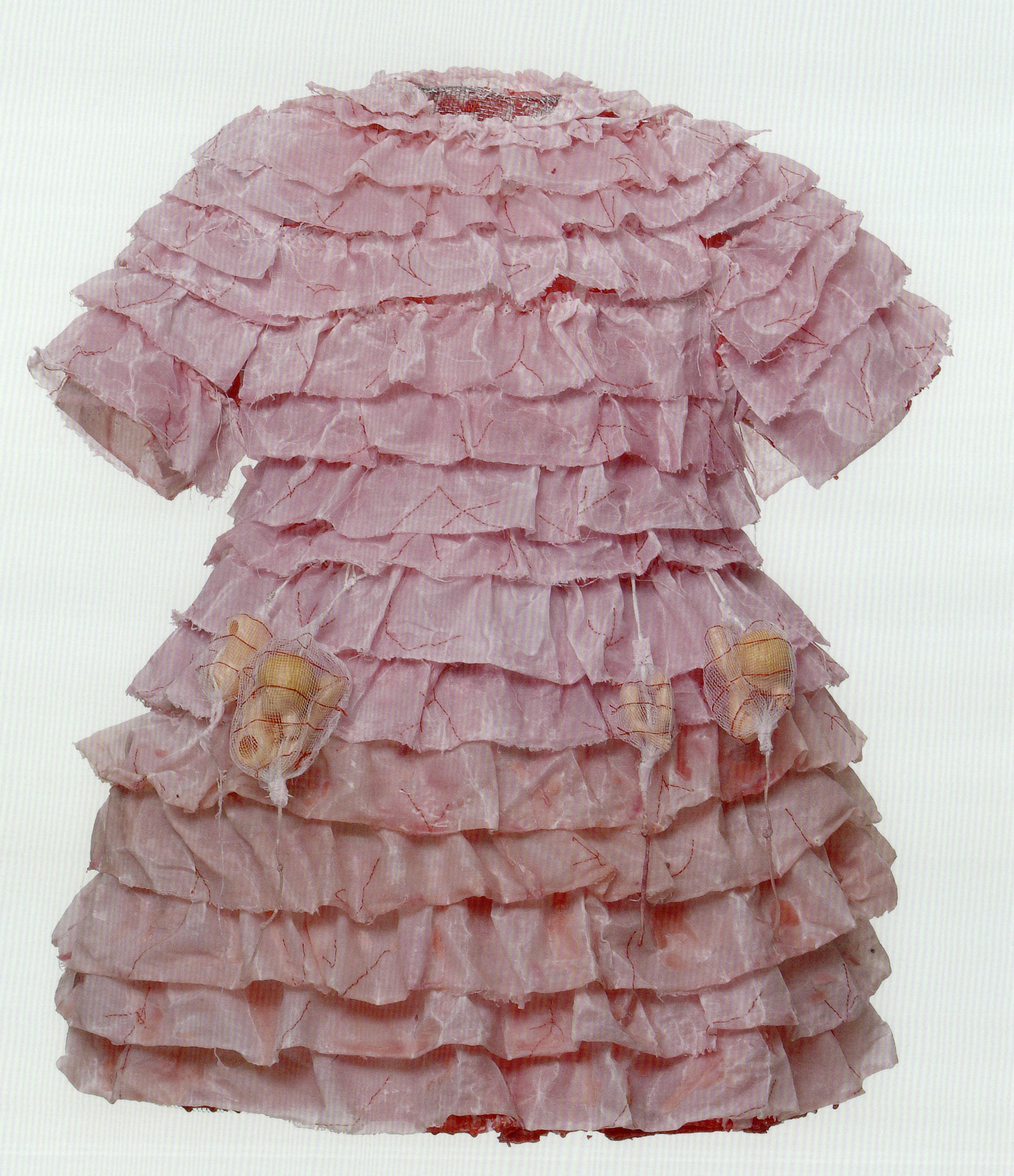

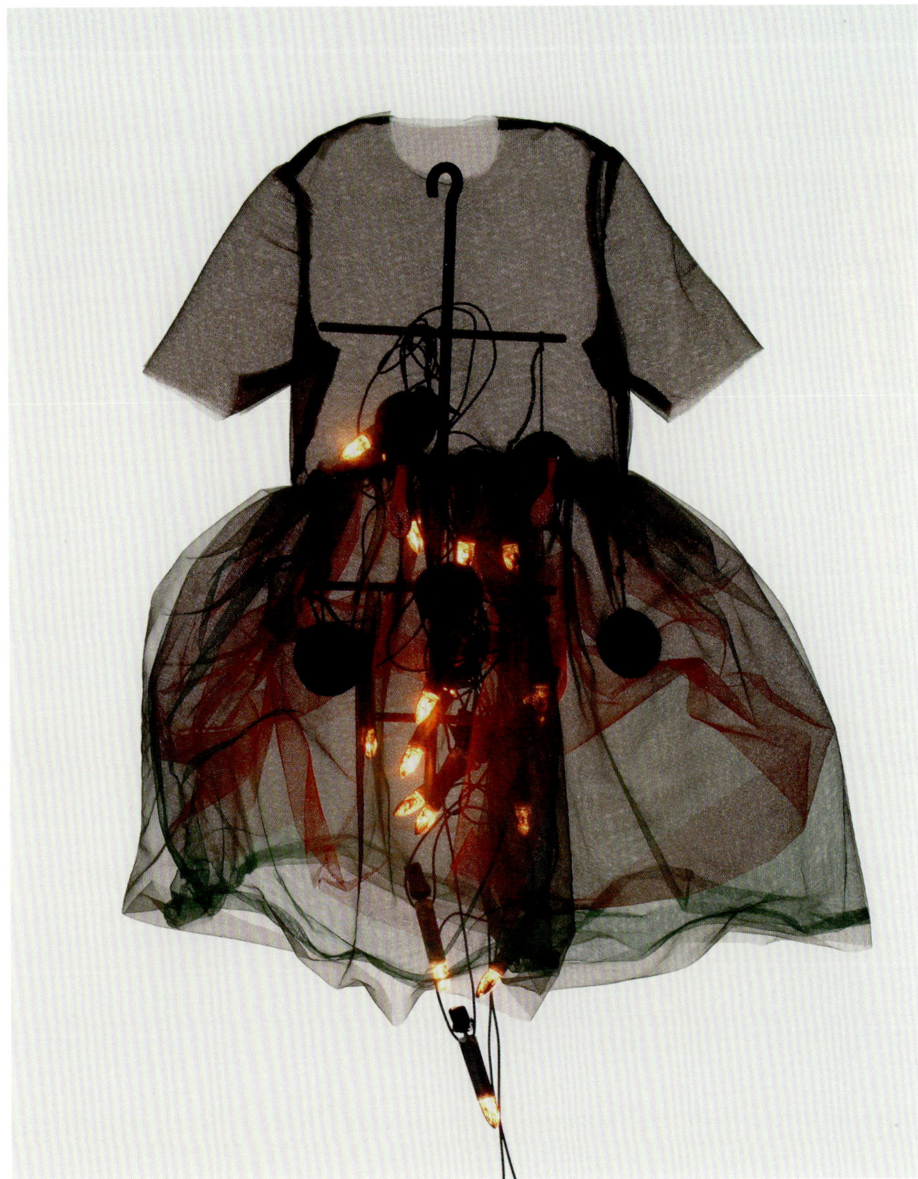

Black Christmas, 2004
Mixed media object, 65 x 40 cm

of Christmas tree lights that have been painted black. The baubles that call to mind Christmas decorations have been replaced by black balls of yarn, a subtle effect that shifts the meaning from recognisable signs to metaphors of a subjective state of mind. These allusions to Christmas festivities, to the most symbolically charged holiday on the Norwegian calendar, hint at broken expectations and a sense of collective coercion. Similar holiday symbols, in the guise of black and greyish Christmas tree lights, flags, balloons, and birth-day candles, are materials that are integrated in several other sculptures with the same theme. The transparent dresses can be interpreted as harbingers of future womanhood, articulating a type of objectivisation that evokes the underlying conflicts in Nora's revolt in Henrik Ibsen's *A Doll's House*. Ibsen's play associates death and destruction with Christmas celebrations in general and the Christmas tree in particular. Nora looks forward to decorating the tree for her family with glitter, stars, and candy, especially since it is the first Christmas the family will be celebrating with its head financially above water. While preparing for Christmas, she thinks about her husband, the bank direc-tor Torvald, whose refined aesthetical taste induces him to idealise a world of purity without death and decay, without the hideous or repulsive. In giggling

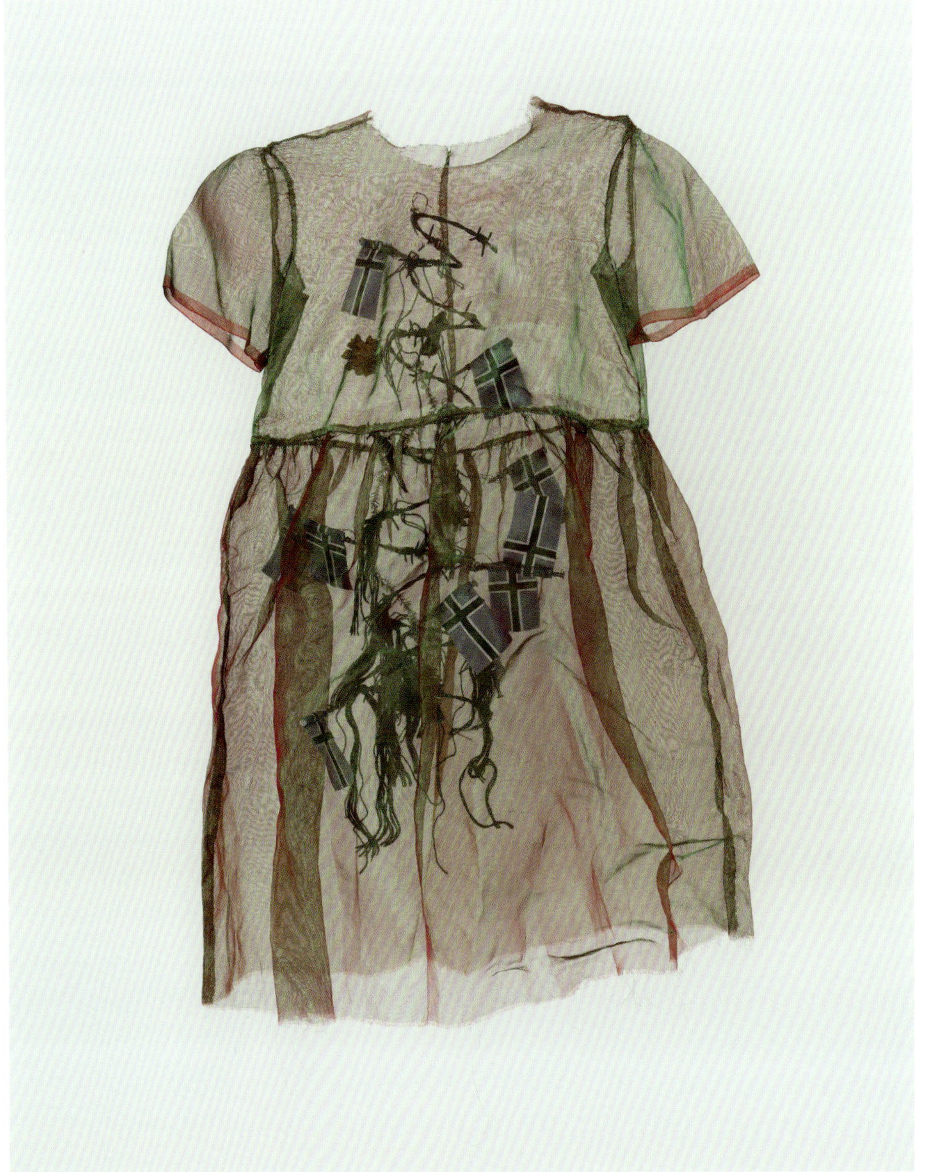

defiance, Nora tells a pair of house guests that she feels like saying something a bit shocking to Torvald, namely to exclaim *Død og pine!* (lit. "Death and agony!", a mild oath at the time). Even as Nora here wants to conjure up what Torvald's repressiveness forbids, she also foreshadows the dissolution that will take place in the bank director's home during the Christmas season.[13] Nora is treated like a child, like a little doll mother that Torvald has all sorts of pet names for, like "my little songbird", something that makes it clear that she is not really a person but his property. Torvald's description dehumanises her as a trapped animal: she is the songbird, or else the *lille hjælpeløse tingest*, the "helpless little creature". *Black Christmas* can be interpreted as a revolt against the traumas lurking beneath the polished facade, traumas that intensify during this holiday but that here rebel and show their twisted side.

The art of the 1990s witnessed an increasing interest in the philosophical and aesthetic tools and theories of Surrealism. These themes tended to be strongly tied to questions of gender and identity. It might be interesting to touch on some of the expressions that were contemporaneous with Mørland's works. In his study *The Return of the Real* from 1996, Hal Foster sees several trends within the body art movement in the light of Jacques Lacan's psychoanalytical philosophy. According to Foster, a new interest in the traumatic and vulnerable is expressed in the way the body is portrayed in the art of Cindy Sherman, Kiki Smith, and Mike Kelley, who use a variety of methods to address trauma through the abject and fragmented body. In Foster's interpretations, the discourse surrounding these artists circles on gender and identity, related to AIDS, homophobia, gene technology, and how society's repression of the body's aging and mortality represent a major part of the taboos that the artists explored. Their techniques were highly organic, and elements that were conventionally regarded as hideous or perverse became key tools that sought to challenge ethical and aesthetical norms concerning gender and identity.[14] In Mørland's work, childhood-related trauma alludes to the female artists of the 1990s who focused on gender and identity as related to their own upbringing. Kiki Smith's works *Little Sisters* and *Skirt* from 1990 both express a tender melancholy, using the materials in a poetic fashion to highlight the connection between fabrics and the female universe.[15] Fabrics signal certain values and traditions that were previously identified with the domestic practice of women. Handicraft takes time and effort, but within cultural history it was dismissed as non-productive work. Mørland's use of materials such as tulle and cotton induces the viewer to identify the dresses as expressions of these culturally contingent factors. She has also designed monumental, outdoor installations featuring this motif in plastic, fabrics, and biodegradable materials. At the Kjerringøy Land Art Biennale in Nordland county in 2013, she erected a monumental dress of seaweed on a nearby beach. One of the biennial's ambitions that year was to invite artists to enter into a dialogue with the Northern Norwegian wilderness and use materials that slowly wear down when exposed to the elements and the shifting seasons.

The inspiration: Surrealism's strategy of liberation

Whether as an artist, art historian, or curator, Astrid Mørland has been particularly interested in female Surrealist artists, above all Leonora Carrington, Frida Kahlo, and Paula Santiago. In 1990 she curated the exhibition *Instinct: Open Intimate Closed Rooms* at Bergen Kunstforening, where she placed artists such as Meret Oppenheim, Leonora Carrington, Remedios Varo, Dorothy Cross, and Paula Santiago in a dialogue with three Norwegian contemporary artists – Gitte Dæhlin, Vilde von Krogh, and Elisabeth Mathisen – who all bear a clear kinship with the imagery and methods of Surrealism. This exhibition helped the Norwegian public rectify the misconception that Surrealism was the exclusive domain of male artists. The thrill of meeting Carrington in Mexico and Santiago in Bergen also helped to reinflame Mørland's interest in the artists who have influenced her own artistic practice so strongly. Many of these Surrealist pioneers have been highlighted at comprehensive retrospectives since 1990, culminating in 2020 with *Fantastic Women*, the largest ever exhibition of female Surrealist artists from Europe, the United States, and Mexico,

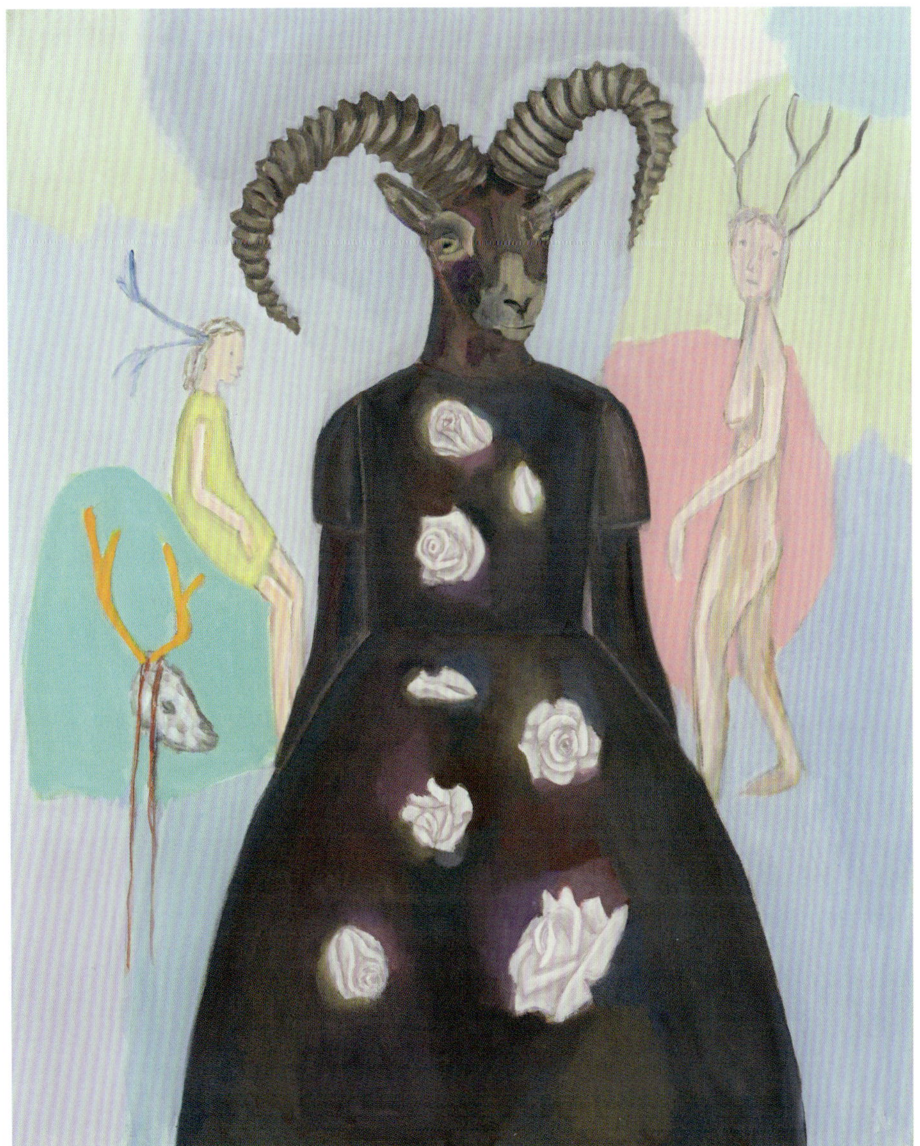

Black Buck 2, 2020
Oil on canvas, 92 x 70 cm

which showcased thirty-six artists and a total of 260 works. Running first at Schirn Kunsthalle Frankfurt and then at the Louisiana Museum of Modern Art in Humlebæk, *Fantastic Women* reappraises key issues concerning the Surrealist movement, for example the notion that women and their bodies were solely an object explored by male artist subjects.

The female Surrealists defined interesting perspectives in regard to gender identity, mythologisation, and self-staging, even as they were highly active in this political and revolutionary movement. This is somewhat paradoxical, for even as no other movement has cultivated women, femininity, and female sexuality in texts, manifestoes, and artworks from the vantage point of the male subject more than Surrealism has, there is also no other artistic movement that has liberated women to such a degree as Surrealism. Following the devastating experiences of the First World War, the Surrealist movement was united in the view that the demoralising structures underpinning the state, such as the existing family unit, needed to be reassessed, since they represented a patriarchal, repressive social structure.[16] Even though the movement protested stridently against militarisation and conventional codes of masculinity, many writers have called attention to the negative side of Surrealism's fixation on women, who were typically conceived of in the passive woman-child role as fetishised

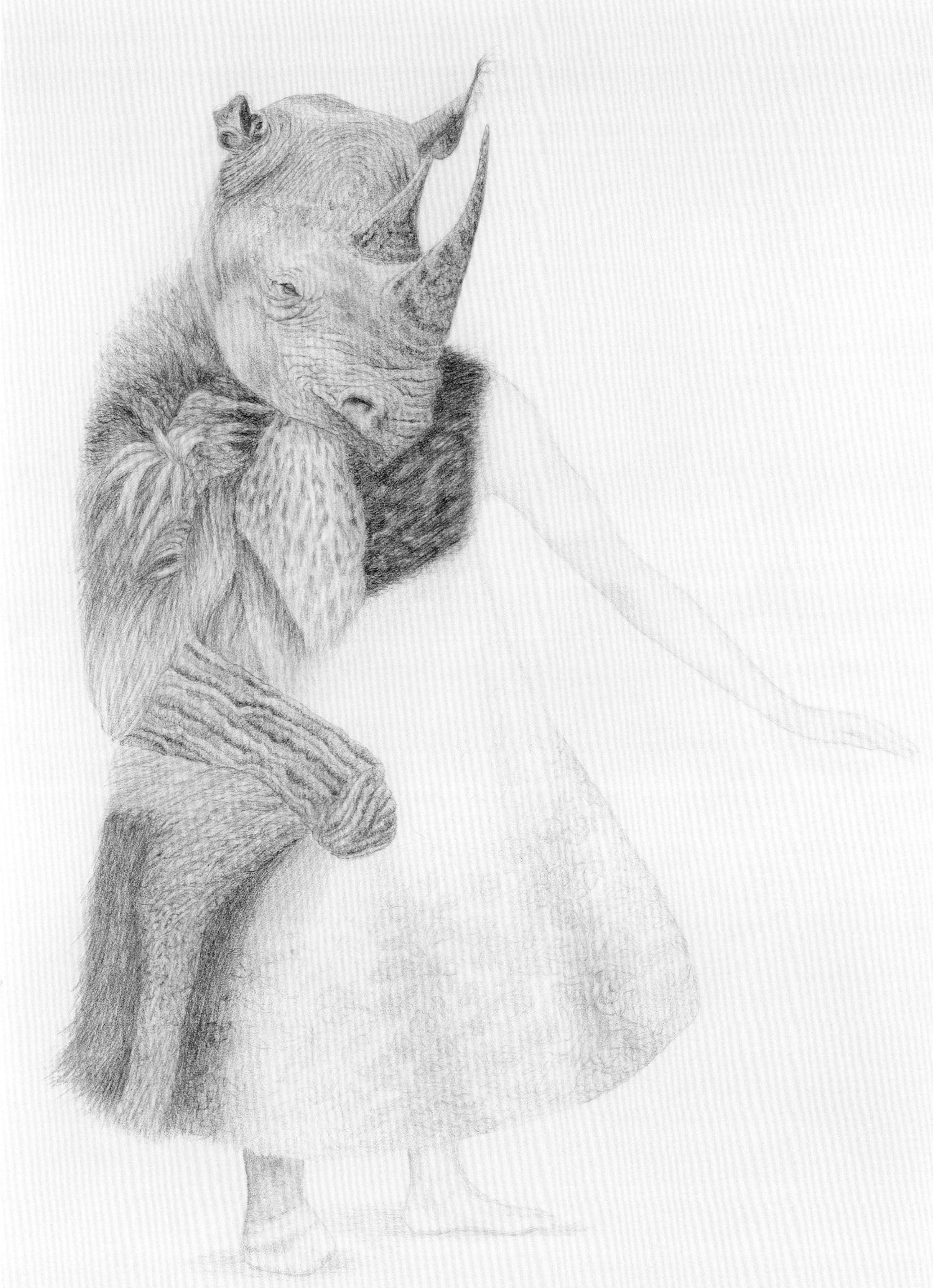

in Breton's novel *Nadja*. Women were often portrayed as muses, venerated as goddesses with magical abilities, or degraded as prostitutes.[17] The first writer to analyse how Breton and other Surrealists viewed women was Simone de Beauvoir in *The Second Sex* (1949). There, Beauvoir emphasises that women in male Surrealist works have no other mission than to be the object of love, and that this desire is not enough to give them subjecthood, since it is the man who defines the desire – essentially, the woman serves as a poetic base to fuel the male artist's desire. But is she also poetry to herself? Beauvoir's answer is that no, Breton does not refer to the women as subjects.[18] From a modern perspective, Beauvoir's critique may seem one-sided, given that many later writers such as Penelope Rosemont have studied how the Surrealist movement was open to women participating and how women were quantitatively well-represented both at exhibitions and as contributors to journals and publications.[19] Another interesting aspect of the emphasis on individual freedom was that the Surrealists also developed their artistic and political strategy through collective processes such as *cadavre exquis*, which served to set up hybrid, surprising encounters through collective drawings. The happenstance of such collaboration bolstered the movement's theoretical underpinnings, and the democratic form also subverted what at the time was the role of the artist. This experimental and inclusive attitude was manifested by Breton's contribution to the *Exposition surréaliste d'objets* at Galerie Charles Ratton in Paris in 1936, where he teamed up with his wife, the artist Jacqueline Lamba, to present objects that were juxtaposed with works by self-taught amateur artists and everyday items that were treated as equally valuable and presented in display cases, like a modern-day cabinet of wonders.[20]

Fabulous creatures: from the Minotaur to the Last Guardian
Fabulous creatures and legendary beasts turn up in various mythical universes and play a prominent role in different religions and folktales. The deities of many pre-Christian religions, such as those found in the ancient Egyptian pantheon, combine human traits with those of mammals, insects, and birds. Typically, the god's body was human, while the headdress symbolised the god's divinity. In Greek mythology we find centaurs, the Minotaur, and the Medusa, mythical creatures that were frequently used by Surrealist artists such as Leonora Carrington. The Minotaur and its labyrinth became instrumental to how Surrealism conceived of the relationship between art and politics in the 1930s. Ever since its founding in 1920, Surrealism sought to use art to reveal a repressed libido in the form of structures of desire that criticised existing social norms. By systematically interweaving Marxism and Freudian psychoanalytical theory, the Surrealists argued that the subconscious had political dimensions that impacted social relations far beyond the individual and domestic sphere. The visual is not only political on an illustrative level; rather, as Theodor W. Adorno claims, what makes art unique is the way its form and

structure uncompromisingly call attention to social tensions.[21] Surrealist art revitalised mythical creatures in a way that promoted the development of modern mythologies, inspired by the poet Lautréamont (1846–1870), whose works drew on a multiplicity of cultures, in contrast to National Socialism's later racist recasting of our mythical heritage. In such a perspective, Surrealism's widespread use of mythical creatures and human-animal hybrids may be seen as an attempt to reclaim collective archetypes and symbols that could oppose the bourgeoning ideological currents of National Socialism and communism.

The Minotaur was a fabulous creature that intrigued many Surrealist artists and that also named the movement's flagship journal *Minotaure* (1933–39). The Paris-based journal was launched in June 1933 with a cover by Pablo Picasso featuring the Minotaur superimposed over a cubist labyrinth collage made of paper bits. In Picasso's depiction, the monster's brutishness has given way to a majestic, classical masculinity, a self-portrait or alter ego that the artist also portrayed in his 1935 *Minotauromachy* etching in the *Vollard Suite* series (1930–37), with the monster's feral, frantic appearance reflecting Picasso's stormy private life and foreshadowing the imminent Spanish Civil War. When Astrid Mørland includes fabulous creatures in series such as *Buck with a Floral Dress*, *The Last Guardian*, and *Bull with a Floral Dress*, they bring to mind the Minotaur in that they show a symbiosis between human bodies and animal heads. The Surrealists' use of the Minotaur as a political metaphor is reimagined by Mørland as a symbol of our present-day melancholic sorrow over climate change, as endangered species emerge in her works from a collective oblivion, with certain areas of the painting being blurred out as though the species are on the verge of vanishing forever into a doomed invisibility. In *Rhino with a Floral Dress*, the creature's head is ponderous, and the protective fur structures from various animals can be interpreted as an attempt to shelter it from human extermination. Even the rhinoceros's mighty head and thick hide cannot protect it from being included on the IUCN Red List of endangered species. Although the international trade of rhino horns has been banned since 1977, poachers still hunt for the magical potency of these horns, a threat that is countered by authorities putting the animals in a coma and sawing their horns off, making it pointless for poachers to kill them. In Mørland's *Rhino with a Floral Dress*, the humanoid rhino has been given a female appearance, showing an intention to inscribe the feminine into the traditional reception of how the Minotaur and the rhinoceros can be associated with the male sexual drive, as in Picasso's series of etchings, *Minotauromachy*, whose subject can be interpreted as his alter ego. At the same time, Picasso chose to depict not Theseus's heroic fight and defeat of the Minotaur but rather the monster's potential threat, which foreshadowed the expected Fascist nightmare that would soon take over Europe.[22] The Minotaur mediates between the conscious and the subconscious, between the public and the private, between inner and outer reality. The journal *Minotaure* presented a critique of the rationalist, in-

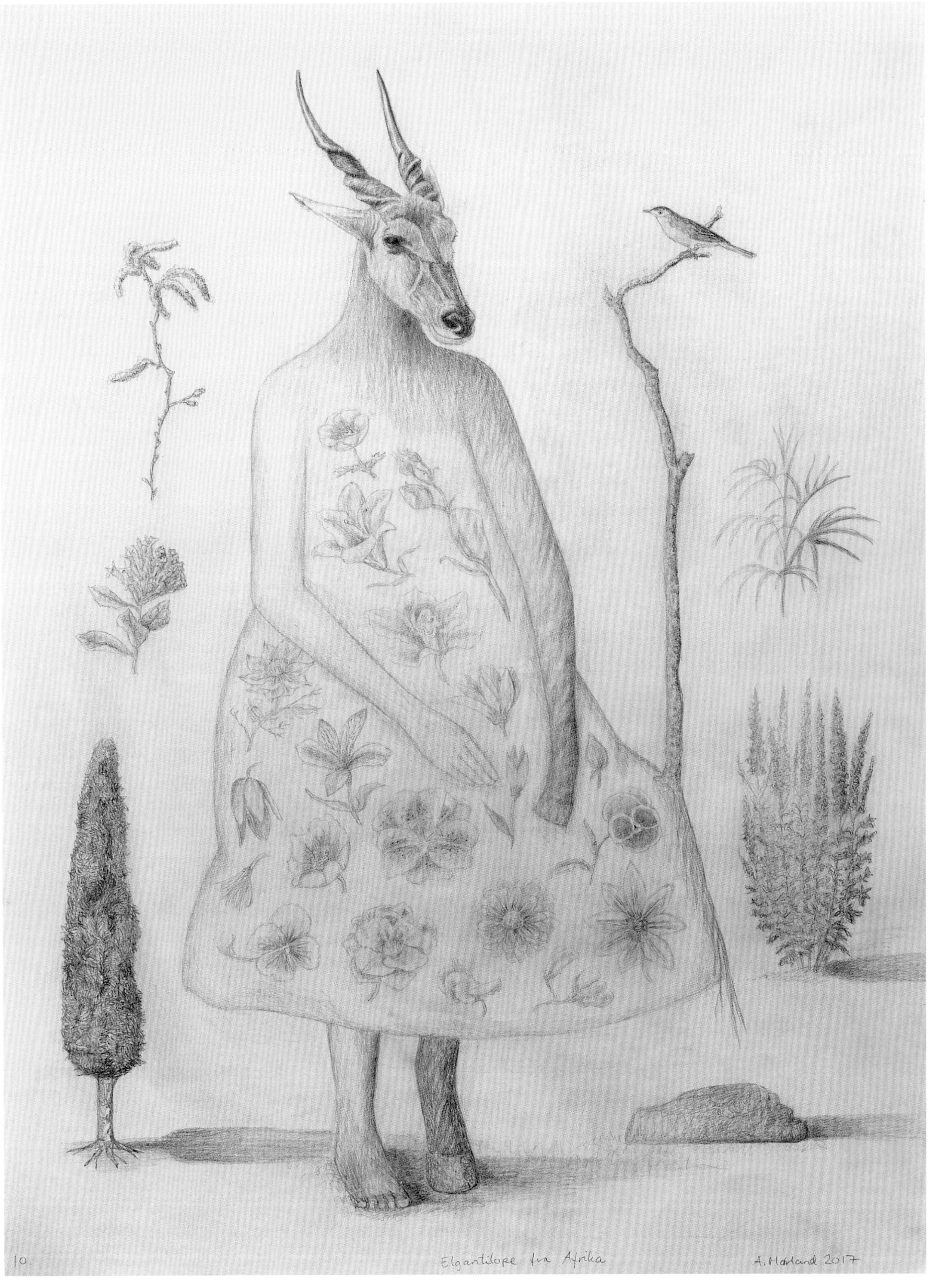

10.
Elgantilope fra Afrika
A. Morland 2017

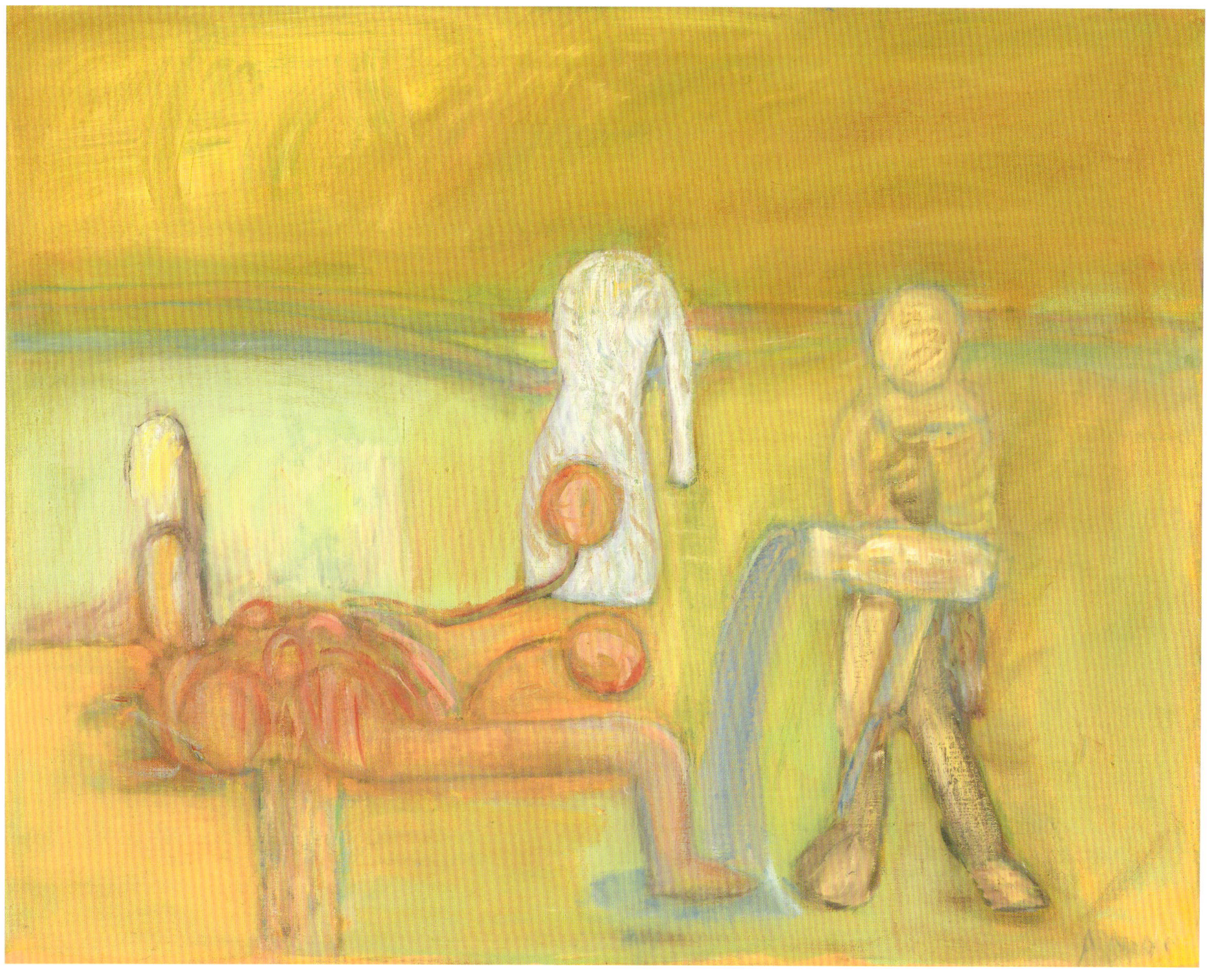

strumental social order that could lead Europe into a catastrophic world war, and that threatened to do so.

Another type of war is heralded by Mørland's fabulous creatures, pertaining to the massive loss of the earth's flora and fauna. In these creatures, autobiographical elements are mixed into a disconcerting contemporary drama, with the loss of biodiversity and autobiographical narratives playing out on the dresses like friezes or like containers of the intimate stories of our lives. The painting of the black, dress-wearing buck is full of contrasts on different levels, such as between the innocent, motherly, and protective elements and the black melancholy of the dress and its decoration of faded roses. The mythical hybrids serve not least as metaphors for the power of transformation, as a venue for metamorphoses and the enigmatic connection between humanity and nature. Mørland's *Last Guardian* shows interesting parallels with Picasso's cover for *Minotaure*, but the majestic, heroic, and virile are related not to a masculine virility but to a feminine figure that wavers between emergence and withdrawal and that suggests a martyrdom of animals. In *Bull with a Floral Dress*, the Minotaur stands frontally in the pictorial plane, where the feminine, delicate, and tender replaces the virility

White Dress and Body Organs, 2000
Oil on canvas, 82 x 102 cm

Yellow Girl with Antlers, 2004
Oil on canvas, 130 x 130 cm

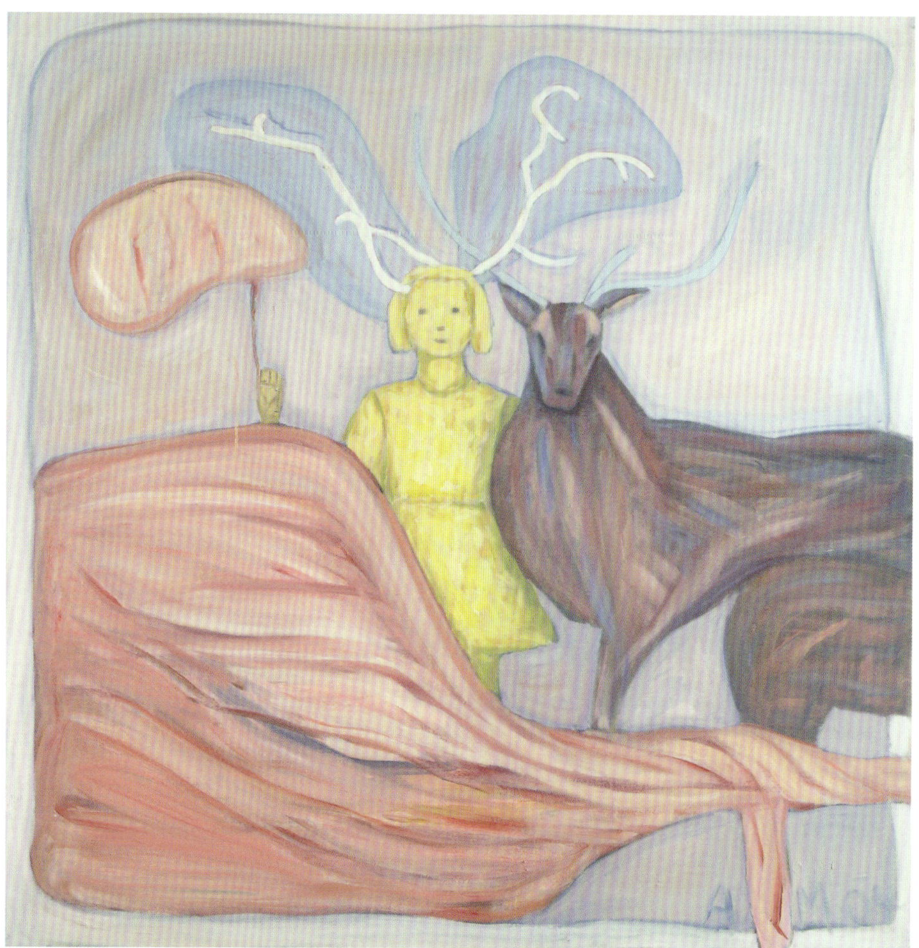

and masculinity that the mythical creature originally symbolised. This figure shares certain traits with how Carrington inscribes the Minotaur into her own mythology-inspired iconography. In *And Then We Saw the Daughter of the Minotaur* (1953), for example, she depicts her two children Gabriel and Pablo in front of a table full of mystical creatures. One such creature that is central to the composition is the Minotaur's daughter, who is clad in an orange mantle that calls to mind the robe of a Buddhist monk. On the table lie glass orbs that hint at a ceremonial rite taking place, while spectral figures dance about in a transcendental light. This feminine version of a Minotaur is highly reminiscent of how Mørland attires and stages her feminine fabulous creatures with animal heads and long dresses. The endangered species inscribe themselves into the history of our collective conscience and into an enigmatic pantheon full of new meanings.

Inspired by Indian myths and Celtic legends, Carrington continued the narrative tradition, using fantastical imagery that has been compared with the work of medieval painter Hieronymus Bosch, an artist whom Breton cited as an inspirator of Surrealism in his first manifesto.[23] What is interesting is that mythical creatures, as well as animals in general, frequently crop up in the female Surrealists' works, as a metaphor, symbol, myth, or alter ego. These creatures represent something untamed, something that refuses to obey patriarchal authority and middle-class customs. In this way, such creatures represent the emancipatory and visionary, something that is also present in the works of Frida Kahlo, Edith Rimmington, Rachel Baes, and Léonor Fini. Carrington frequently painted animal figures, such as the Egyptian goddess

Red Branch, 2005
Oil on canvas, 130 x 130 cm

White Branch, 2005
Oil on canvas, 130 x 130 cm

Behind the Curtain, 2005
Oil on canvas, 130 x 130 cm

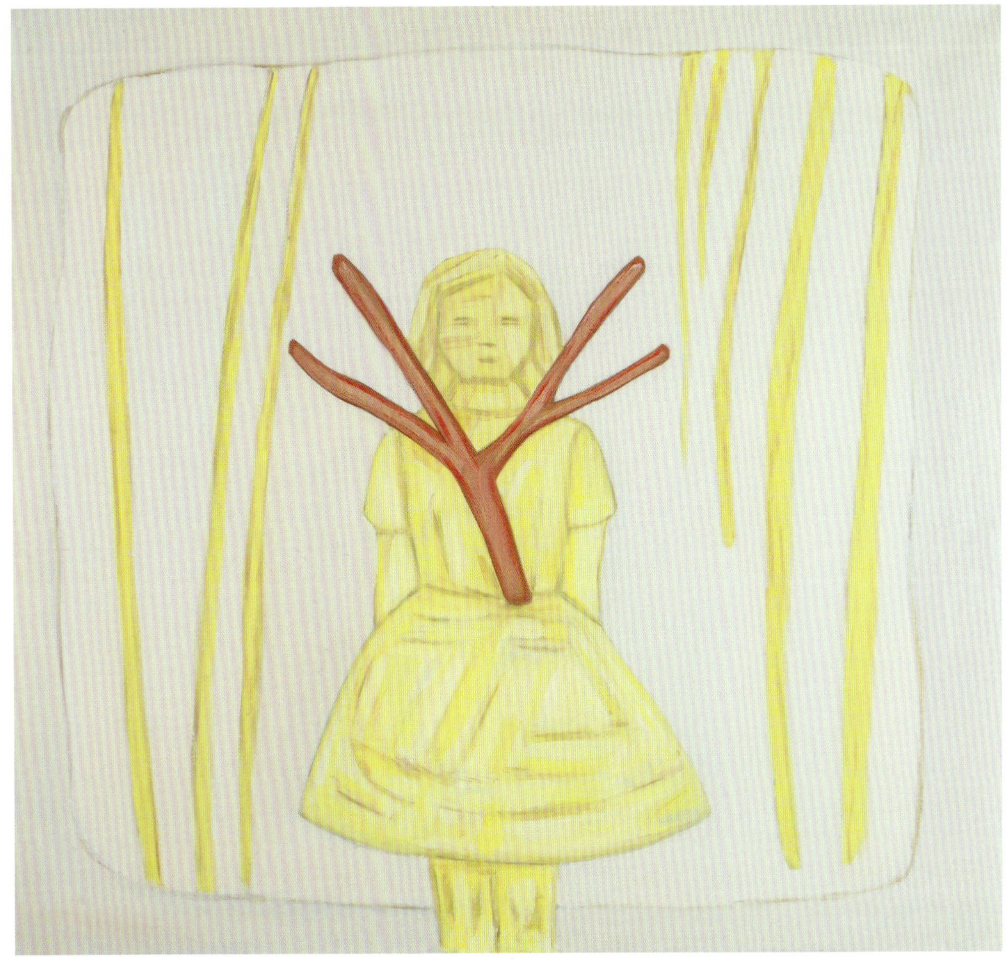

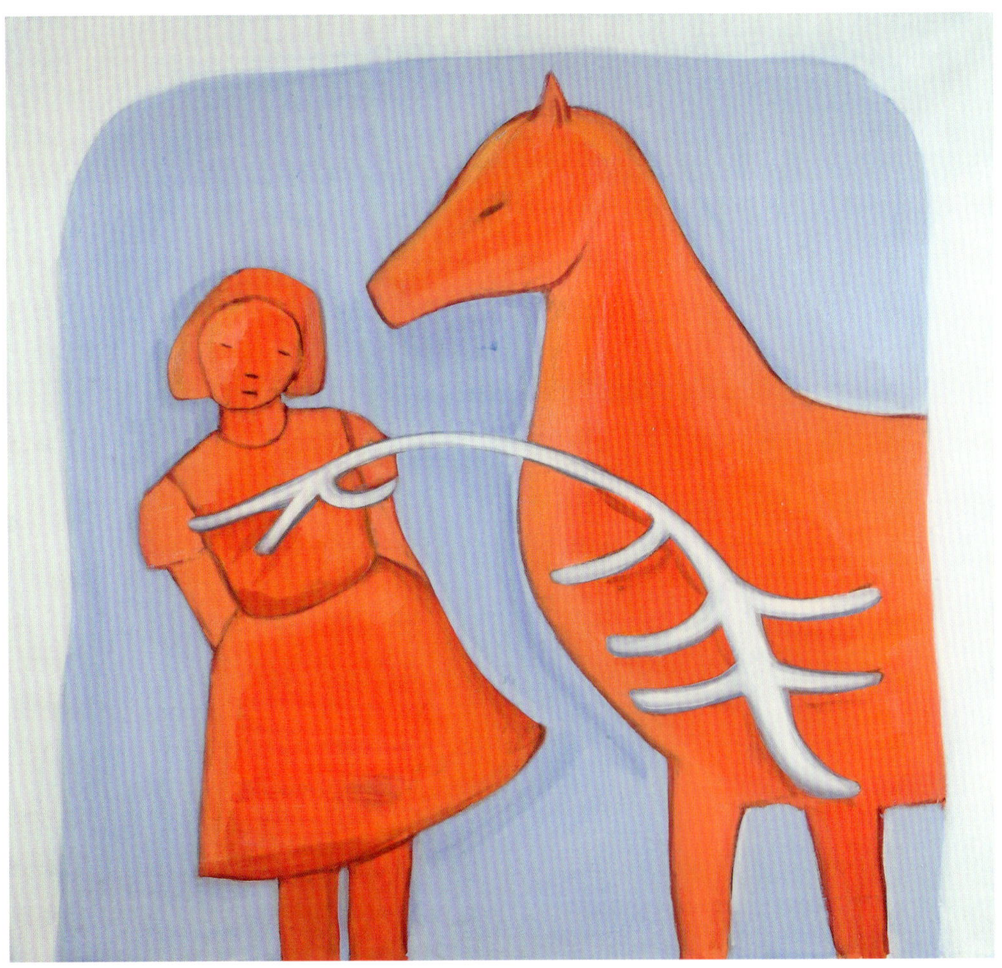

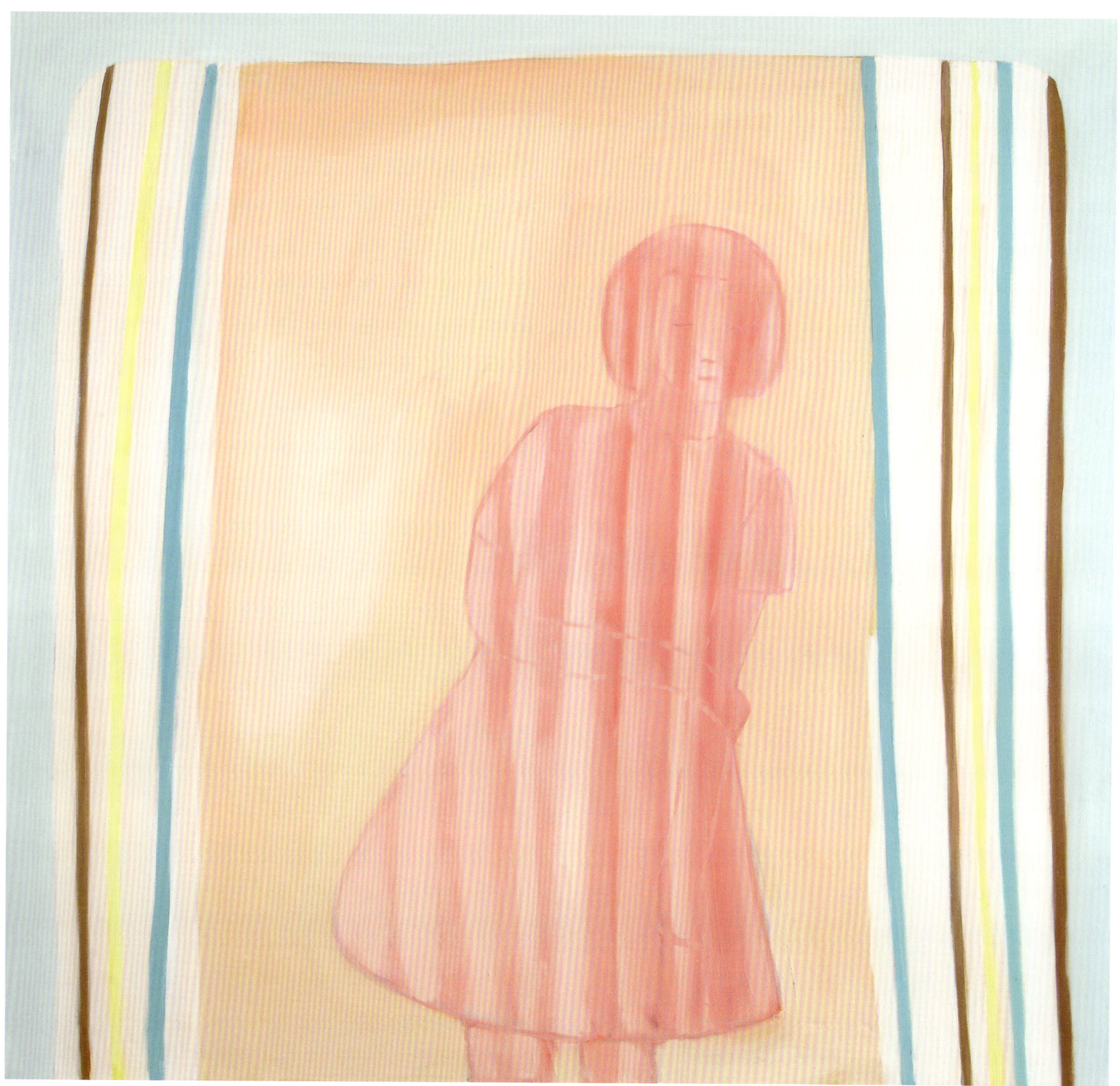

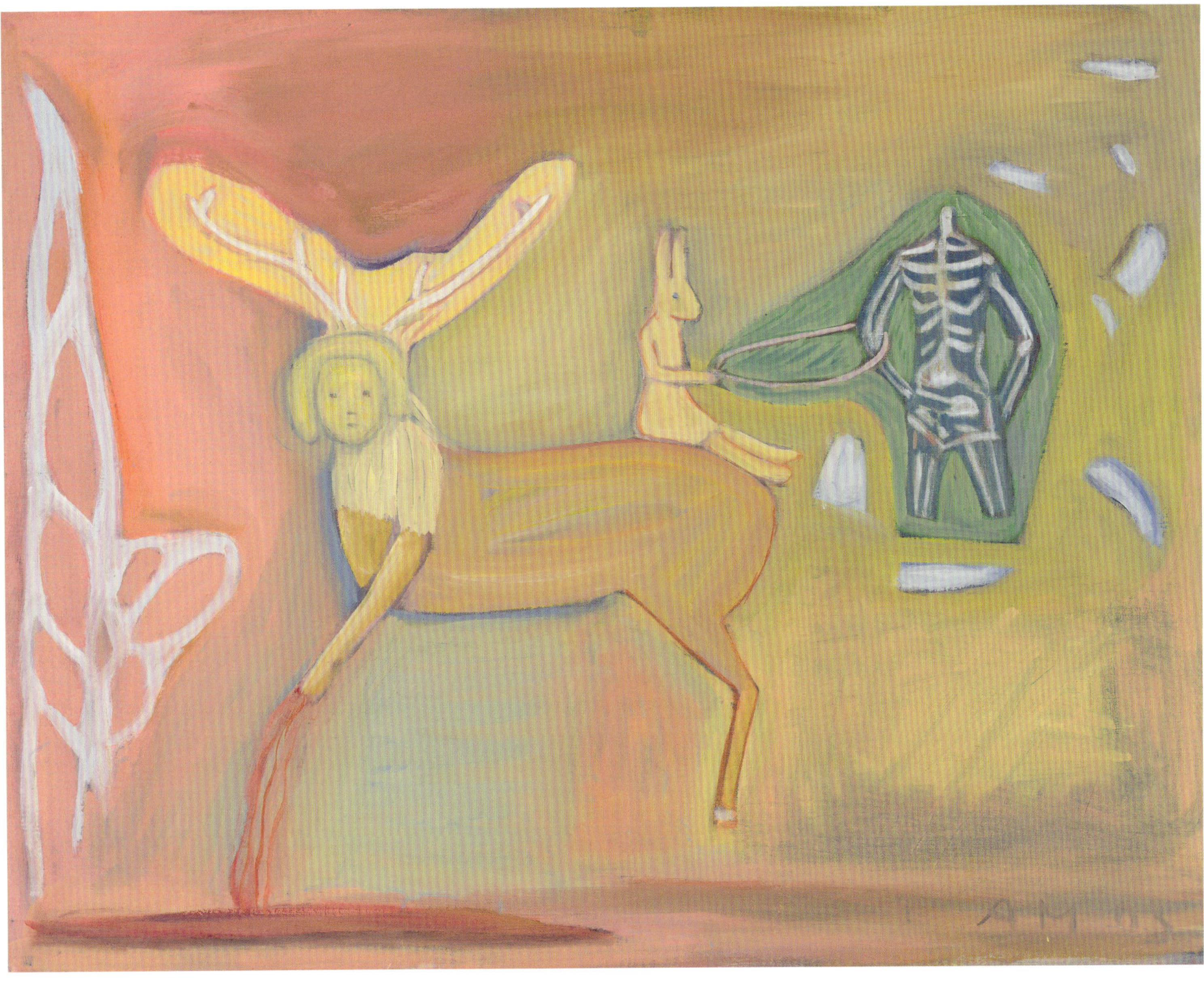

Yellow Girl with Rabbit, 2003
Oil on canvas, 80 x 100 cm

Isis and a catlike woman-lion hybrid, symbolising fertility and regeneration, that features in several of her paintings and sculptures. It is interesting to note the kinship between Carrington's sculpture *La Grande Dame* (*Cat Woman*, 1951), which featured fabulous creatures and insects on the sculpted figure's chest and dress, and the way in which the feminine characters in Mørland's drawings serve as the backdrop for fantastical narratives. Carrington sought inspiration from Celtic myths, which unlike Christianity manifested matriarchal, social structures where "the goddess" was prominent. Frida Kahlo likewise used the Aztec goddess Malinalxochitl, an identification that expressed and wore traditional costumes from the Tehuantepec region, which was famous for its female-dominated culture. As Whitney Chadwick has commented, magic animals were a common motif among many of the female Surrealists, as for instance seen in Carrington's painting *The Inn of the Dawn House* (1936–37), where she portrays herself dressed in nineteenth-century men's clothes in a luxurious manor and where her wild hair alludes to female strength and virility, to a dangerous Medusa accompanied by a hyena. The galloping horse outside the window is her preferred alter ego, while the hyena symbolises her relentless hunger for freedom. The wild woman most definitely does not want

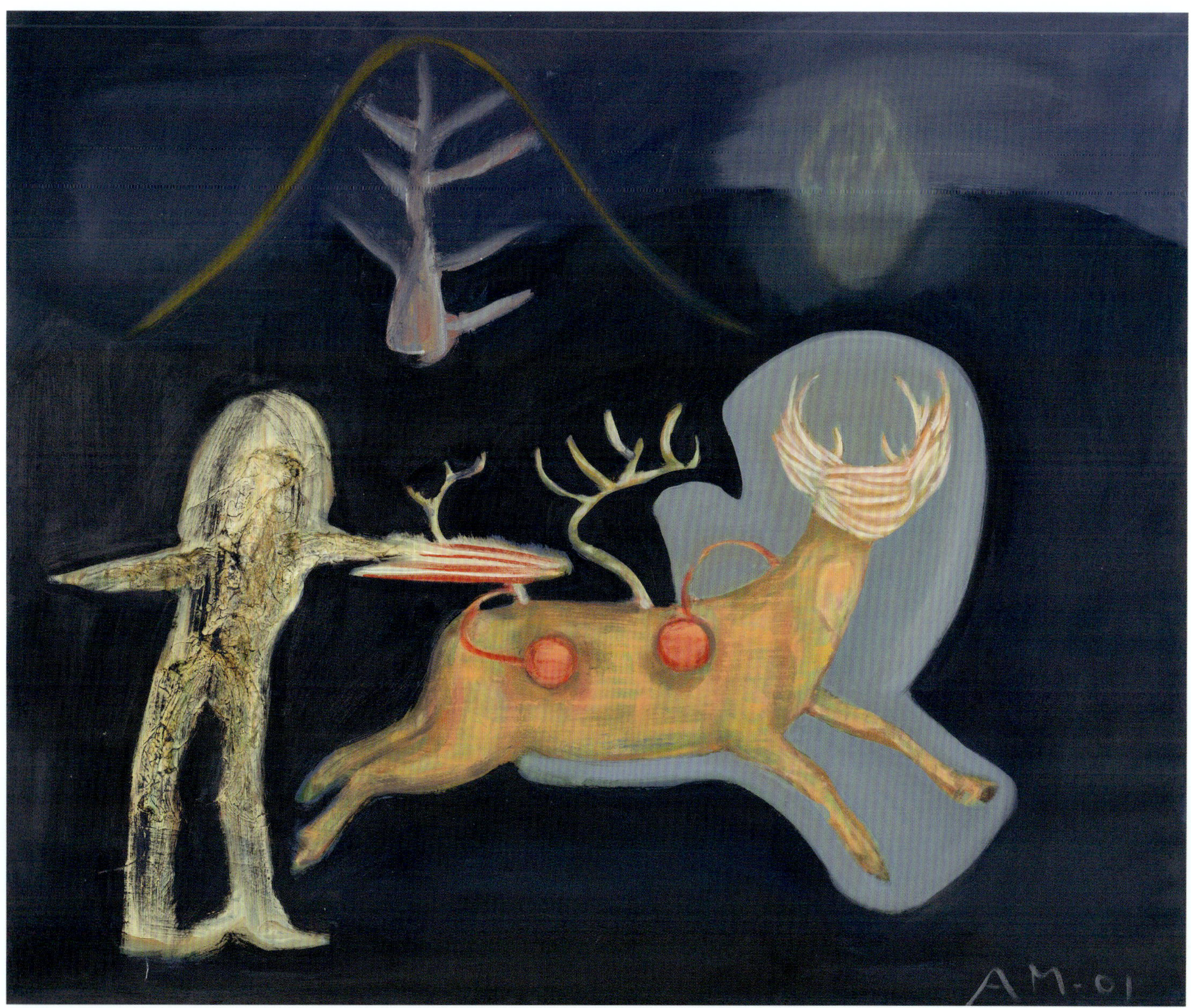

Homage to Frida Kahlo, 2001
Oil on canvas, 98 x 115 cm

to adapt to the middle-class conventions that are reflected in the interior's immaculate curtains and Victorian furniture. Both the woman and the hyena have been alienated and trapped in a petty bourgeois universe, one that also comes to the fore in Carrington's short story "The Debutante" (1939). Mørland's narrative universe emerges in part from this tradition, where the fluid state of the fabulous creatures transcends the gender conventions' framework narrative and realises the sought-after freedom.

The deer's branches: martyrdom through a night-time song

A deer with a human face is a prominent theme in many of Astrid Mørland's paintings. In many works this motif is combined with a little girl, as in *Yellow Girl with Antlers*, where the girl stands in the centre in close contact with a deer that gazes straight at the viewer, just as she does. The girl seems to have borrowed magic powers from the deer, since white antlers are branching out from her head, surrounded by two luminous, bluish fields that evoke butterfly wings. The antlers become interwoven and similar. The girl may be seen as a self-representation, given the 1950s-style dress that alludes to the artist's childhood. She holds an organ-like balloon that, like the foreground structure,

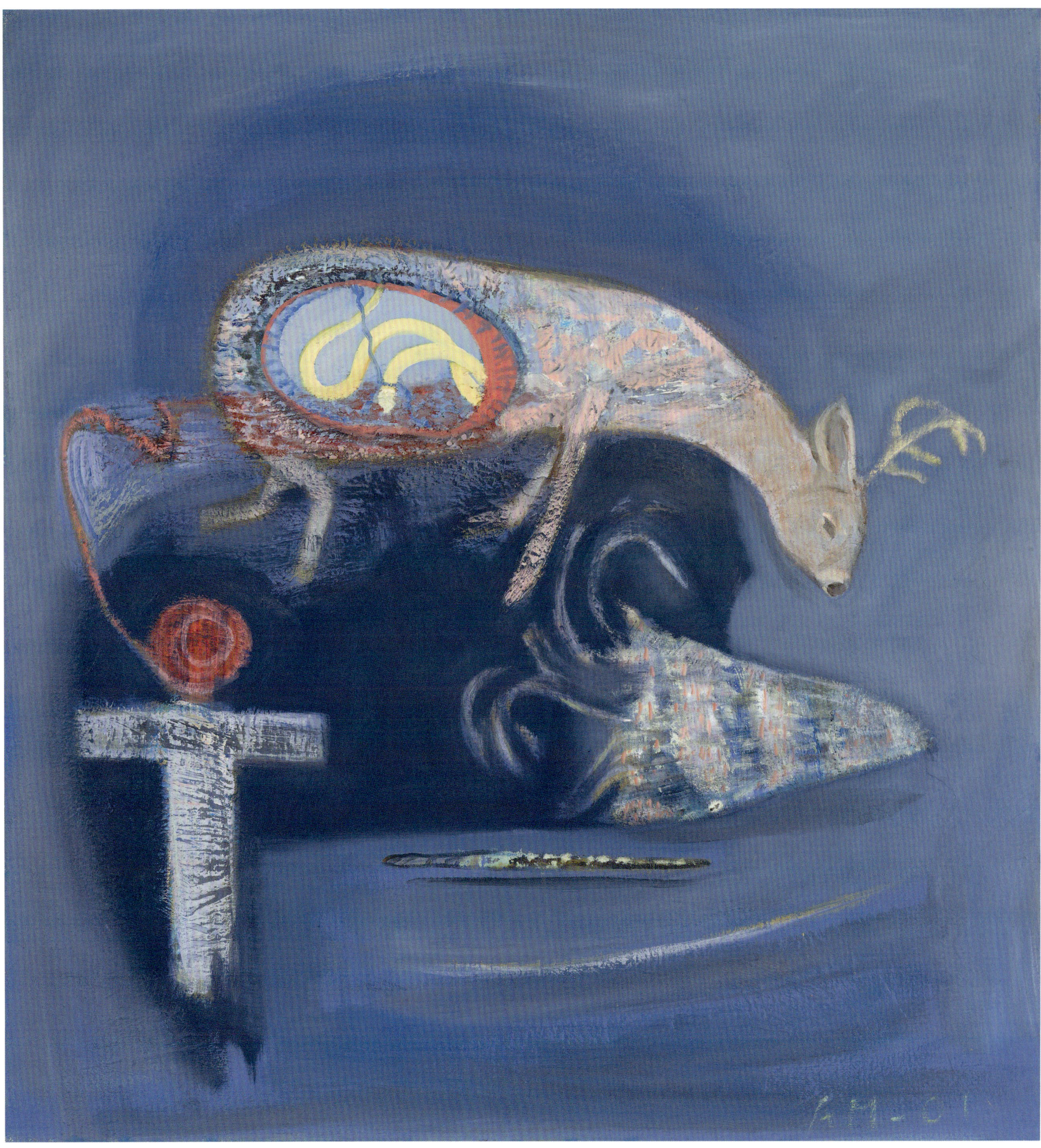

Deer with Open Chest, 2001
Oil on canvas, 110 x 95 cm

evokes the inner body's sinews and muscles, thus weaving the ephemeral and the spiritual together in a transcendental world. The deer places itself like a jigsaw piece close to her waist, and this fluid, ever-changing identity between human and animal is an exchange that seems to afford the girl a stoic power. In *Yellow Girl with Rabbit*, luminous antlers, which are encircled by a golden shape that resembles wings, grow forth from the deer's head, providing a fluctuating, upward movement that suggests a metaphysical journey. One of the deer's legs also serves as the girl's hand, which has been injured, as seen from the blood streaming down into a pool on the ground. The imagery conjures a narrative of suffering, a martyrdom that is all the more apparent when considering the deer's status within Christian iconography as a symbol of Christ. The rabbit that sits atop the deer drags death along with it, thus closing the circle. *Homage to Frida Kahlo* incorporates a stylised adaptation of Kahlo's painting *The Wounded Dear* (1946), in which the Mexican artist shares her physical and emotional suffering right before a spinal operation that left her bed-ridden for nearly a year. Her right leg would eventually be amputated up to the knee as the result of gangrene. In Kahlo's self-portrait, the artist has morphed into the suffering deer that has been penetrated by nine arrows, standing in an alley amid trees without a visible canopy. The arrows may refer to the martyr St Sebastian, with the branch on the ground in front of the deer alluding to a Mexican funeral rite. In Mørland's homage, the tree and the antlers represent growth and power. The association between these two elements may hint at a closer symbolic kinship, given that many traditions have imbued skeletons and antlers with the same vitality as trees. Mythological deer creatures typically personify growth, rebirth, cycles, and the connection between the ephemeral and the metaphysical. They also incarnate the cycles of nature and the eternal circulation of water. Antlers often hung on the gables of banquet halls and were also fixed to the ceilings of crypts and mausoleums. In *Homage to Frida Kahlo*, the antlers are placed on the buck's back, and two red fertility symbols that resemble fallopian tubes may prompt the viewer to reflect on Kahlo's own martyrdom of a lost pregnancy and physical suffering. In *Deer with Open Chest*, the buck seems to float in a cosmic space where its intestines have been painted in yellow and red. The animal seems to collapse into death, before it sinks down into the velvet night. The fact that a crucifix-like shape is so prominent in the juxtaposition with the deer may allude to its metaphorical power as a symbol of resurrection.[24]

In *Buck and Orchid* the buck head represents an endangered species. The head has been given a three-dimensional, plastic appearance, standing in contrast to the surface-oriented background, while the fabulous creature's dress, painted with dissolved brushstrokes, mediates the contrasting idioms. This visual-grammatical contrast sets up a dynamic interplay between abstraction and figuration. The dress itself is adorned with an orchid and a branch with blue drops that continue to trickle beneath the palm of the buck's hand and

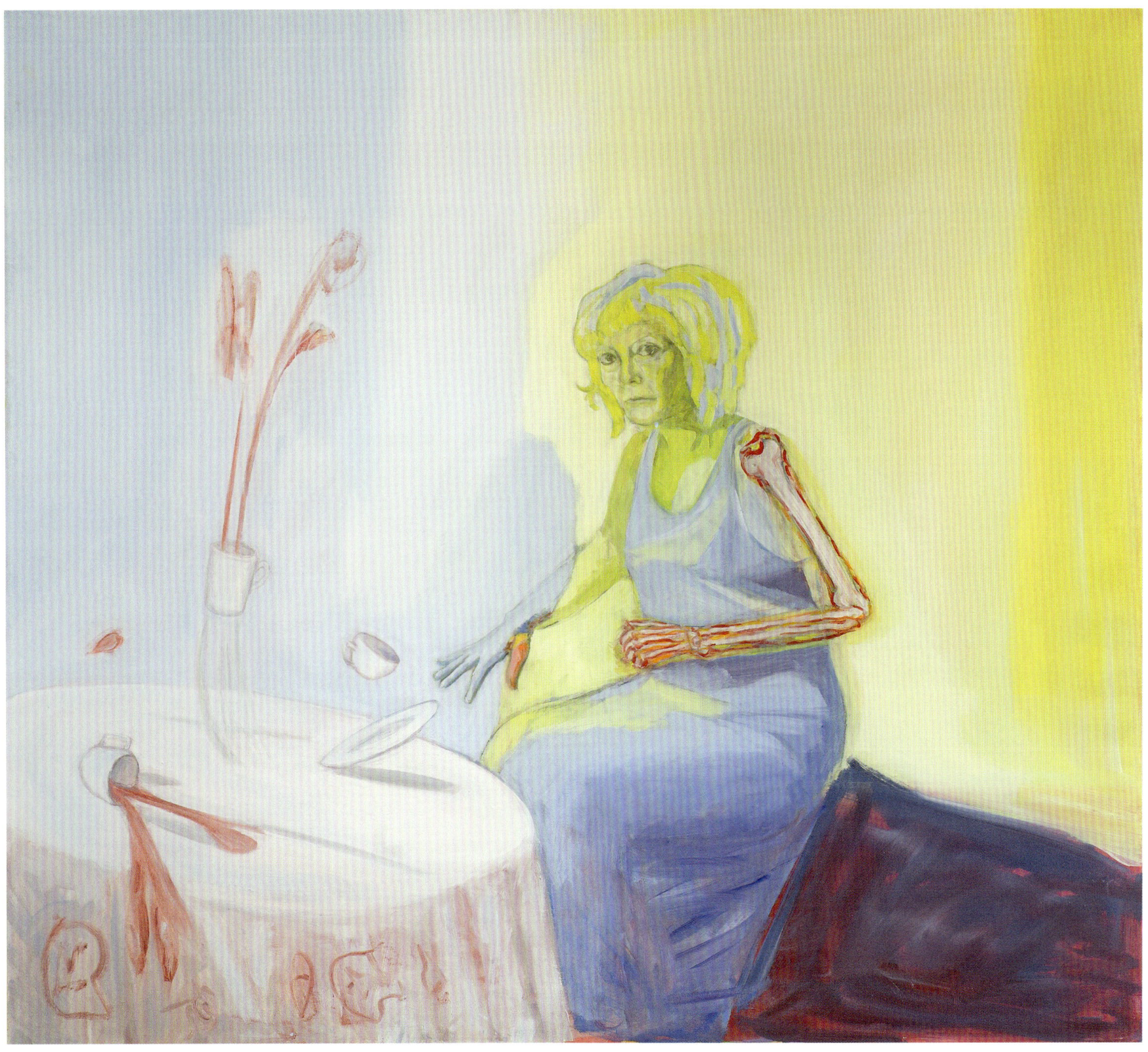

down towards the ground. The skeleton on the left-hand shows a sitting girl with a fragile, transparent body that seems to levitate weightlessly against a blue background, while the botanical species have been meticulously rendered in a style that recall an herbarium, where the underlying empirical, scientific investigation of the species' particular traits has been reimagined in a surrealist style. It is as though Mørland is pointing out that the loss of biodiversity is a loss for humanity as well. We are put on an equal footing as living beings, as inhabitants of the same earth, and the identification puts a critical spotlight on how natural resources are exploited. In the series of drawings titled *The Last Guardian*, a mystical narrative featuring various human figures plays out on the titular character's dress. Roots, trees, and hollow trunks operate alongside lilies, flowers, and even a colon from an anatomical wall chart. The scientific gaze contrasts strongly with the displacement and condensation that is accrued in the fabulous creatures, where rocks and plants grow forth from their bodies.

Yellow Gaze, 2013
Oil on canvas, 120 x 130 cm

It's Not My Cup of Tea, 2011
Oil on canvas, 65 x 70 cm

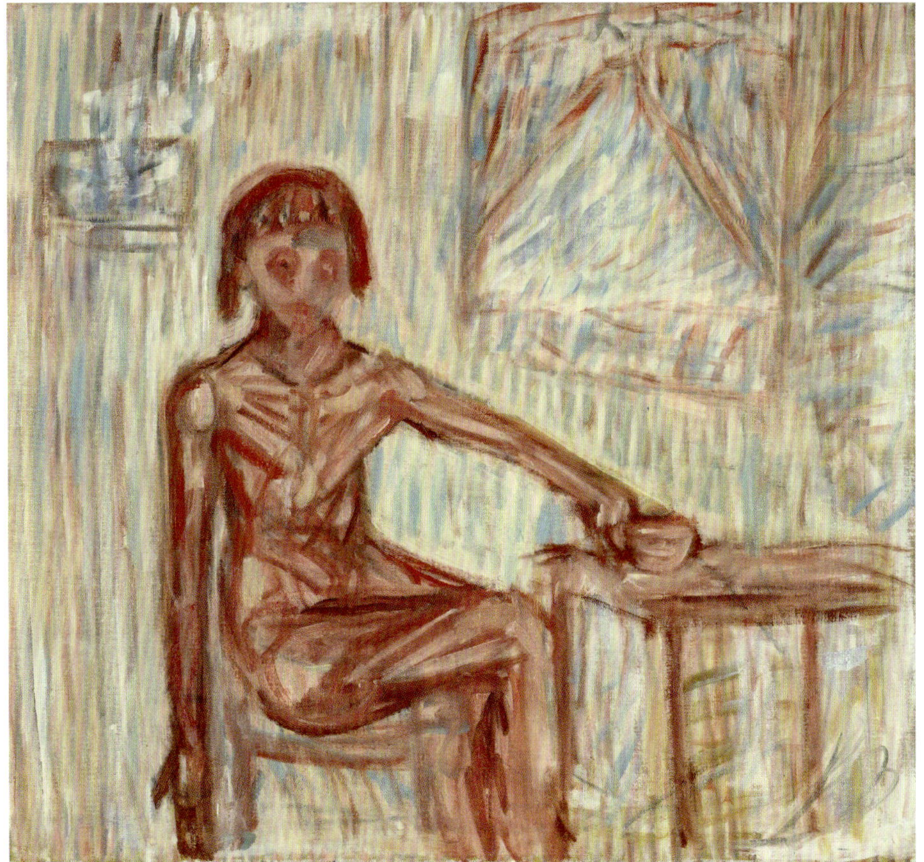

It may be instructive to refer here to Remedios Varo's painting *The Creation of the Birds* (1957), where a mythical being, half woman and half bird, is surrounded by magic objects and devices that are a modern interpretation of St Jerome in his studio. Similarly, the scientific worldview's objective accounts have been taken over by the irrational in Mørland's work, where botanical and anatomical wall charts, and their wealth of detail, are used as an instrument to open up a wondrous room of possibility. A bestiary is a type of medieval text where fables about either real animals or mythical creatures became moral allegories of the Christian gospel. For her part, Mørland creates new, modern-day depictions, a contemporary bestiary where fabulous creatures can be interpreted as allegories of the loss of biodiversity and humanity's conflict with nature.

Melancholic metamorphosis

In Mørland's works, the body is frequently destabilised, moving about in hybrid constellations and morphing between animal, tree, and human, between man and woman, between life and death. The body is exposed to a transformation in the painting *Yellow Gaze*, which was presented at the *Munch by Others* exhibition in 2013. Mørland based this painting on Edvard Munch's interior *Melancholy (Laura)* (1899), an empathetic and insightful depiction of his sister Laura. In Munch's original, Laura, suffering from a mental disorder, is shown staring anxiously ahead of her with an empty, dismal gaze, while the anxiety itself seems to course throughout the blood-red patterns that spread hallucinatorily out from the table's centre.[25] In Mørland's adaptation, this metaphor has incorporated an additional surrealist element. The table and its service have been taken over by a poltergeist that hovers above the table's surface, while a cup on the table spills out a blood-like fluid that is repeated both in the tablecloth's pattern and in the open skeletal arm devoid of the protective skin layer. Mørland portrays herself as the mentally unstable woman, who scarcely seems to react to the mystical levitation that is going on. An intense, sourish light permeates the painting's material components, interacting with the red shade of suffering. The ground beneath her seems to become destabilised, and the only thing anchoring the figure to reality is the intense gaze with which she rivets the viewer. The transparent and delicate, the fragile and unstable, evince a hallucinatory state where boundaries are dissolved and where the person's anxious gaze seems to just wait for the next psychotic cataclysm.

Loss and melancholy are recurring themes in Mørland's works, as explored in a societal context. The mourning of loss and death has become displaced in our culture, especially because old age and our physical and mental ailments are now so institutionalised. Art manages to bring the existential feeling of loss back to the sphere of melancholy as an object of meditation and reflection. One salient example is Munch's *Between the Clock and the Bed*, where the artist's introspection offers a moving portrait of old age and death. By appropriating Munch's work in her own painting *Dawn*, Mørland stages herself within what we may call the narrative of the male artist genius, only with Munch's original contemplation of old age and death now taking place from a woman's perspective. The depicted woman's shrunken body, wanly bluish face, and dark eyes conjure up a shadowy look, even as a rebellious spark remains in her thick, Medusa-like hair. For this composition, she has added some of her own art to Munch's studio home at Ekely; a long-sleeved dress with blue mussels is also shown on the right, while Munch's iconic bedspread from *Between the Clock and the Bed* has been repurposed as Mørland's skirt. This feminist reworking addresses how difficult it is for women to be admitted into the narrative of the canonised genius. The woman's face has been sapped of inner life, and her body has stiffened in a frozen posture that is repeated in the sleeves of the girls' dress. Social alienation, sorrow, and depression have always been closely linked to the state of society, but in our individualistic era we risk privatising these states.[26]

Throughout history, art has highlighted melancholy as a creative state of mind, one that likely has engendered more texts, interpretations, and pictorial conventions than most other emotions.[27] According to the intellectual historian Karin Johannisson, the multitude of words used to capture the concept of melancholy, such as "dejection", "despondency", "sadness", "gloom", and "downheartedness", all have in common that they refer to a sense of loss.[28] The concept of melancholy also involves emotions such as emptiness, paralysis, and an absence of feeling present in the world. Older texts about melancholy describe the mental state as a fear of losing yourself because of dramatic bodily transformations. Such metamorphoses – as though the body were made of glass and could be broken upon the slightest touch, or as though it suddenly morphed into clay and could crack open – are interesting parallels

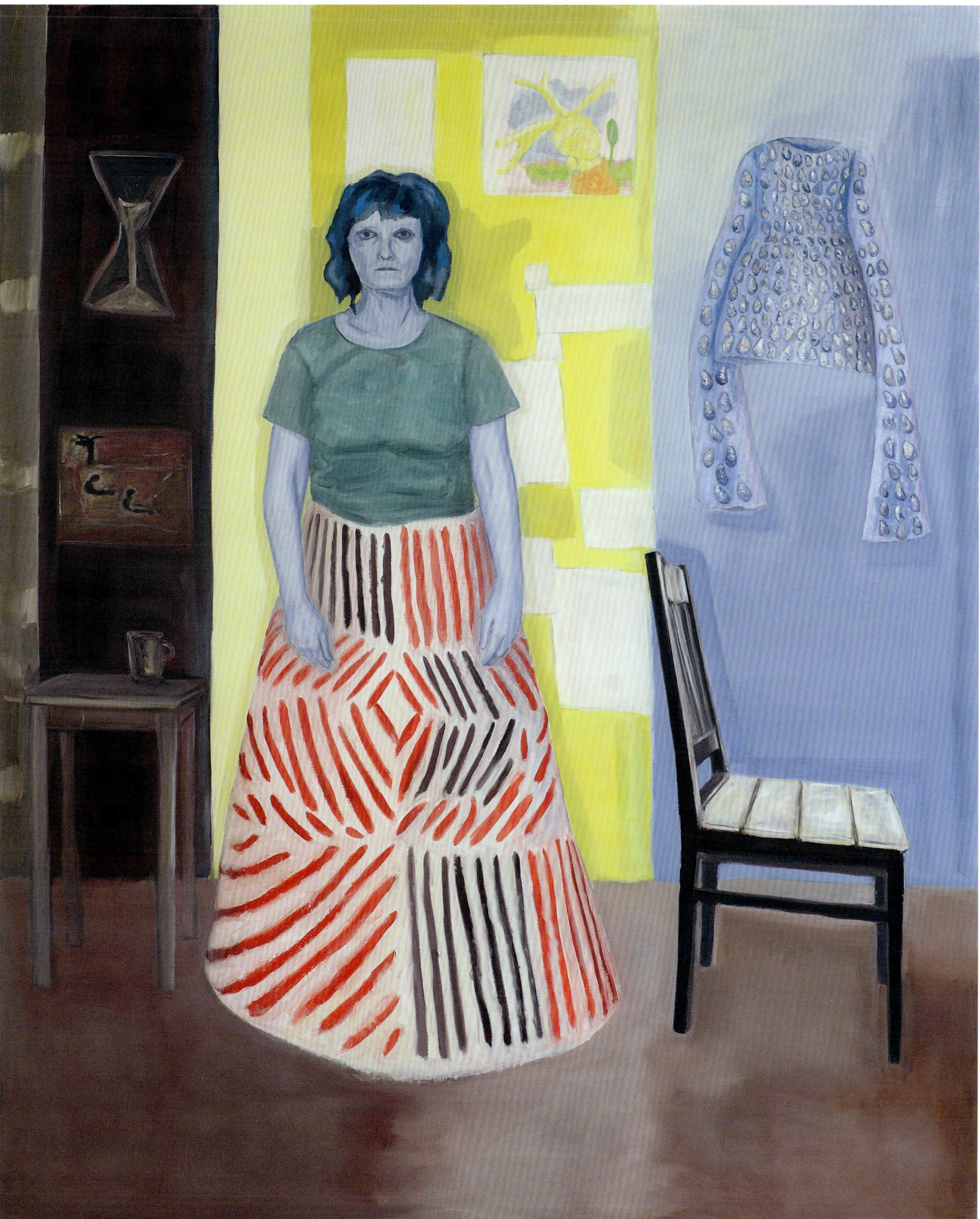

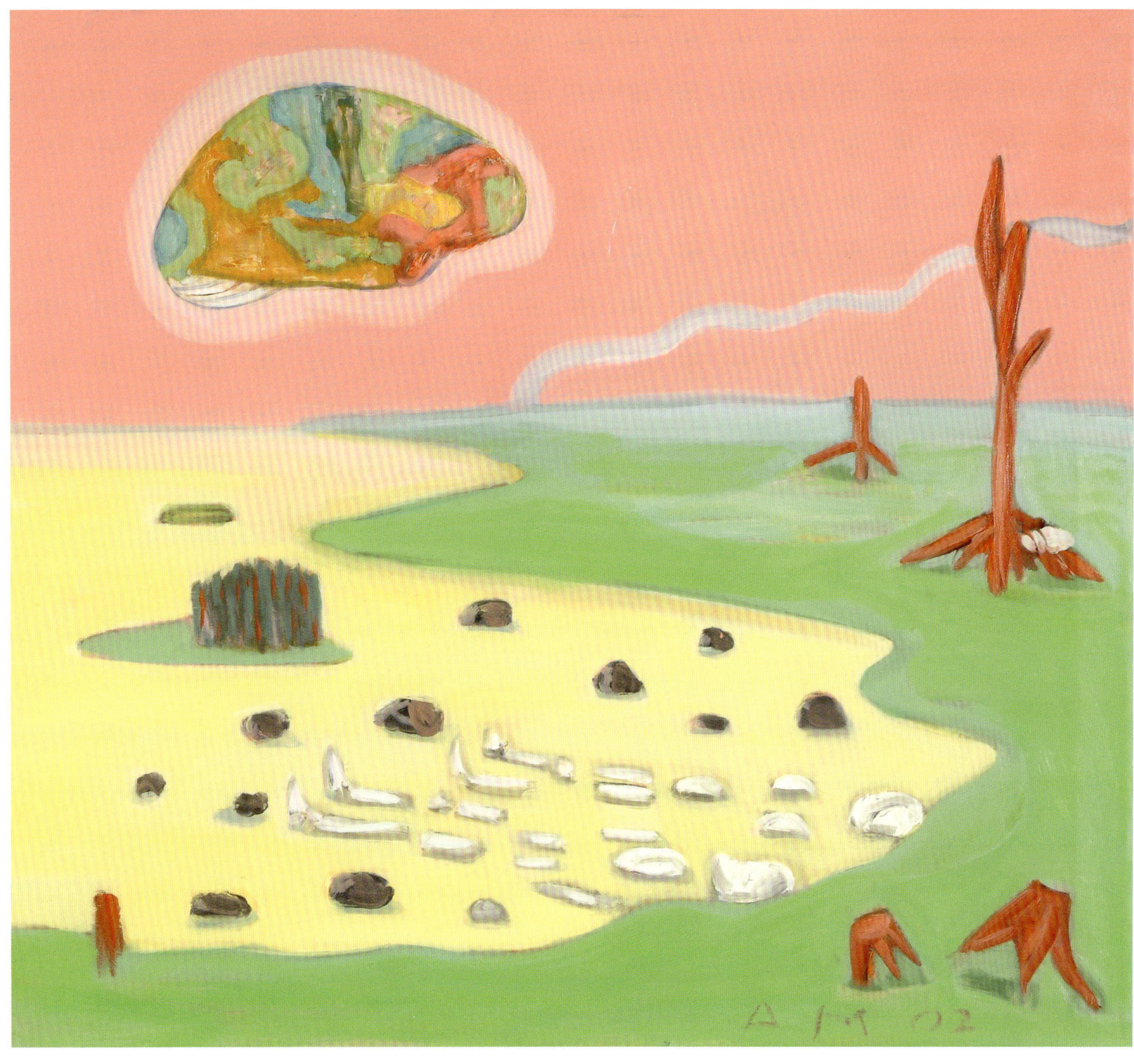

Yellow Beach, 2002
Oil on canvas, 70 x 75 cm

Woman Power 1, 2005
Oil on canvas, 110 x 90 cm

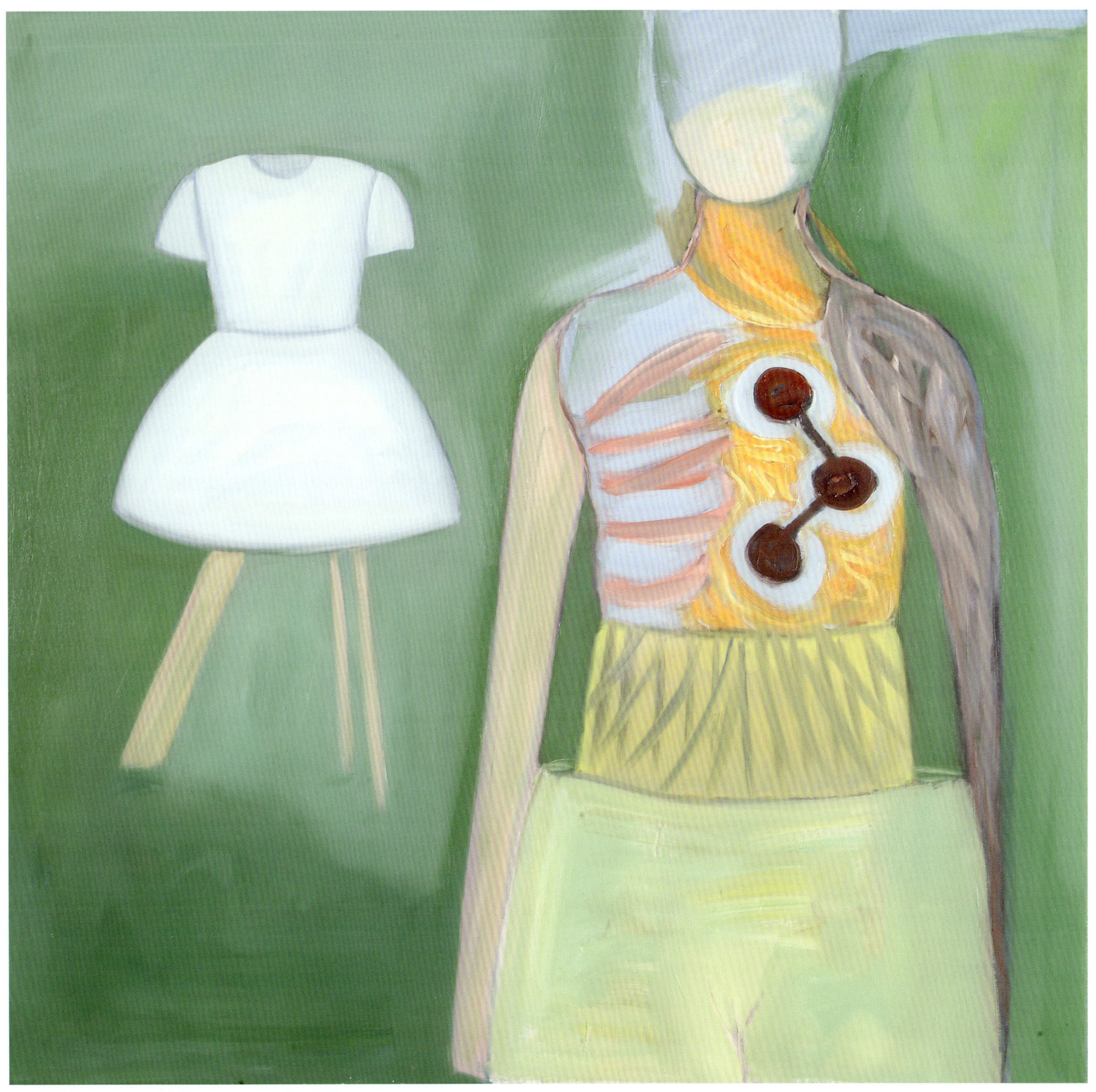

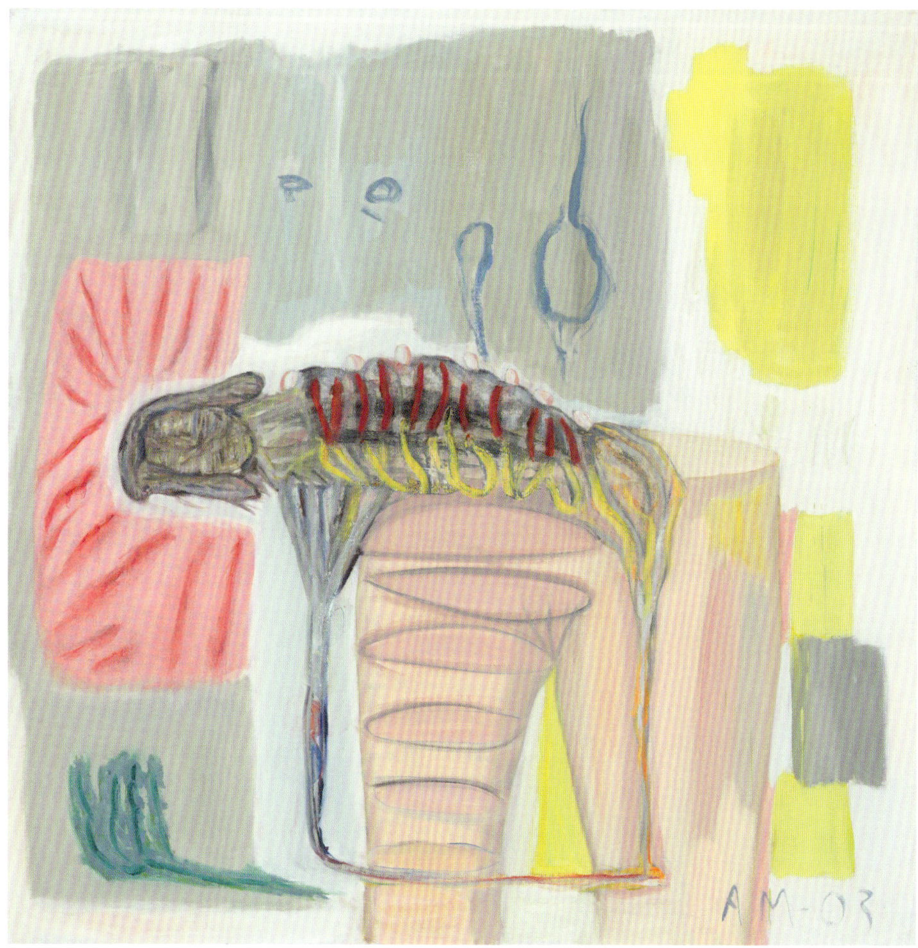

Nada Nada 3, 2003
Oil on canvas, 120 x 120 cm

Woman Power 2, 2005
Oil on canvas, 110 x 90 cm

when looking at the many metamorphous states that Mørland's treatment of the inner and outer body refers to. The girls' dresses that are made from wax allude to such a fragility, where the slightest touch could lead to cracks forming. At the same time, the material evokes the exposure of wounds and bodily fluids. In Surrealist art, metamorphosis was cultivated as a distinct visual grammar and linked to the subconscious – by theorising that "what one sees in an object is another, hidden object", Surrealists could use metamorphoses to refer to a deeper layer in the subconscious human psyche.[29]

Orchids, red landscapes, and a bleeding island

The series of drawings titled *Skin & Orchid* juxtaposes detailed drawings of various orchids with faces suffering from rashes, infections, and sores. Medical science's schematic categorisation of skin diseases such as cholera, syphilis, smallpox, and leprosy is what gave Mørland the idea to juxtapose the faces with the morphology of orchids, as based on botanical wall charts. Typically associated with pure beauty, orchids belong to the largest plant family. But despite its longstanding history and its hardiness, the species is threatened by the massive global decline in various types of bees such as bumblebees. The orchids' beauty gives them a melancholic undertone and is contrasted with faces marred by various skin diseases that are commonplace in the refugee camps of Bangladesh, Yemen, and Somalia because of the lack of water. The loss of biodiversity is seen in connection with the refugee crisis and the millions of people who have been forced to flee their homes and who are threatened by diseases that were eradicated from Europe 150 years ago.

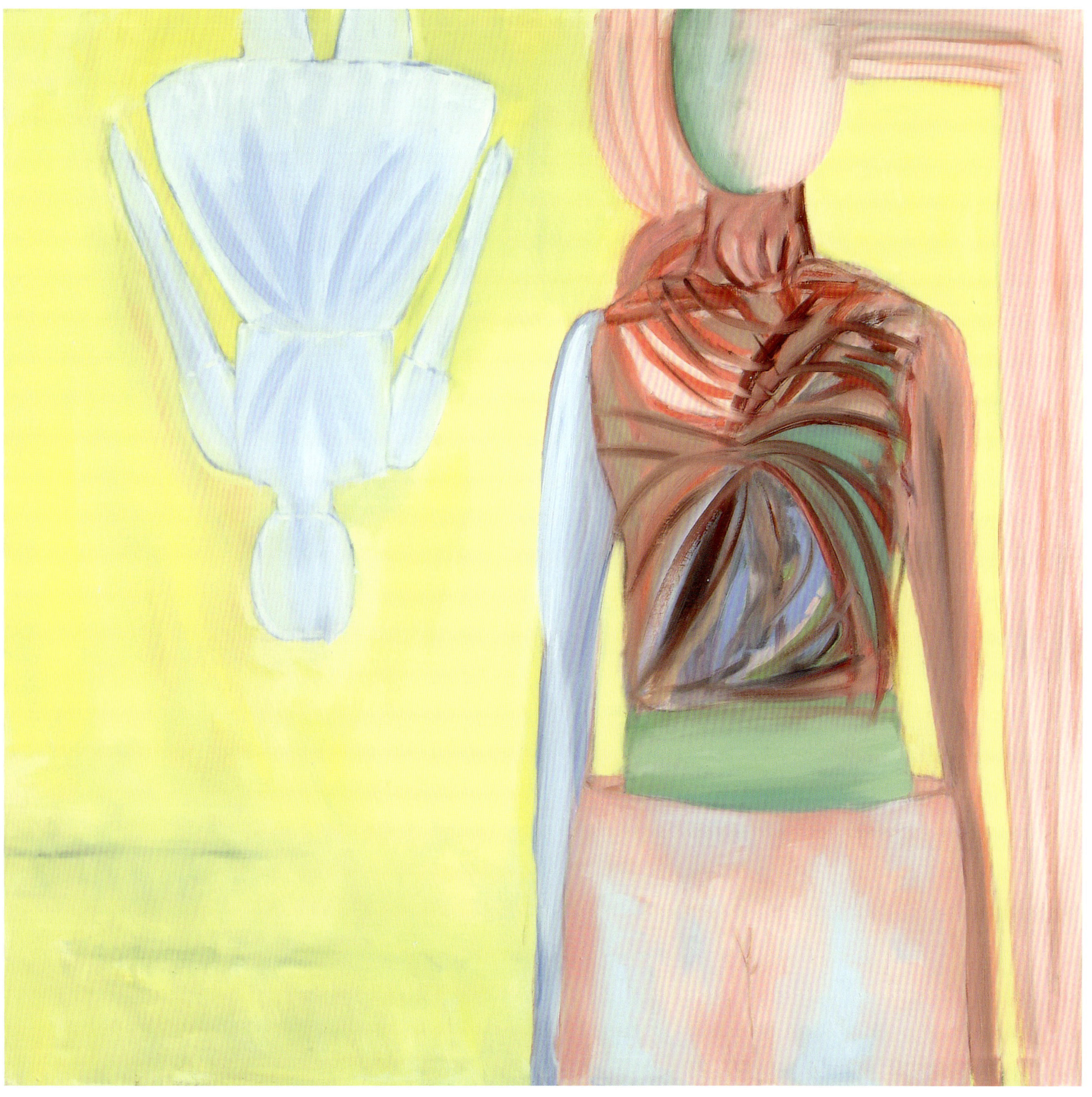

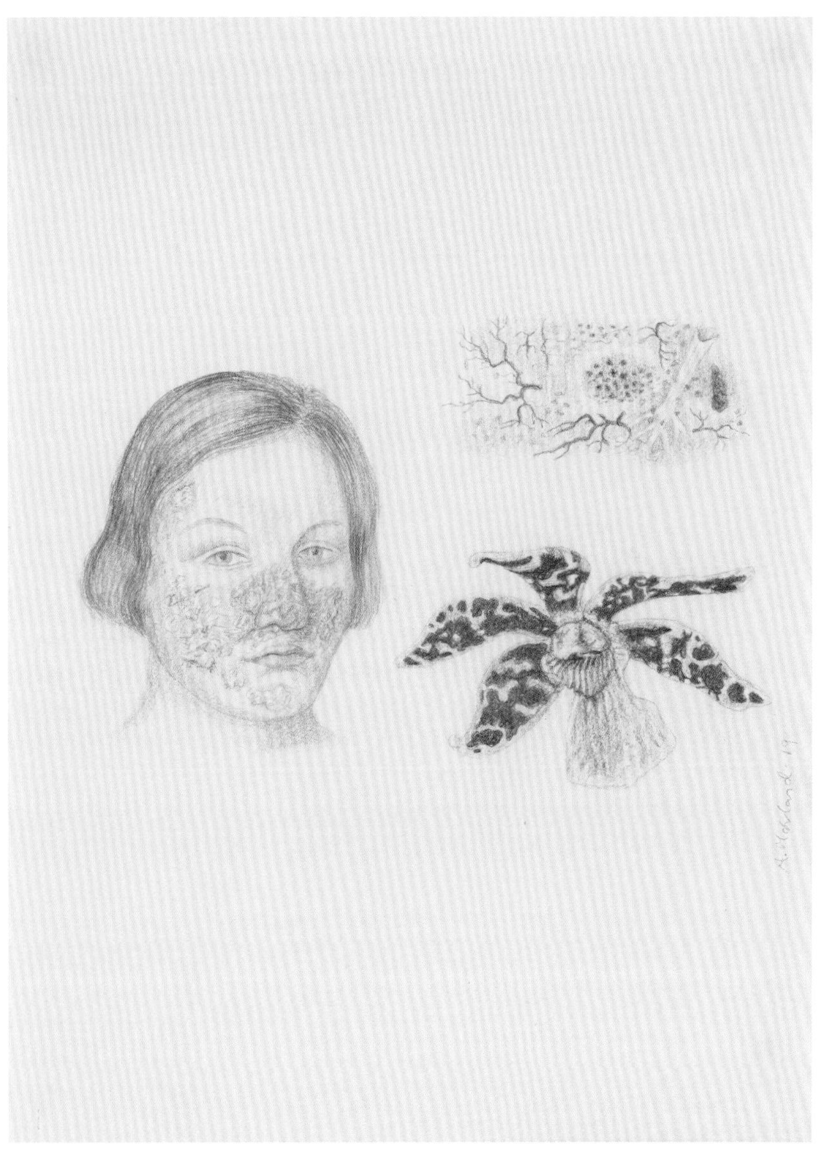

Skin & Orchid 1, 2018
Pencil on paper, 32 x 23 cm

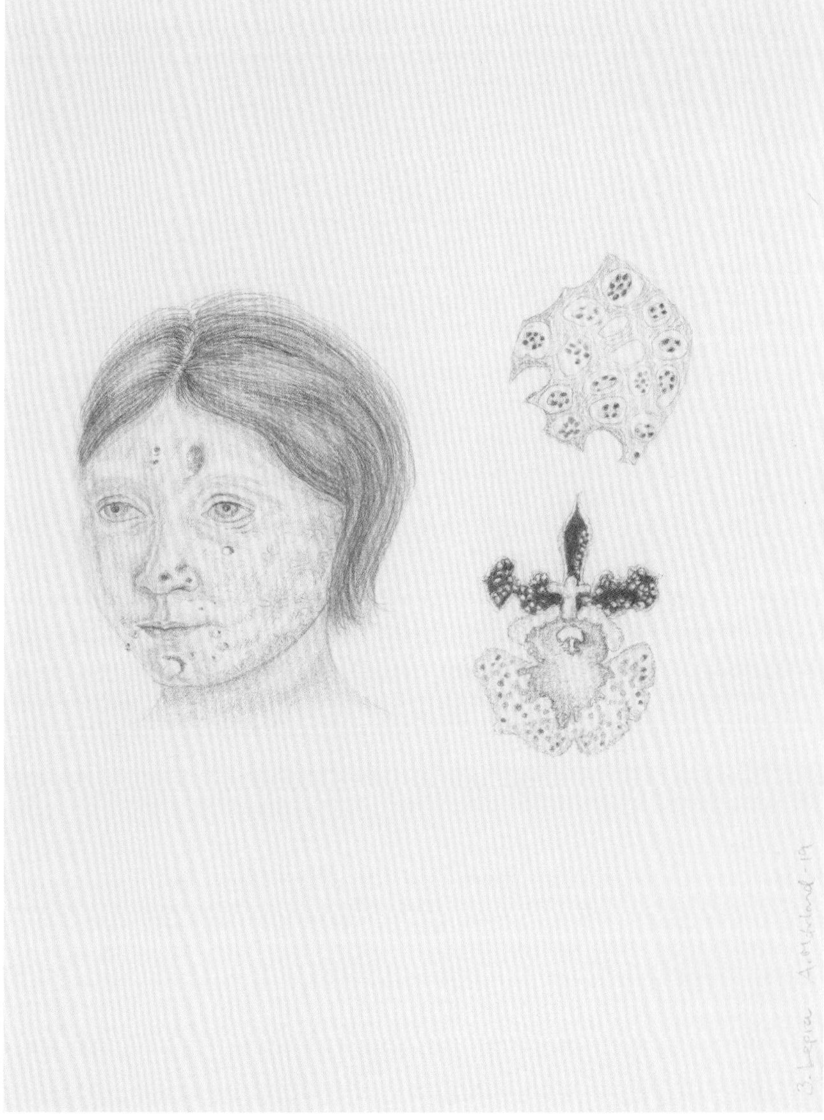

Skin & Orchid 2, 2018
Pencil on paper, 32 x 23 cm

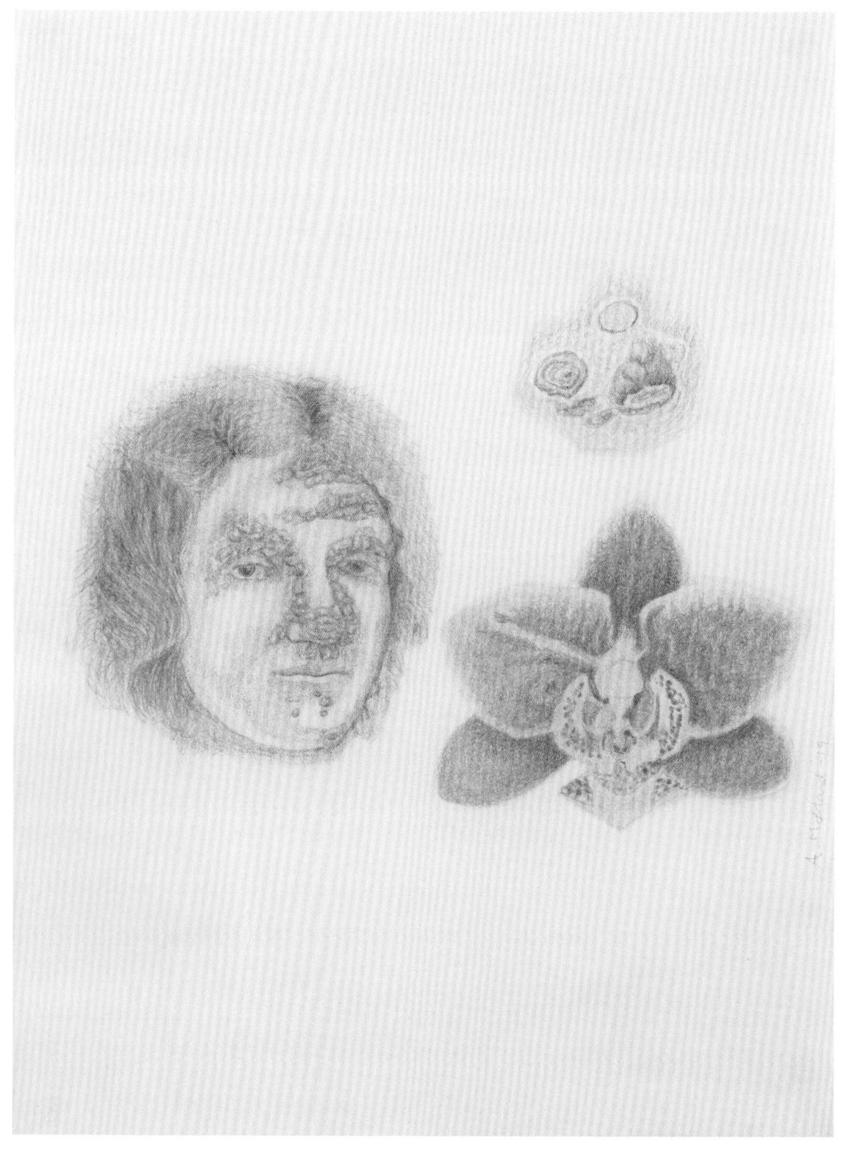

Skin & Orchid 3, 2018
Pencil on paper, 32 x 23 cm

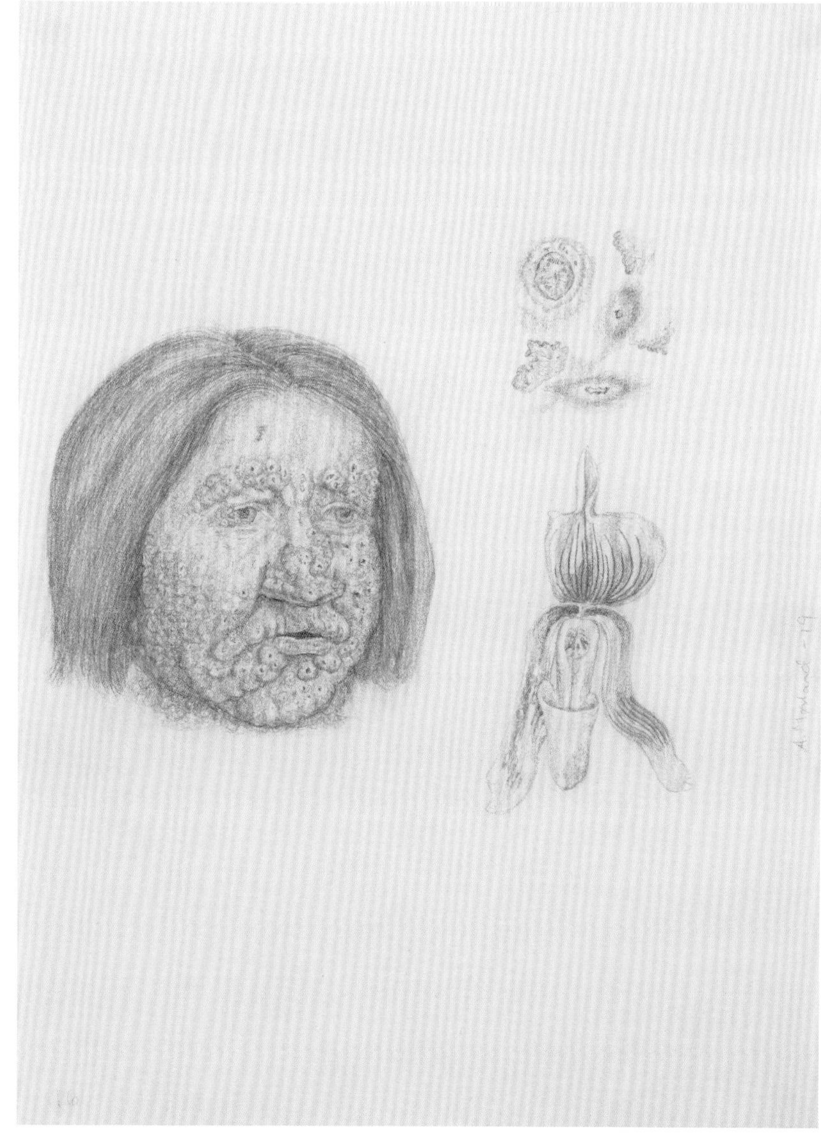

Skin & Orchid 5, 2018
Pencil on paper, 32 x 23 cm

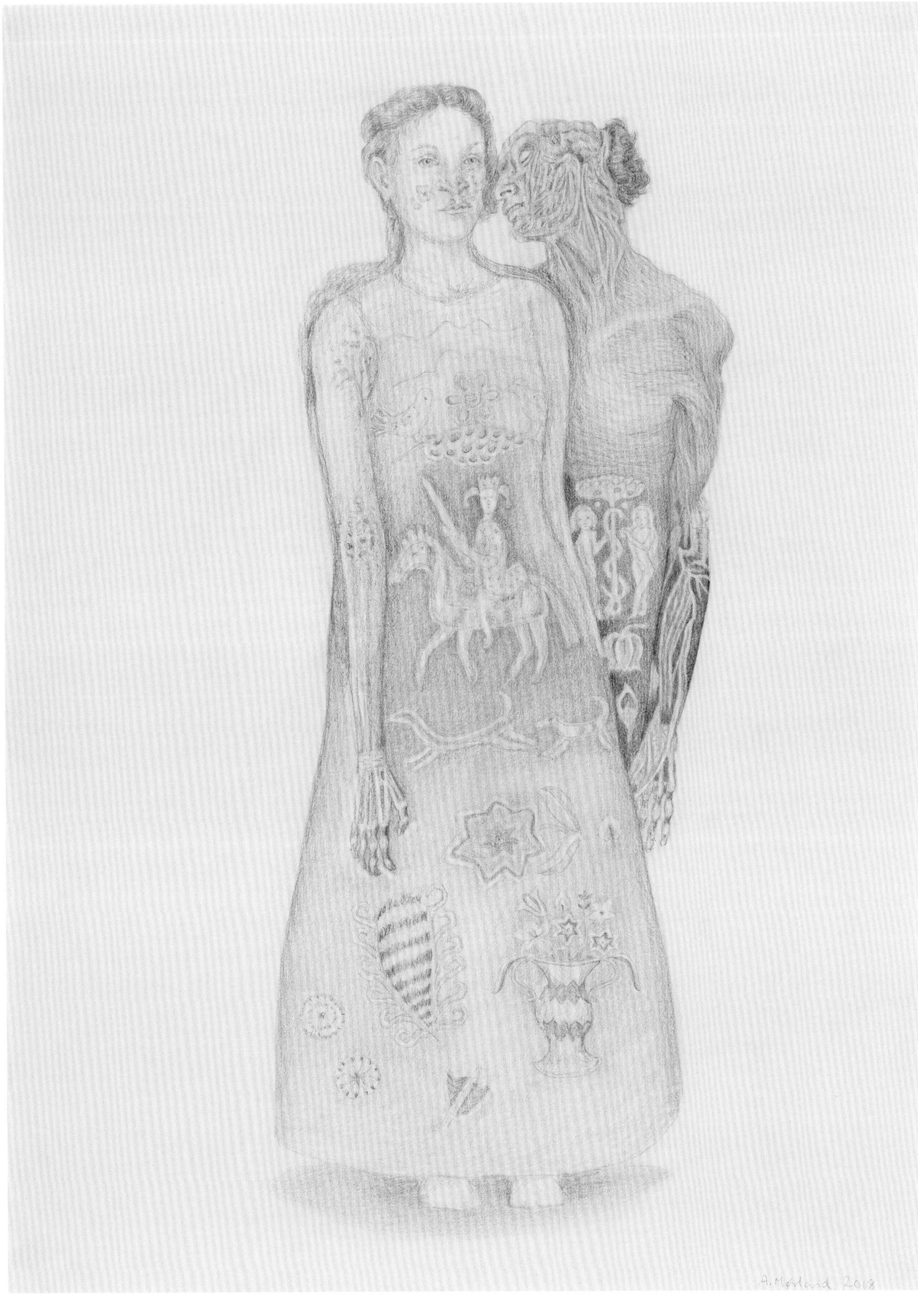

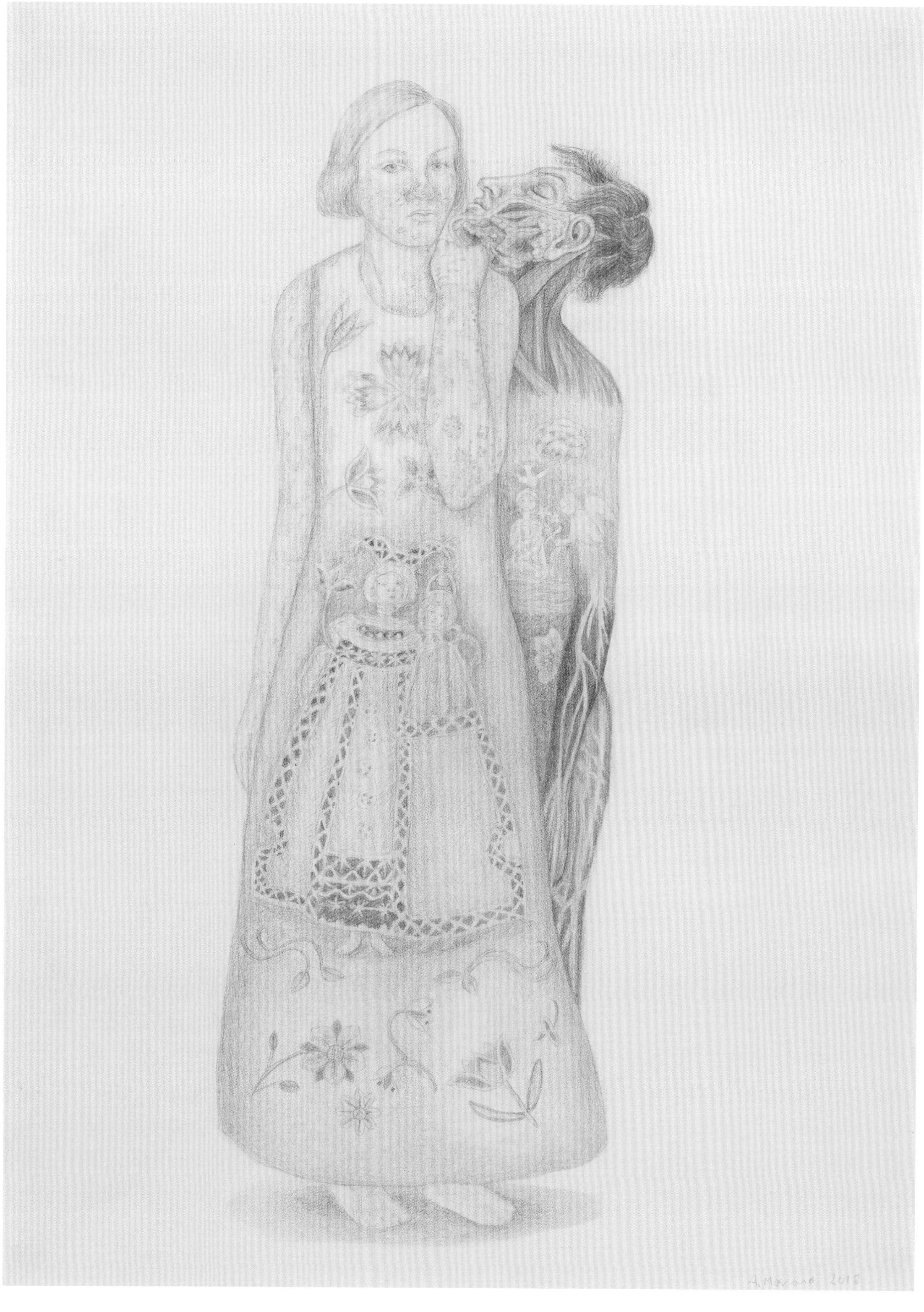

Couple 1, 2018
Pencil on paper, 60 x 40 cm

Couple 2, 2018
Pencil on paper, 60 x 40 cm

Pages 84–85
Red Dress, Black Roses 1, 2020
Oil on canvas, 120 x 90 cm

Red Dress, Black Roses 2, 2020
Oil on canvas, 120 x 90 cm

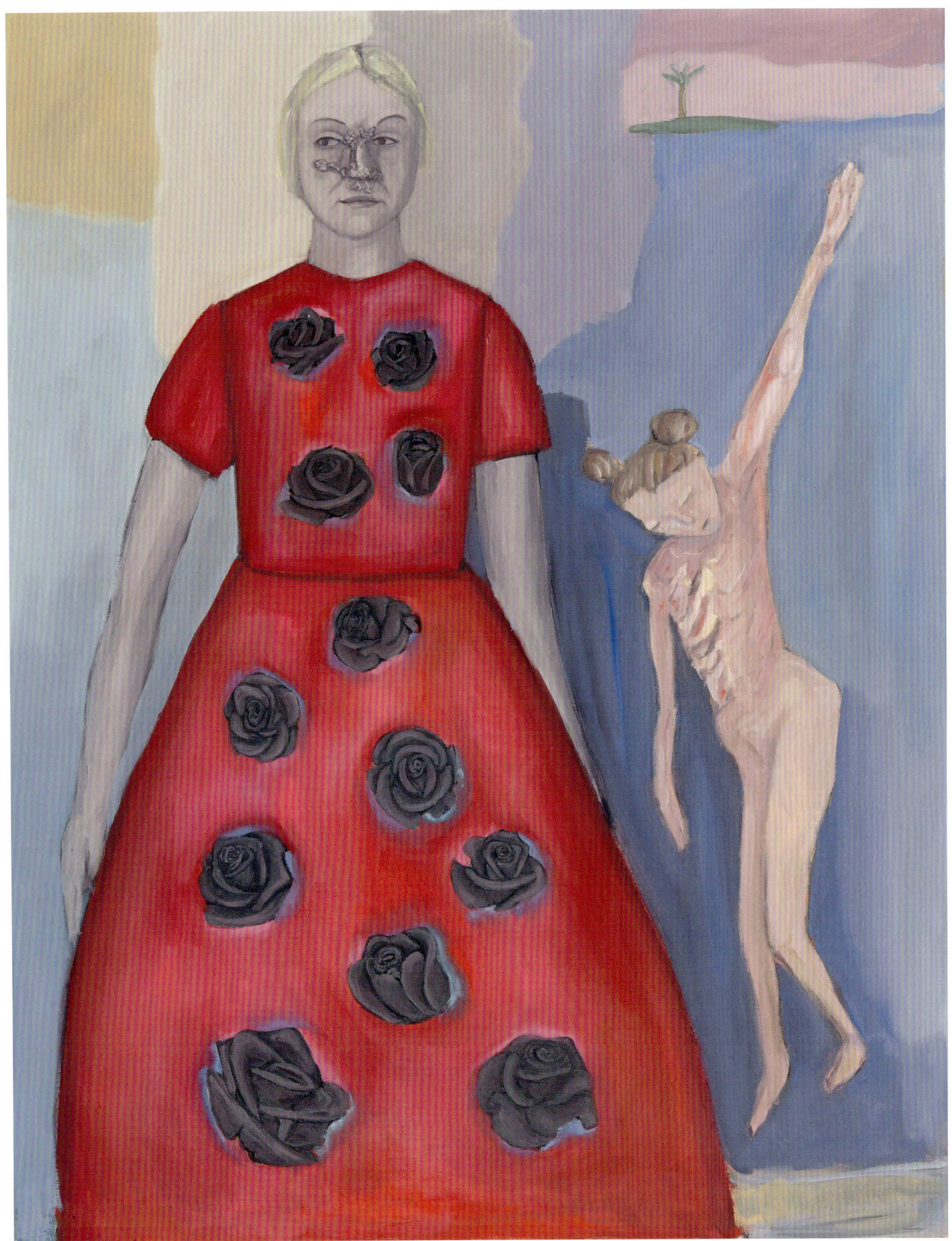

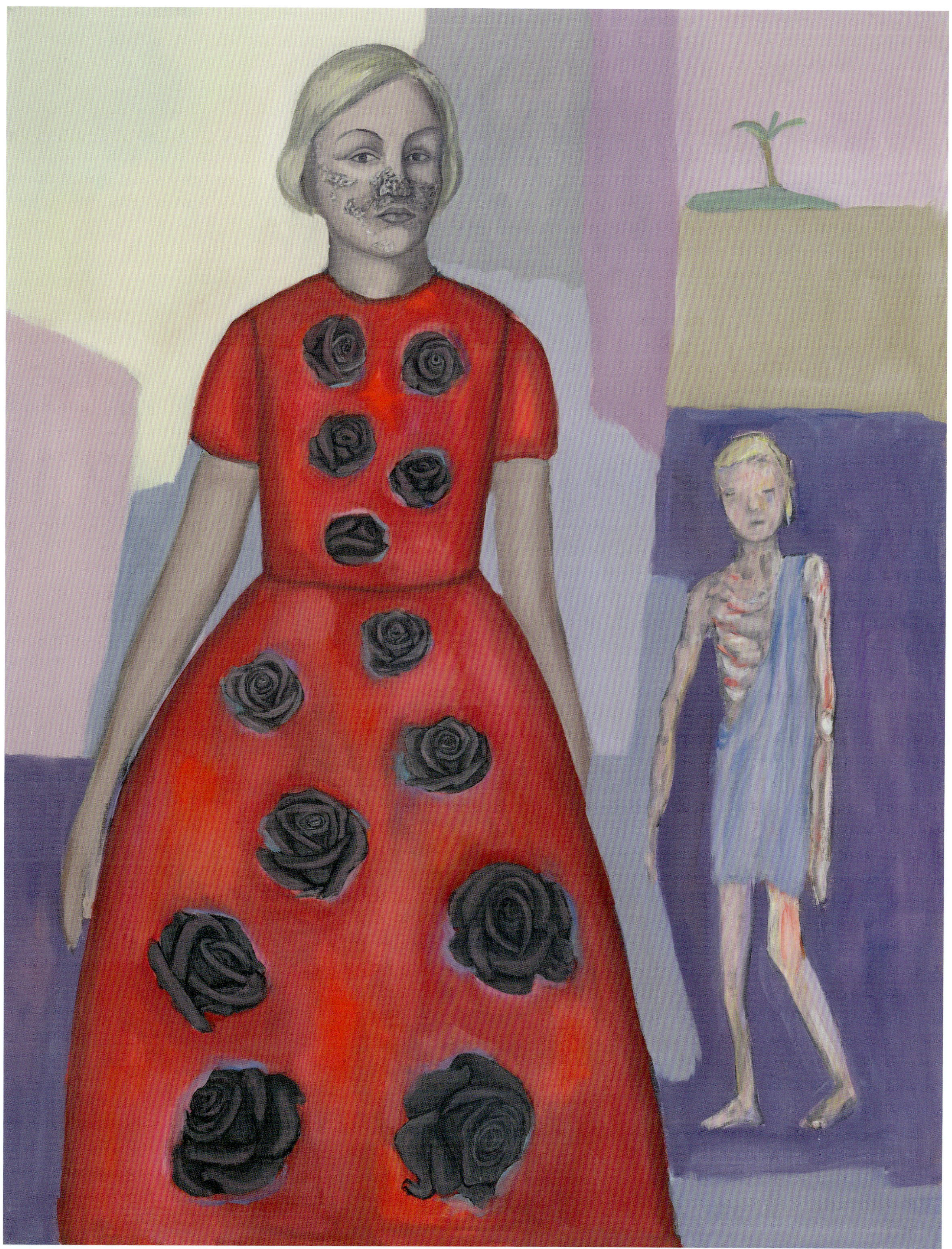

Red Landscape 1, 2011
Crayon on paper, 42 x 30 cm

The unease that we feel when seeing the deformed and dissolved faces expresses a contrast with the West's perfectionist ideal of beauty, even as it comments on human vulnerability in a world of climate change induced war and natural disaster. According to the latest IPCC report, a million animal and plant species are threatened by extinction at an alarming rate never before seen in human history. Loss of biodiversity is now a global crisis of the same magnitude as the climate crisis, two themes that are woven together in *Skin & Orchid*, given that today's migration includes millions of climate refugees. In this manner, nature is juxtaposed with human vulnerability.

The *Red Landscape* series features drawings that refer to five scenes of war that have left deep wounds in the history of civilisation: Sarajevo 1914, Rhineland 1936, Thua Thien-Hue 1968, Tora Bora 2001, and Benghazi 2011. The works were inspired by the collage technique, using images culled from various sources: old anatomical drawings, antique armour, fragments of a dress, numerical series, and landscapes referring to the sites where the scenes of war took place. Mørland was impressed by the collages she saw at the Kunstgewerbeschule in Basel in 1973 where she first encountered original works by Meret Oppenheim, Max Ernst, and Paul Klee. At the school in Basel, she created surrealist collages as models for her paintings. It is precisely this type of composition that has typified her works, perhaps above all her drawings, where the dialogue between whole and fragment is apparent. A clear parallel to this technique is Surrealism's experimentation with automatic writing and drawing, which opened up subconscious impulses by allowing the pen to flow across the paper. Similarly, the collage technique, where the artist would assemble pictures from different arenas of life without too much premeditation, opened up new worlds of expanding our consciousness. The Surrealists spent a good deal of time designing seamless transitions, and in Mørland's drawings the hybrid figures and transitions between humans, animals, and plants are indeed seamless. In the *Red Landscape* series, the various components have an inner logic centring on the topological basis that meets fragments from the body's inner anatomy and its defence system in the guise of age-old armour. Fragmentation is an essential aspect of the drawings, where the elements hover about in the pictorial plane unencumbered by the laws of gravity, like collective remembrances of past events. Evoking Arnold Böcklin's painting *Isle of the Dead*, the landscapes and the ocean take on a symbolic meaning. They are left untouched by the devastation of war, but its red-pastel appearance gives the topography a status as a silent witness from afar. The pastel technique entails that the landscapes seem veiled, with the name of the site and the number of killed inscribed as notes on the right-hand side. The body's inner anatomy is depicted in shades of pink, red, and grey, referring to how the catastrophe and suffering of war can fade but never be completely erased. These nuances become a barometer of how individuals and groups process their sorrow. Above these snippets from anatomical wall charts float pieces of armour that insist on protecting and preserving life.

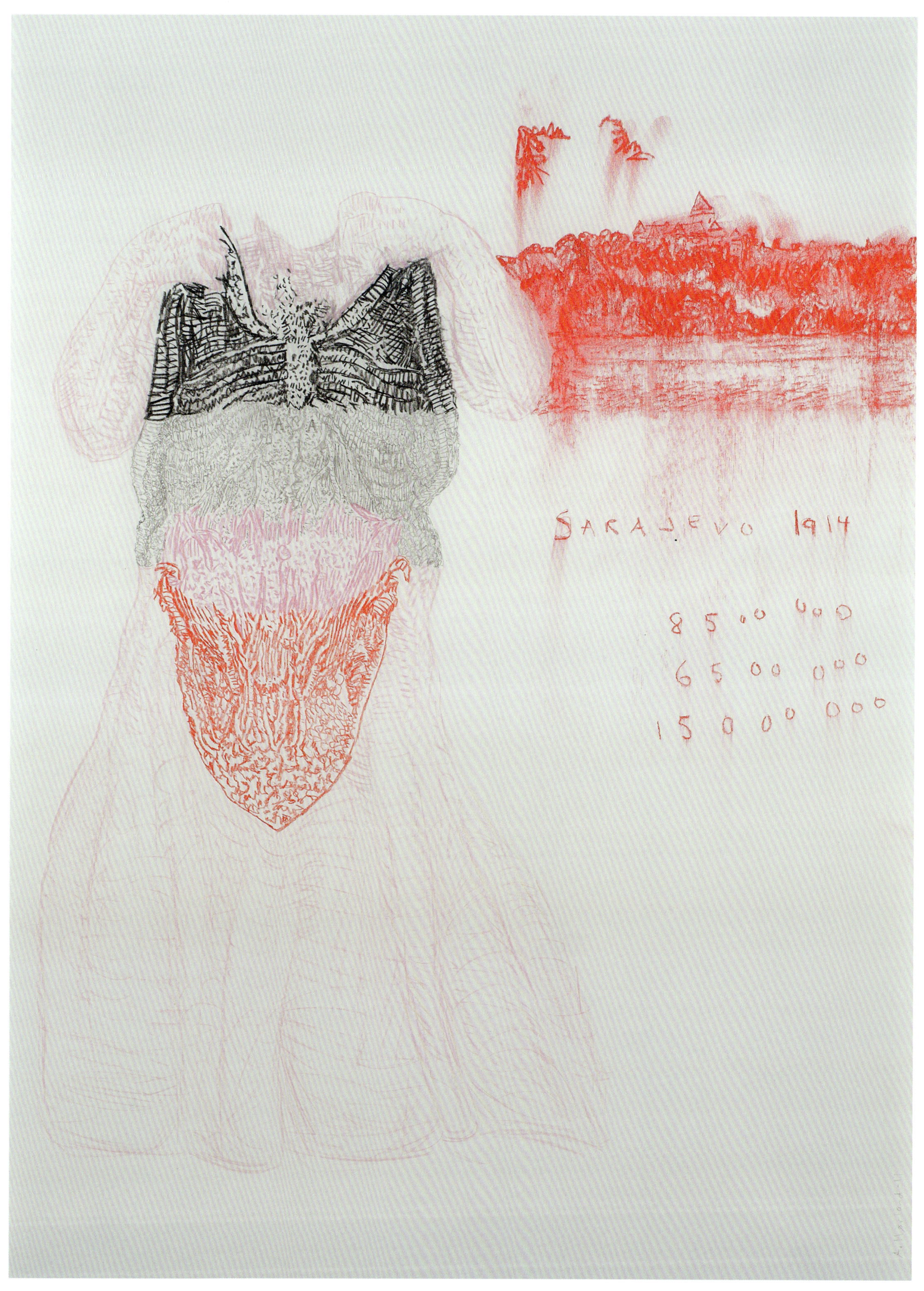

SARAJEVO 1914
85 00 000
65 00 000
15 0 00 000

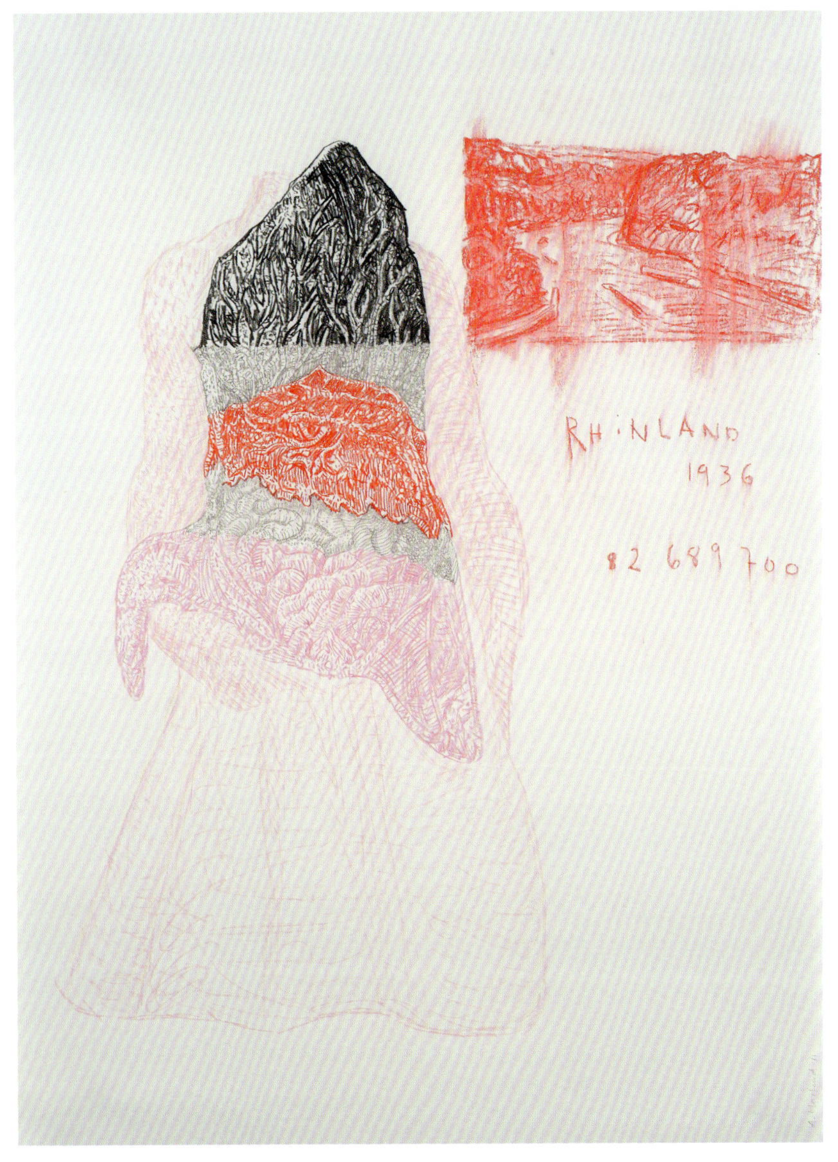

Red Landscape 2, 2011
Crayon on paper, 42 x 30 cm

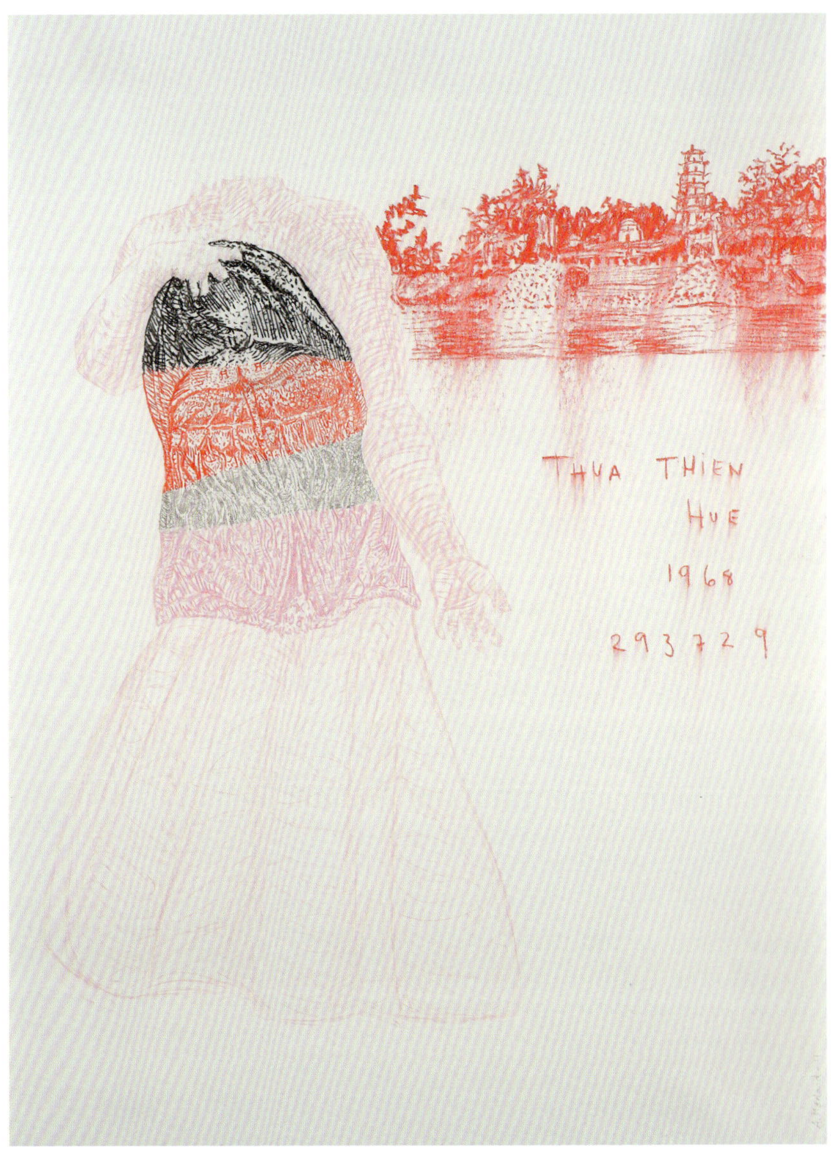

Red Landscape 3, 2011
Crayon on paper, 42 x 30 cm

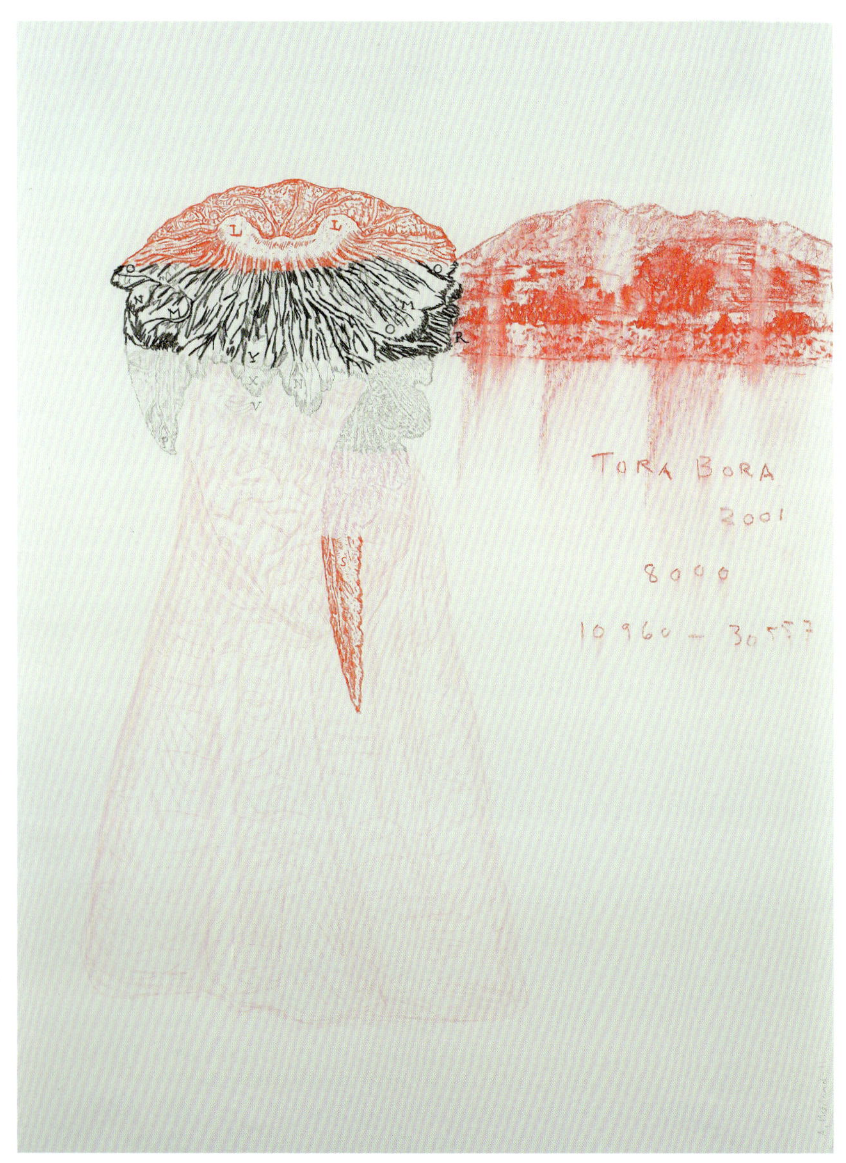

Red Landscape 4, 2011
Crayon on paper, 42 x 30 cm

Red Landscape 5, 2011
Crayon on paper, 41 x 33 cm

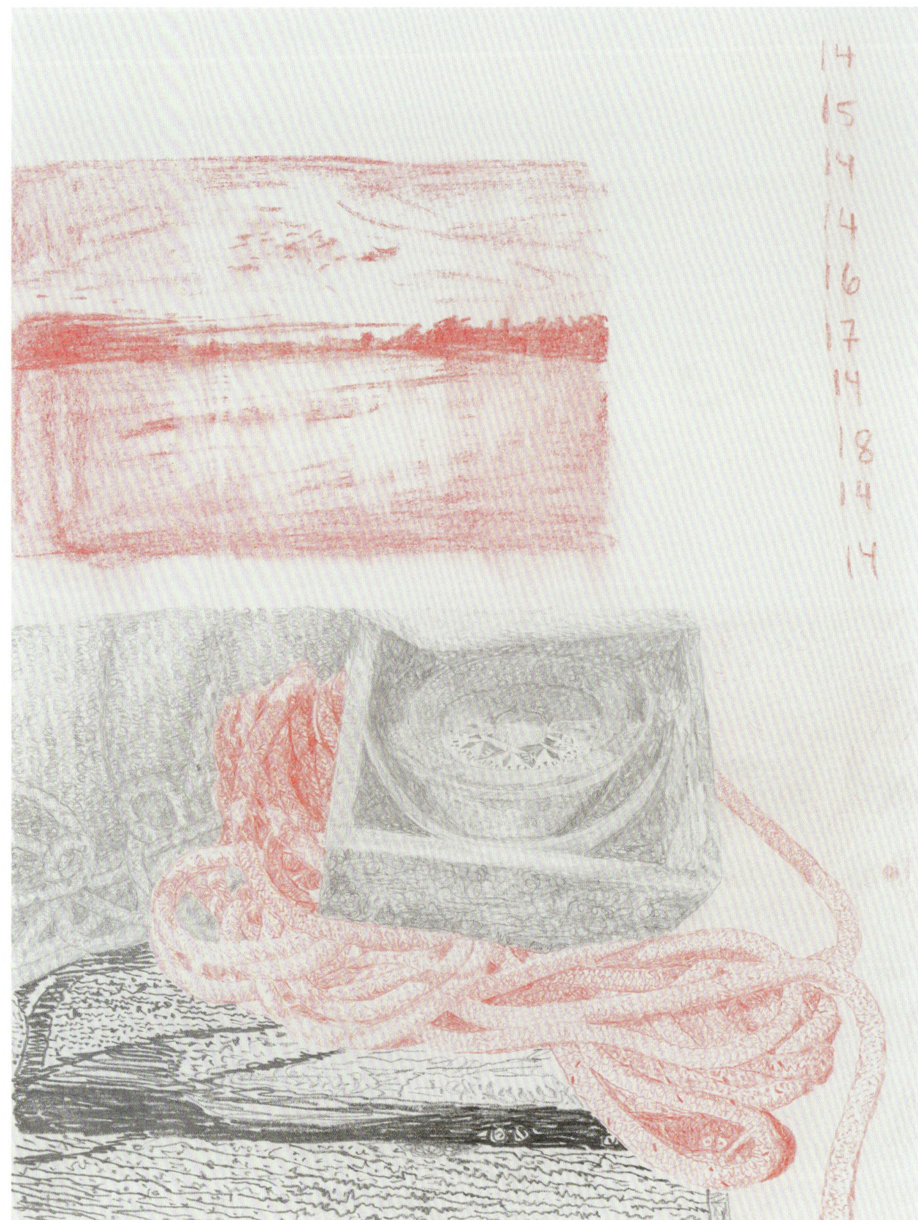

Red Landscape, Summer 1, 2011
Crayon on paper, 41 x 33 cm

The dress alludes to a similar protection of the child, becoming in this universe a feminine contrast to the masculinity of all warfare. The untouched landscape is slowly coloured red by the losses of war. This sets up an interesting contrast between horizontal and vertical components where the body's anatomy is juxtaposed with the sites' topography and where the inner body branches off into rivers and landscapes. In *Thua Thien*, one of the hands seems to lift the skin up to offer a glimpse into the body's inner anatomy of intestines and sinews, which may recall how traditional anatomical models could show seemingly untouched facial expressions, where the elegant gestures of the hand allowed a glimpse into the gashed body.

Mørland continues to explore this theme in the series of drawings titled *Red Landscape*, in this case as a response to the 22 July 2011 terrorist attack against the Government Quarter in Oslo and a political summer camp on the nearby island of Utøya. The three components that are juxtaposed here are fragmentary scenes from the inside of a sailboat. We see an old compass and some rope in a jumble at the bottom of the deck, hinting at the exact place Mørland was on that fateful day. Instead of the number of killed, the ages of

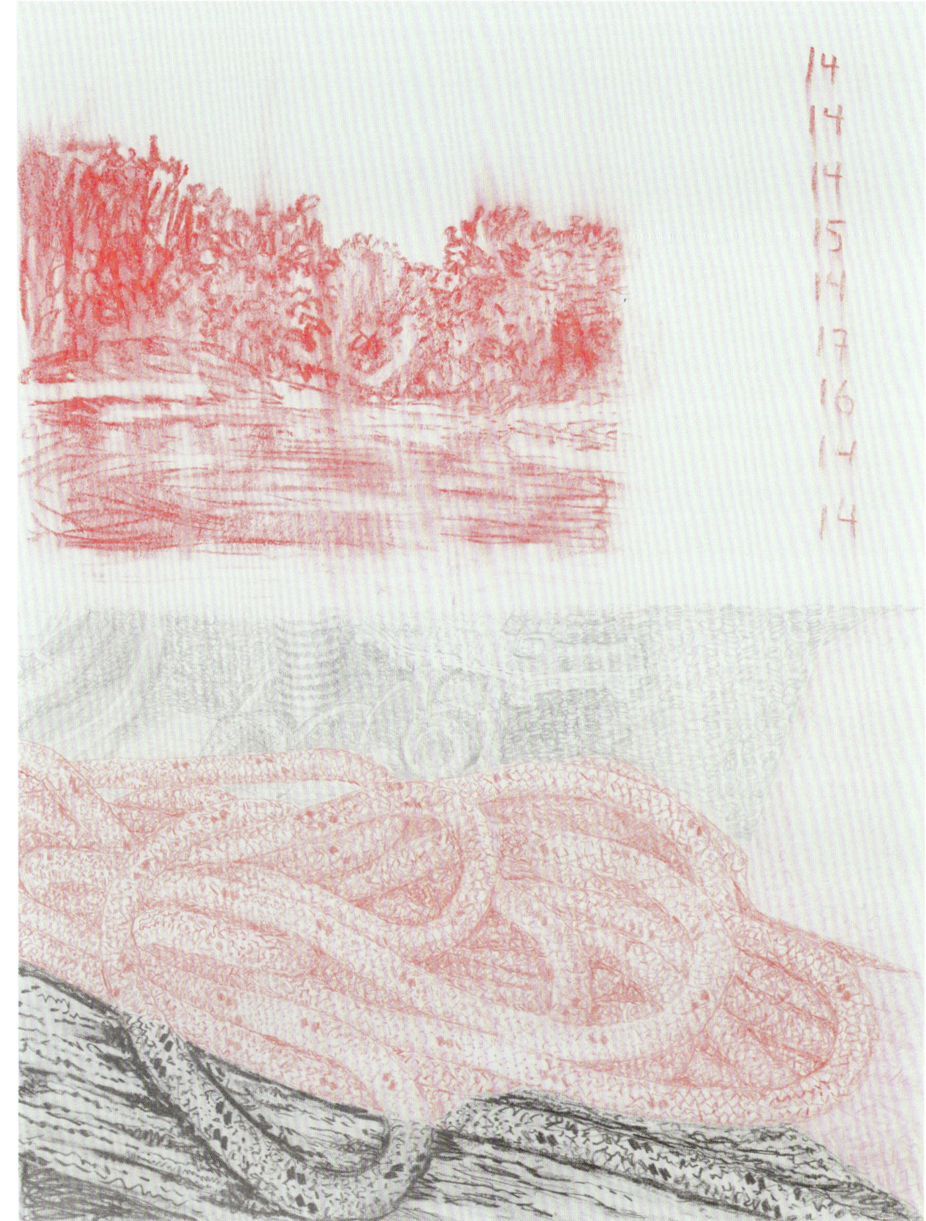

Red Landscape, Summer 2, 2011
Crayon on paper, 41 x 33 cm

the victims are written down. Moreover, the imagery prompts the viewer to think of all the civilians who used their own boats to save the young people trying to swim to safety from Utøya, and of how the death and merciless suffering caused by the terrorist attack impacted these civilians. Mørland's interpretations convey the decisive moment and show how mundane items, such as a sailboat's ropes and compass, may become coloured by traumatic experiences, even as the bleeding island of the suffering may be discerned in the background as the silent witness of nature.

[1] Terje Nordby, "Heltenes fødsel", in *Forvandlinger: Et moderne møte med greske myter* (Oslo: Andersen & Butenschøn, 1999), 40.

[2] Ingrid Pfeiffer, "Fantastic Women in Europe, the US, and Mexico", in *Fantastic Women: Surreal Worlds from Meret Oppenheim to Frida Kahlo*, ed. Ingrid Pfeiffer (Frankfurt am Main: Schirn Kunsthalle Frankfurt; Humlebæk: Louisiana Museum of Modern Art; Munich: Hirmer, 2020), 29.

[3] André Breton, "Political Position of Today's Art" (1935), in *Manifestoes of Surrealism*, trans. Richard Seaver and Helen R. Lane (Ann Arbor: University of Michigan Press, 1972), 210.

[4] Salvador Dalí, "Mine festninger", in *Kunstnere om kunst*, ed. Stian Grøgaard (Oslo: Oktober, 1993), 72.

[5] Siri Meyer, "Kunst og psykoanalyse", accessed 21 September 2020, https://www.sirimeyer.no/kunstessays/kunst-og-psykoanalyse; Freud

Delimbed, 2004
Mixed media object, 60 x 40 cm

Museum, "The Dream-work", accessed 21 September 2020, https://www.freud.org.uk/learn/discover-psychoanalysis/the-interpretation-of-dreams/the-dream-work/.

[6] Peter Thielst, *Kønnet, kroppen og selvet: Idehistorier om det europæiske menneske* (Copenhagen: Gyldendal, 1990), 109.

[7] Hal Foster, *Compulsive Beauty* (London: MIT Press, 1993), 81.

[8] Mabel Lang, *Cure and Cult in Ancient Corinth: A Guide to the Asklepieion* (Princeton, NJ: American School of Classical Studies at Athens, 1977).

[9] Hal Foster, *The Return of the Real: The Avant-Garde at the End of the Century* (Cambridge, MA: MIT Press, 1996), 127–28.

[10] Tone Lyngstad Nyaas, "Abjeksjon, kropp, fragment: Kiki Smith, utvalgte verker 1986–1994" (*cand. philol.* thesis, University of Oslo, 2000). See also Jésus Fuenmayor, Kate Haug, and Frazer Ward, eds., *Dirt and Domesticity: Constructions of the Feminine* (New York: Whitney Museum of American Art, 1992).

[11] Astrid Mørland, *Instinct: Open Intimate Closed Rooms*, trans. Anne Louise Sawkins (Bergen: Bergen Kunstforening, 2000), 22.

[12] Leena-Maija Rossi, "Att re-turnera blicken", in *Konst, kön och blick: Feministiska bildanalyser från renässans till postmodernism*, ed. Anna Lena Lindberg (Stockholm: Norsteds förlag, 1995), 211–25.

[13] Merete Morken Andersen, "*Et dukkehjem* (1879)", in *Ibsenhåndboken* (Oslo: Gyldendal, 1995), 122.

[14] Foster, *Return of the Real*, 127–28.

[15] Helaine Posner, *Kiki Smith* (New York: Bulfinch Press, 1998), 74.

[16] Breton, "Political Position of Today's Art", 213.

[17] Pfeiffer, "Fantastic Women", 28.

[18] Simone de Beauvoir, *The Second Sex*, trans. and ed. H. M. Parshley (London: Jonathan Cape, [1949] 1953), 267.

[19] Penelope Rosemont, *Surrealist Women: An International Anthology* (Austin: University of Texas Press, 1998), 40–45.

[20] Ingrid Pfeiffer, "Surreal Objects Yesterday and Today", in *Surreal Objects: Sculptures and Objects from Dalí to Man Ray*, ed. Ingrid Pfeiffer and Max Hollein (Ostfildern: Hatje Cantz, 2011), 15–33.

[21] Theodor W. Adorno, *Prism*, trans. Samuel Weber and Sherry Weber (London: Spearman, 1967), 32; Theodor W. Adorno, "Theses on Art and Religion Today", *Kenyon Review* 7, no. 4 (1945): 678.

[22] Robin Adèle Greeley, "The Minotaur in Its Labyrinth: Art and Politics in the Surrealists' World", in *Monsters & Myths: Surrealism and War in the 1930s and 1940s*, ed. Oliver Shell and Oliver Tostmann (Baltimore: Baltimore Museum of Art; Hartford, CT: Wadsworth Atheneum Museum of Art; New York: Rizzoli Electa, 2018), 95–99.

[23] Mørland, *Instinct*, 12–13.

[24] *Physiologus* is a didactic Early Christian tome that depicts legendary creatures, which are attributed either malevolent or benevolent qualities. The tome was meant to instruct its readers on how they could use such creatures as guides to finding the path to salvation. *Physiologus* describes the deer as the implacable enemy of the snake, thus becoming an allegory of Christ combatting Satan.

[25] Poul Erik Tøjner, *Munch med egne ord* (Oslo: Forlaget Press, 2000), 102–11.

[26] The sociologist Émile Durkheim investigated the concept of alienation already in the late nineteenth century in connection with the dissolution and transformation of social norms and structures. As related to today's individually oriented society, we find that an all-embracing desire, not least for material goods, has driven individuals into a spiral of needs, where a restless quest for gratification leads people to vacillate between apathy and euphoria, between dejection and agitation.

[27] Karin Johannisson, *Melankolske rom: Om angst, lede og sårbarhet gjennom tidene*, trans. Monica Aasprong (Oslo: Cappelen Damm, 2010), 65.

[28] Ibid., 29.

[29] Jacques Meuris, *René Magritte*, trans. Michael Scuffil (Cologne: Benedikt Taschen, 1991), 51.

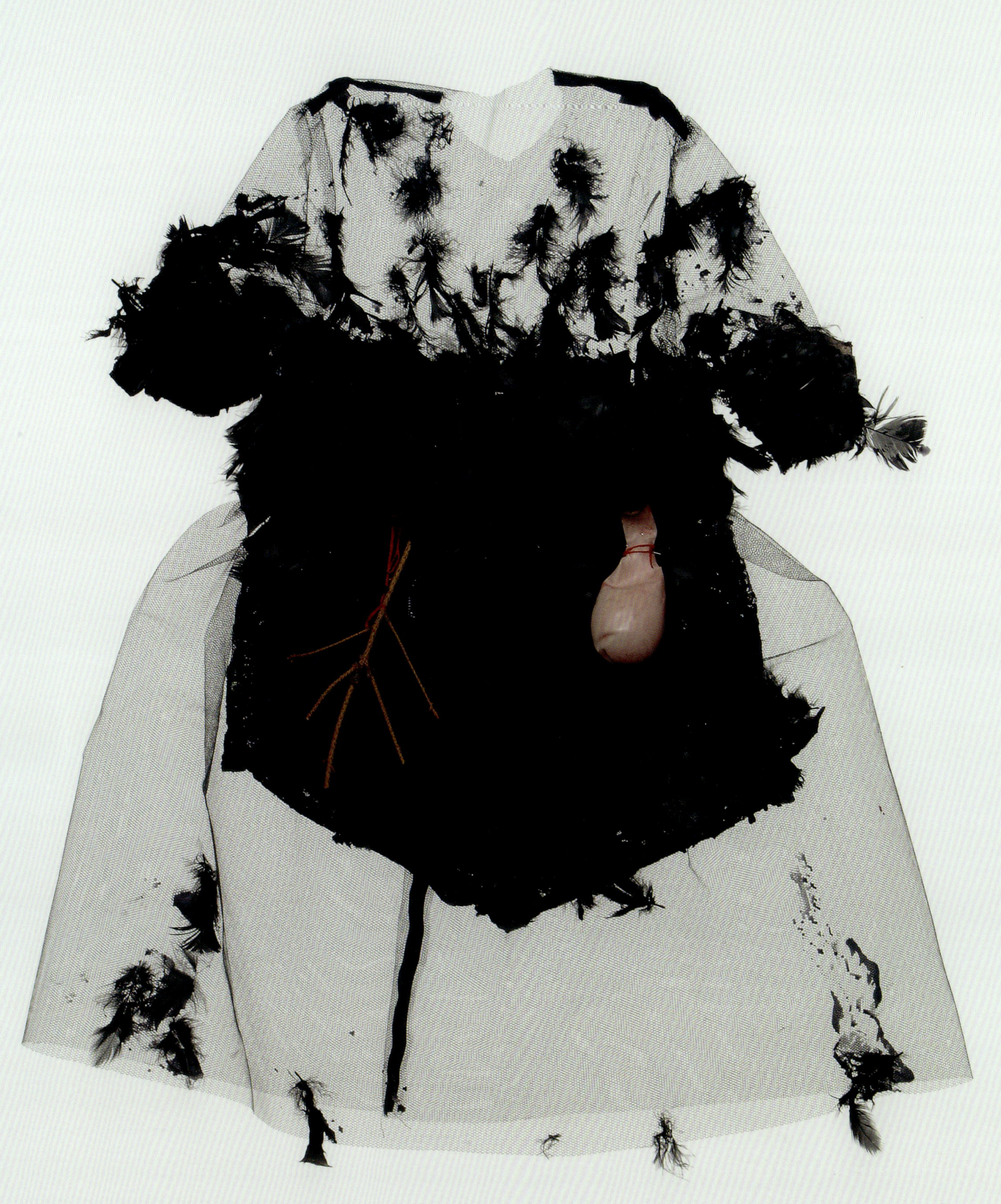

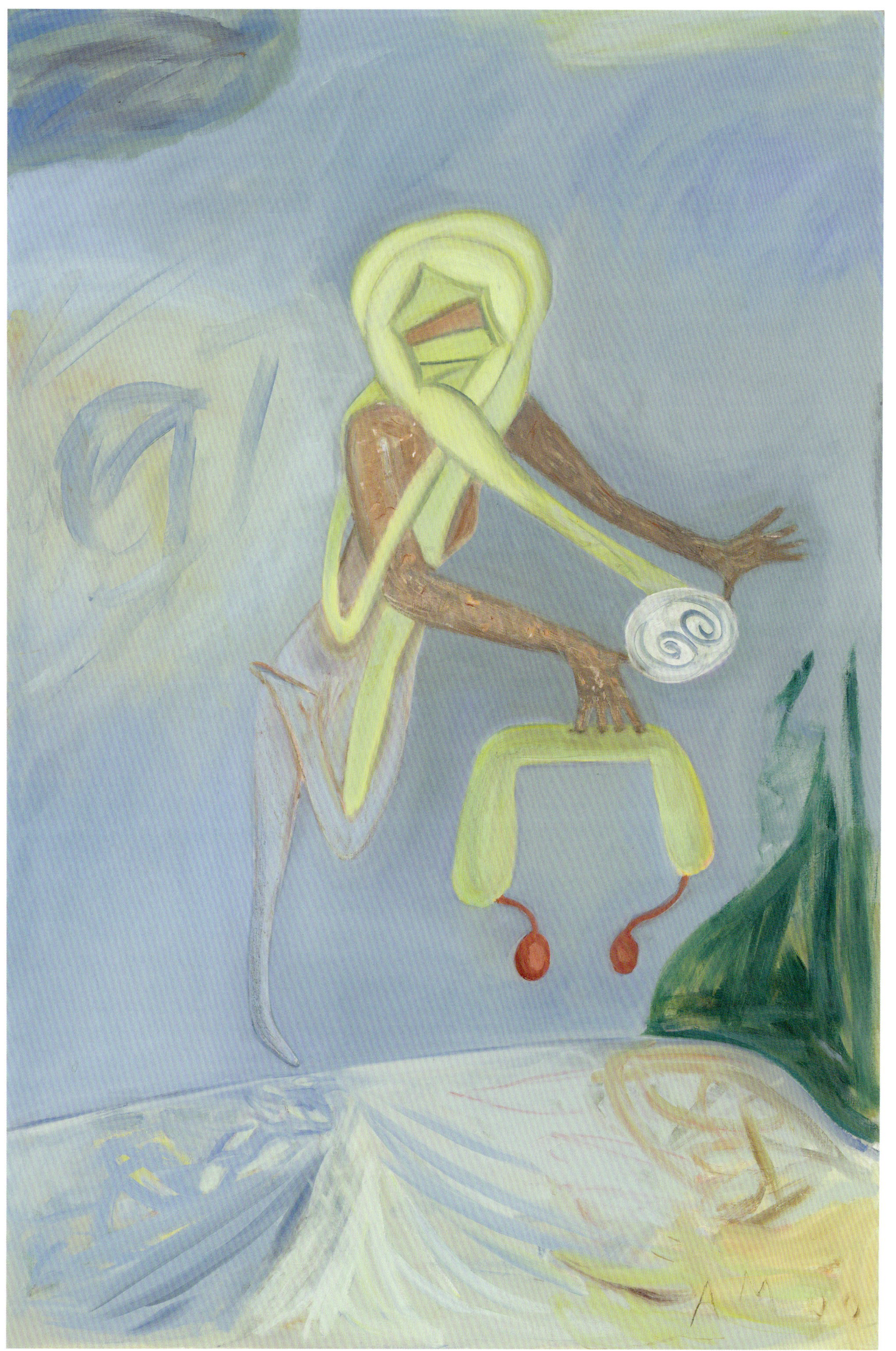

The Symbiosis between Humans and Nature

Irene Haslund

In the painting *Above the Earth*, a face is covered, concealed. What does it mean for the various perspectives in the picture that this face is concealed? When some of the details are blurred out, when you cannot see a person's entire face, their expression becomes more mysterious, making it easier to invest some of your own self in the picture. In that case, the latter is no longer of someone particular but of people in general. And when something is missing, something else becomes visible. By virtue of being veiled, the image becomes distilled into an essence. Concealment obscures trivialities, and the expression and mood become more prominent. The veil gives a sense of a mental state. Is there something we are hiding in our lives? Are we hidden to ourselves? We ask to see and to be seen. We each walk around with our own face, but we cannot see that face.

There is a tension in the covered and the uncovered. There can be power in keeping something out of sight, allowing it to elude our grasp. When something is concealed, underlying, or wrapped up, it often piques the onlooker's curiosity. The gaze's desire to see everything, but be obstructed, can in itself become an impetus. What we are denied is what tastes the best. Distance increases desire. It is when we are not presented with readymade answers that our imaginations are truly let loose.

Heraclitus (c. 540–470 BC) is known for the aphorism "nature loves to hide". Nature expresses itself enigmatically, since the world is in itself an enigma. In the concealed there is a notion that we will never get to the bottom of what it is we are wondering about. As we engage with the world, there will always be a few mysteries that remain unresolved. All the while, the world remains the object of our curiosity. Existence itself is concealed. Heraclitus teaches us about the paradox of existence: even though all of nature or reality is present, it nevertheless eludes being fully comprehended. The painting *Above the Earth* arguably touches upon such a way of thinking, showing us as it does a wordless language. How can we live in a world that is so fundamentally paradoxical? Heraclitus seems to warn against inferring too much meaning from it all. He advises us not to project a deeper meaning into the cosmos: "Life is a child amusing himself, playing a game of draughts. The kingship is in the hands of a child."

The figure in *Above the Earth* holds something in his or her hand, as though trying to get a handle on existence – is it a toy? a symbol? Symbols can be perceived as concrete, visible representations of something abstract that does not immediately lend itself to being represented. It is a sign that brings something into the light, even as it hides something else that yet has not been revealed. That which is hidden or secret and invisible is protected by the sensuousness of the symbols. The symbol refers to a movement among people where it

Above the Earth, 2000
Oil on canvas, 150 x 110 cm

brings about a change in those who start using it. It makes it possible for the invisible to be revealed through concealment.

Black Stones. The picture depicts a feminine figure lying with her hands behind her back. Her face looks mummified. Her head and neck rest on a root. The roots have been severed and are entwined around the figure's shoulders. Her body undulates like a beach between the green terrain and the blue sea. Is she Mother Earth? The green terrain is somewhat barren and scarred. Perhaps because it has been exploited and wounded? The sky above looks polluted. One of the roots extends upwards like a smokestack. The inlaid picture to the right is perhaps showing the fertile soil that once was: a more vibrant colour, a tree growing. Is this about nature's rebuke of how humanity has treated the earth? Are the black rocks an oil spill? The earth's bounty has been removed, harvested by people. It is the felled trees that can resuscitate her.

When looking at the picture, it is impossible not to step into the character and thereby be directly confronted by her. She is alone in the picture, but her body language indicates that someone else is present: she is turning towards some-one who is looking at her, who she addresses and interacts with. In fact, it is me she is looking at. It is me she is leaning towards. It is me she is scaring with her deathlike face. What are you people doing? It is as though Mørland in this picture has painted not only a female figure but also the person looking at the woman. The picture is confrontational; it demands something, something that requires a response. The viewer is faced with a choice, but the choice has not been made yet. Indeed, it is as though longing itself has been depicted here.

Where does longing come from? What is that voice doing in our lives? Longing is always there, close by, like a shadow, usually unobtrusive and mute – like a rock, always accompanying us in the background. Most of us – who either are unwilling or unable to immerse ourselves in the flat, dry intoxication of the present – notice a longing in our lives. It is as though what is present is not quite enough for us; it leaves behind a hunger or a thirst in us for what is absent. Longing is the gateway to letting ourselves be swept away, seduced, and tempt-ed to let go of that part of life that is the here-and-now. It is a warning from inside of us that we, despite all our efforts, do not entirely belong in the world.

Longing helps us to connect the unconnectable together, lets us see the unseen and hear the unheard, be where we cannot be, meet what we can never meet, love what we can never love. Longing is not just about ourselves but about everything else in the world that we are intertwined with and part of. It is about the others, about society and nature, about the superhuman and the spiritual, about the invisible and those who, in different ways, have left us behind. Long-ing can show us how our own and other people's lives are about far more than

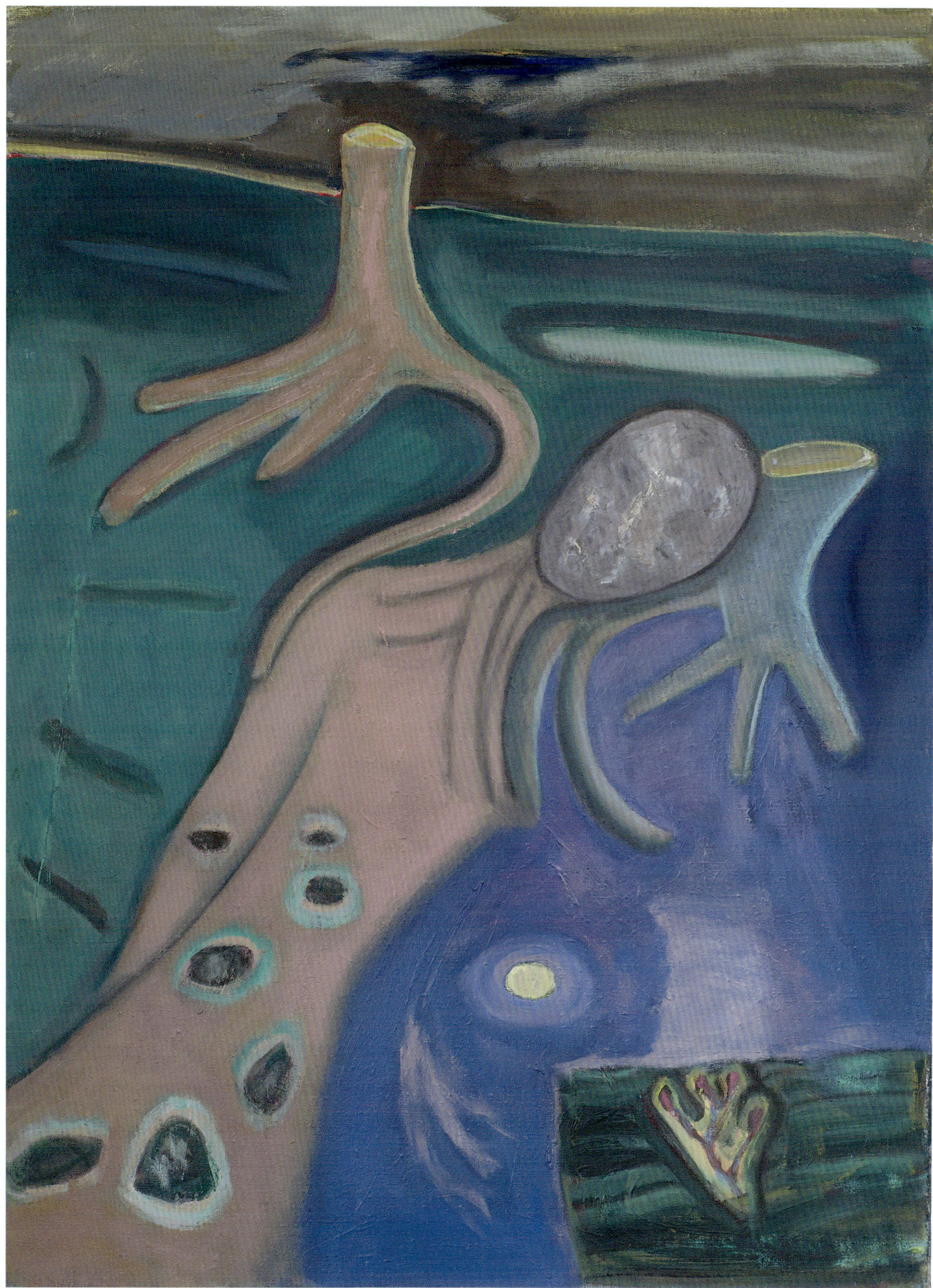

the psychological topics that modern people are so preoccupied with. Longing shows us the way to the gift known as the world – the entire, complex reality we are woven into, the life we live in the company of all other beings.

People, deer, and horns are recurring motifs in Mørland's paintings, as in the series *Buck and Orchid* (1–5) from 2019 and *Black Buck* (1–3) from 2020. In each picture, she teases out something new in an old motif, and does this more and more compellingly each time.

Black Buck 1. The black buck in the middle of the picture has a female shape and is clad in a wide, black dress with large, white roses. In the background, two women stand on each side of the buck: one is naked, while the other is dressed. The woman on the left has two branch-like growths protruding from her head, while the woman on the right has a buck's horn-on her head. The latter seems to be the younger of the two, her hair is longer, and she looks healthier. The two women find themselves at either end of a life cycle: one represents youth and a fertile future, the other represents the autumn of life. A twig is nearby each of the women; the twig by the younger woman looks more luxuriant.

There is something threatening and dominant about the black buck; its horns have an aura of power and arrogance. But there is also something dignified and solemn about it. Its gaze peers out from the sorrow but has yet to free itself from it; it is as though the gaze is declaring that the sorrow is not me but something that has happened *to* me. The woman on the left and the buck look at each other. Have we done something wrong? Are we ourselves what is wrong?

Scientists have actually discovered physical evidence that young people today are developing "horns" on the back of their skull. They have observed some bone growths, hornlike spikes, sticking out from the skulls of these young people, just above the neck. The scientists suggest that these spikes come from the young people craning their heads forward to interact with modern technology, such as smartphones and other handheld devices.

This supports the Norwegian philosopher Peter Wessel Zapffe's notion that humans are a species whose evolution has overshot the target. It is not the first time this has happened: for instance, Zapffe refers to a certain type of deer that allegedly became extinct because its antlers never stopped growing, making it an easy catch for predators – in essence, the animal fell victim to its own horned crown. And it is the same with humans. Zapffe characterises us as "over-equipped". It is our intellectual abilities that serve as our antlers.

Perhaps this quotation from an essay Zapffe wrote in 1933 is apt for Mørland's picture: "So he stands there with his visions, betrayed by the totality of being, in wonderment and fear. Animals as well felt this fear, in thunderstorms and beneath the lion's claw. But man started to fear life itself – started even to fear his own existence."[1]

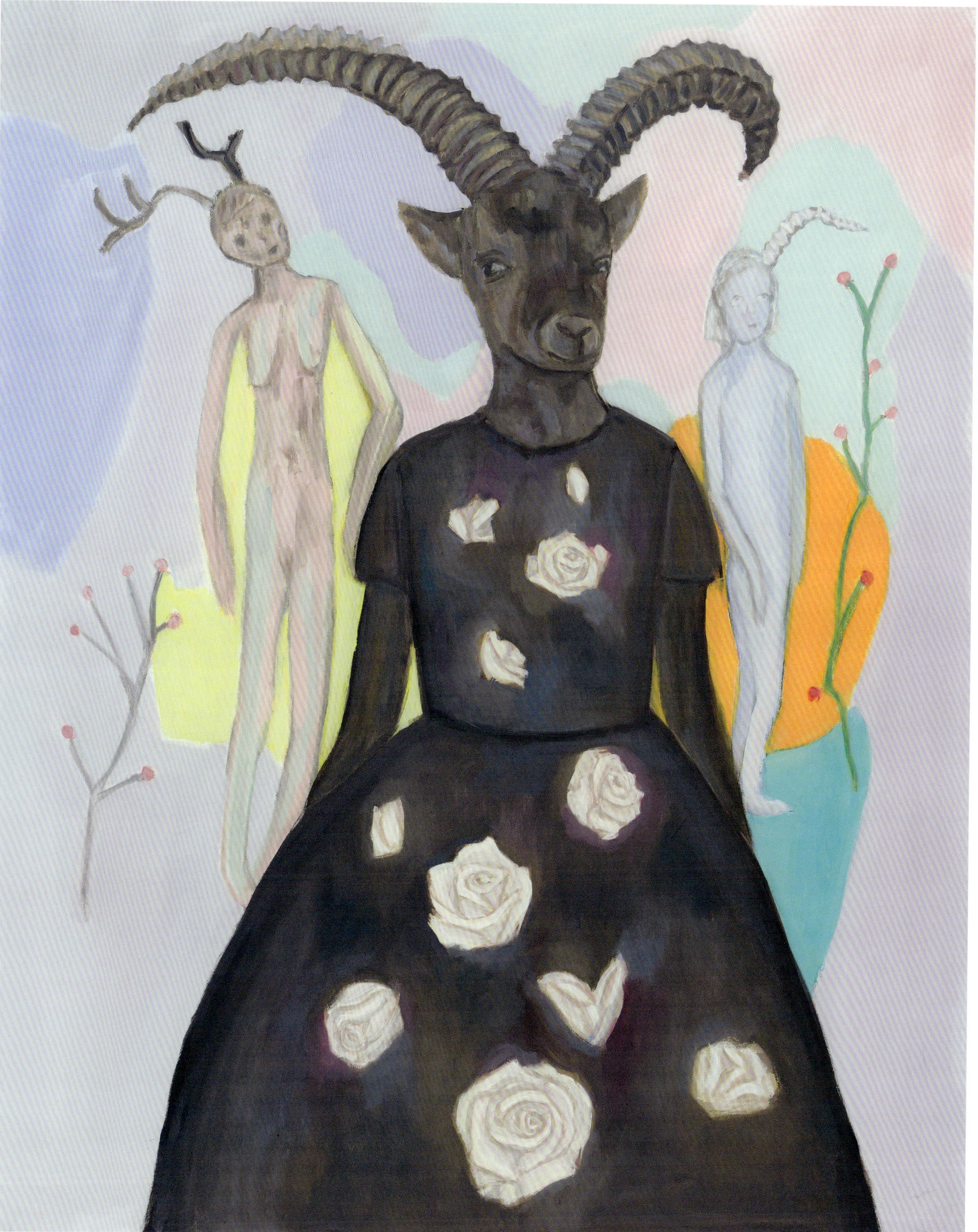

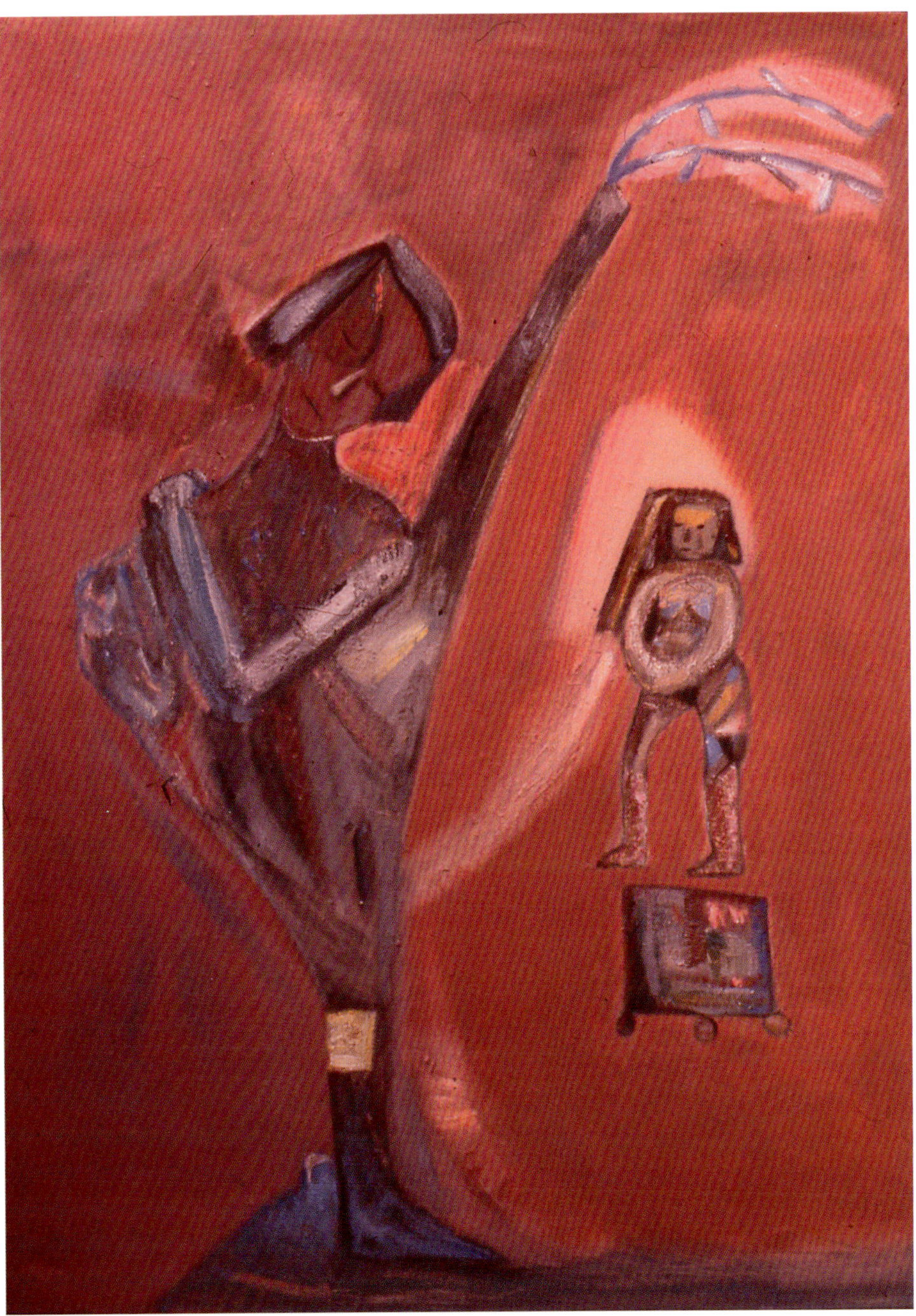

People are burdened by alienation, by fears, by experiences of the absurdity and pointlessness of being. Zapffe therefore argued in favour of humans ending their reproduction.

In contrast to Zapffe's essay, however, Mørland's pictures also speak of creation, growth, and hope. We see this in the roses, the twigs, and the young woman. The insight that we have also gone astray in our evolution makes it possible to see our choices in a new light. The ruins are a symbol of the transient, but they are also suggestive of a new start. The baneful and the beautiful go hand in hand. But with power comes responsibility. The past and the present must be used to save the future.

[1] Peter Wessel Zapffe, "Den sidste Messias" (1933), in *Essays*, ed. J. B. Gundersen (Oslo: Aventura, 1992), 16: "Saa staar han da der med sine syner, forraadt av altet, i undring og angst. Ogsaa dyret kjendte angst, i tordenveir og under løvens klo. Men mennesket fik angst for selve livet – ja for sitt eget væsen."

The Woman, the River and
the Tree 1, 1998
Oil on canvas, 80 x 75 cm

The Woman, the River and
the Tree 2, 1998
Oil on canvas, 80 x 75 cm

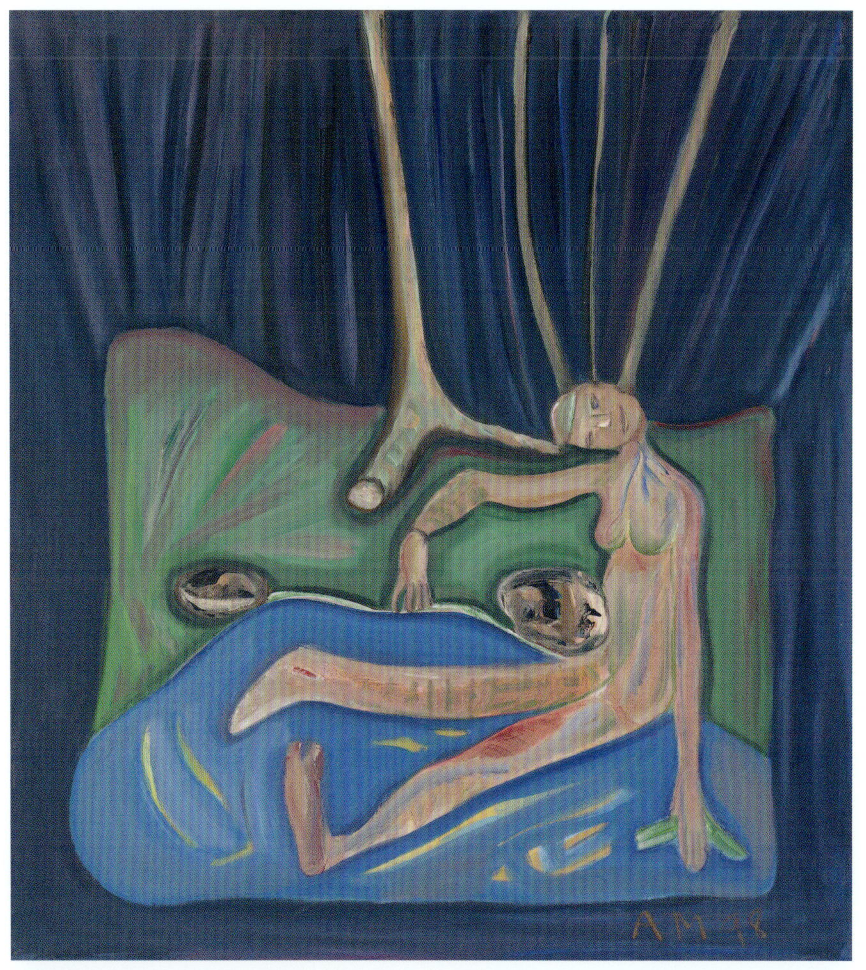

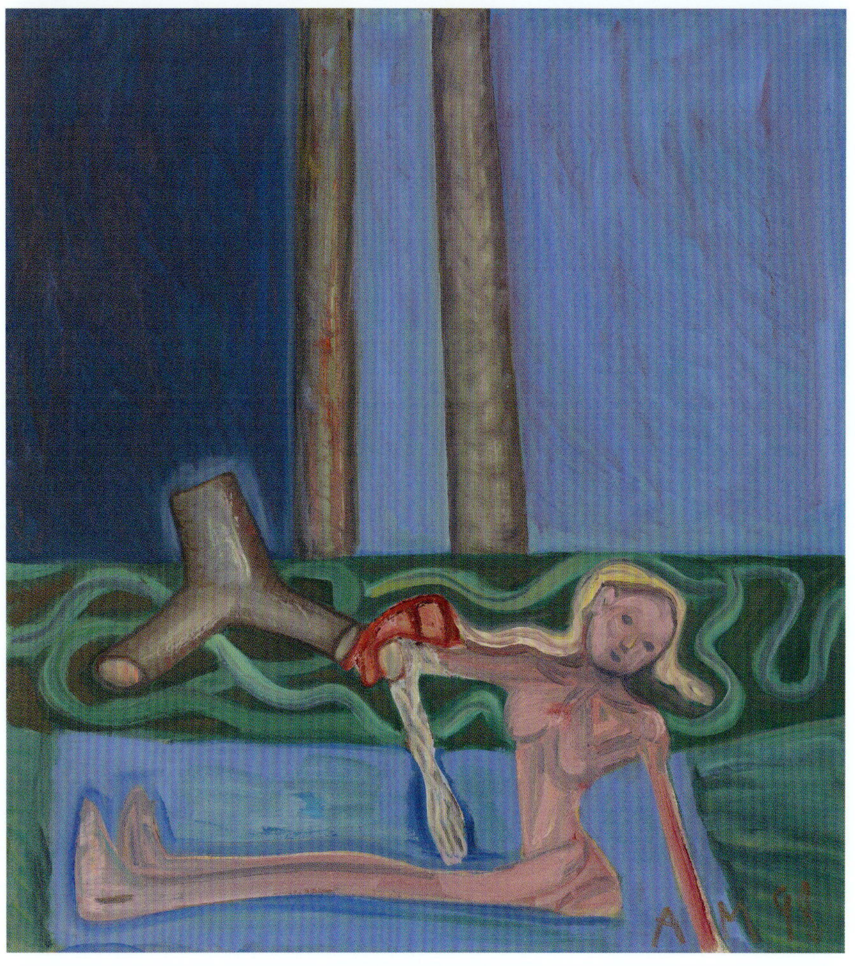

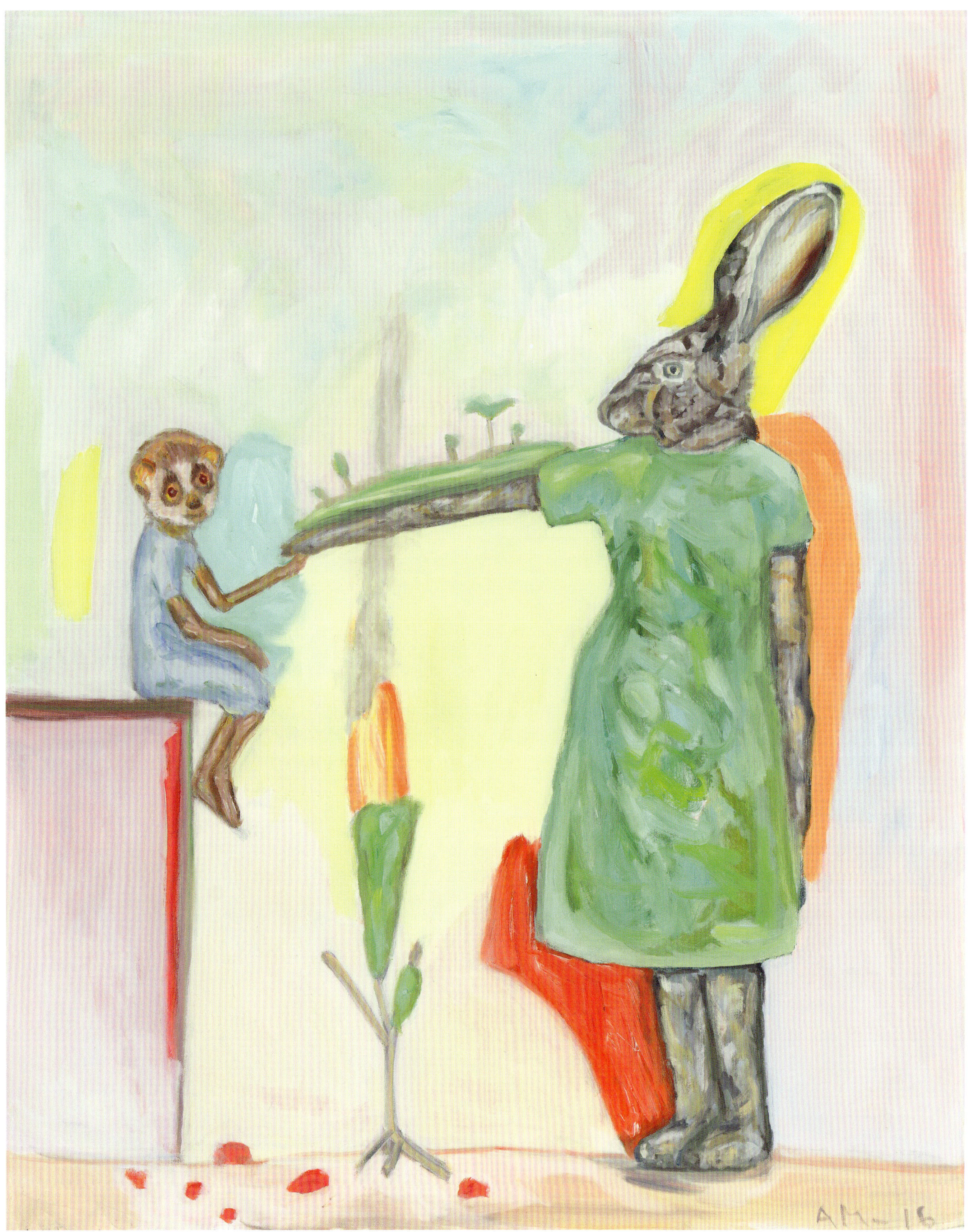

AM~ 16

A Collage of a Moment in Time

Eli Skatvedt

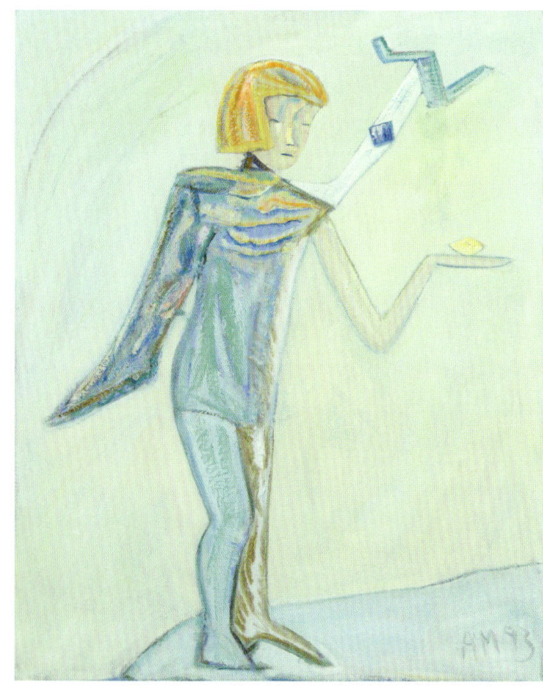

Woman on a Root, 1993
Oil on canvas, 80 x 60 cm

*In a Hundred Years Everything Will
Be Forgotten, Said the Rabbit*, 2016
Oil on canvas, 90 x 70 cm

In order to understand what shapes contemporary society, politically, financially, and sociologically, you must start with an idea. It is precisely such ideas that the artist Astrid Mørland provides us with in her works of art. Humanity as part of nature is not a new theme for the artist, but is rather a philosophical idea she has explored in various ways in her paintings and drawings ever since the 1970s. It was at this time, when Mørland was herself an art student fighting for equality and fair distribution, that an international group of scholars published the report *The Limits to Growth* (1972) on behalf of the Club of Rome.[1] Using computer models, the report investigated humanity's future population growth and resource consumption. The aim of the book was to calculate the upper limit of growth and consumption before human activity would overburden the physical limitations of our planet. The report's calculations made for grim reading.

The crucial connection between humanity and nature in Mørland's art is already apparent in her early works. In the painting *Woman on a Root* (1993), for instance, the artist seeks a symbiosis between humanity and nature, as a female figure stands in the ocean with one of her legs depicted as a root. As she tries to draw nourishment, to put down roots in nature, this alienated woman is met by a wave. One of her arms is thin and bony, the other is a blue wing. The themes of nature versus culture, of dreaming versus being awake, are recurring dichotomies in the artist's work. In the painting *Woman with a Skeletal Arm in a Red Landscape* (1997) we see a female figure sitting in a red landscape. Her skirt is a green field, and her one arm is a bone. Right next to her we see a framework, which may prompt the viewer to associate the woman's skeletal arm – humanity's "framework" – with a building of some kind. Once again we grasp how the artist focuses on humanity living in pact with nature, and not alienated and separated from it, as the woman's inner framework is made visible. The blood-red hue symbolises nature's own cardiovascular circulation. In the series *In a Hundred Years Everything Will Be Forgotten* (2016), the figures depicted in the various paintings and drawings are all animals, but the connection to previous works is nonetheless clear. The schism the artist feels is expressed by the diverse figures of the hare, wolf, bison, and rhinoceros, which may allude to endangered species. As the title implies, the animals give the viewer a hint of the future: there is no way back; we must protect nature; human activity must be changed. Even though it is only recently that Mørland has addressed the climate crisis, for example in various dress-based installations dealing with insect extinction, we understand that the bond between nature and humankind that is on the verge of dissolving has been important for a long time.

In Norway, the environmentalist Erik Dammann published *Fremtiden i våre hender* (*The Future in Our Hands*), a landmark 1972 book that castigated consumer society and materialism and launched a national movement,[2] while the

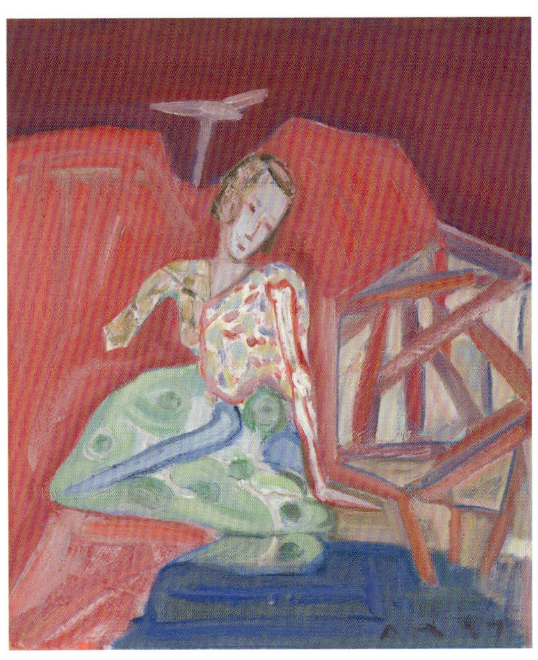

Woman with a Skeletal Arm in a Red Landscape, 1997
Oil on canvas, 50 x 41 cm

philosopher Arne Næss fronted deep ecology and allowed himself to be carried away by the police during the fight against developing the Mardalsfossen Waterfall and the Alta-Kautokeino River for hydroelectric power.[3] It makes an impression to hear the aged Dammann state in a later interview in 2017 that his efforts to change society have been to no avail, but that it has never been more evident that we are at a crossroads where change simply must take place.[4] Internationally, the follow-up study *Limits to Growth: The 30-Year Update* (2004) argues that we have been living on a planet that has been running on empty since the 1990s.[5] And now, in 2020, we have yet to reach the limit set in the original report, but we are well on our way, despite our technological progress. In 2018 a fifteen-year-old Swedish schoolgirl began playing truant from school in order to strike against climate change. Greta Thunberg thereby launched a global movement, and in 2019 she was announced as *Time*'s Person of the Year.[6] Asking us to listen to the world's leading climate scientists, Thunberg concludes that the Paris Agreement's objectives require changes in human activities on a scale that has never previously been seen.[7] We are living at a time when everything is tumbling down around us. Is it any wonder we are worried? What can art contribute with in a world undergoing enormous upheaval because of the climate crisis? Can art take the temperature of a planet on fire?

In 2009 Mørland drew a series of mummies from Greenland. The drawings are of a fairly large scale, and one of them, a *memento mori*, has been created directly onto a white wall, and there is a levity to the linework. The expression is transparent and poetical, in hues of blue, red, and lead grey. The series is titled *What I Am* and joins together disparate elements. The first element is a find made in Greenland in 1972 of eight mummified corpses from 1475, two children and six women. The mummies were dressed in sealskins and bird feathers, and had what they needed to survive in the afterlife. Their facial expressions varied, as though they were smiling or laughing. The other element is a *memento mori* from 1427, a fresco that Masaccio, one of the foremost painters of the Early Italian Renaissance, painted at the bottom of the altarpiece in the Santa Maria Novella church in Florence.[8] Masaccio, who was a master of pictorial illusionism, painted a skeleton in a grave with an inscription in Italian stating, "I once was what now you are, and what I am you also will be."[9] The fresco of the skeleton lying in the grave was painted not only with a sharp contrast between light and shadow, which adds the illusion of volume, but also with a central perspective focused on the foot of the crucifix, which adds spatiality. These illusionist techniques were meant to give the viewer a sense of physical presence. The text describes the circle of life and reflects the viewer's own mortality.

Climate change is likely taking place most rapidly in the Arctic and the Svalbard archipelago,[10] and we are all contributing to these effects since we are all linked through the global ecosystem. In the meanwhile, various members

Wizard, 1999
Oil on canvas, 56 x 68 cm

Indigenous, 1999
Oil on canvas, 68 x 57 cm

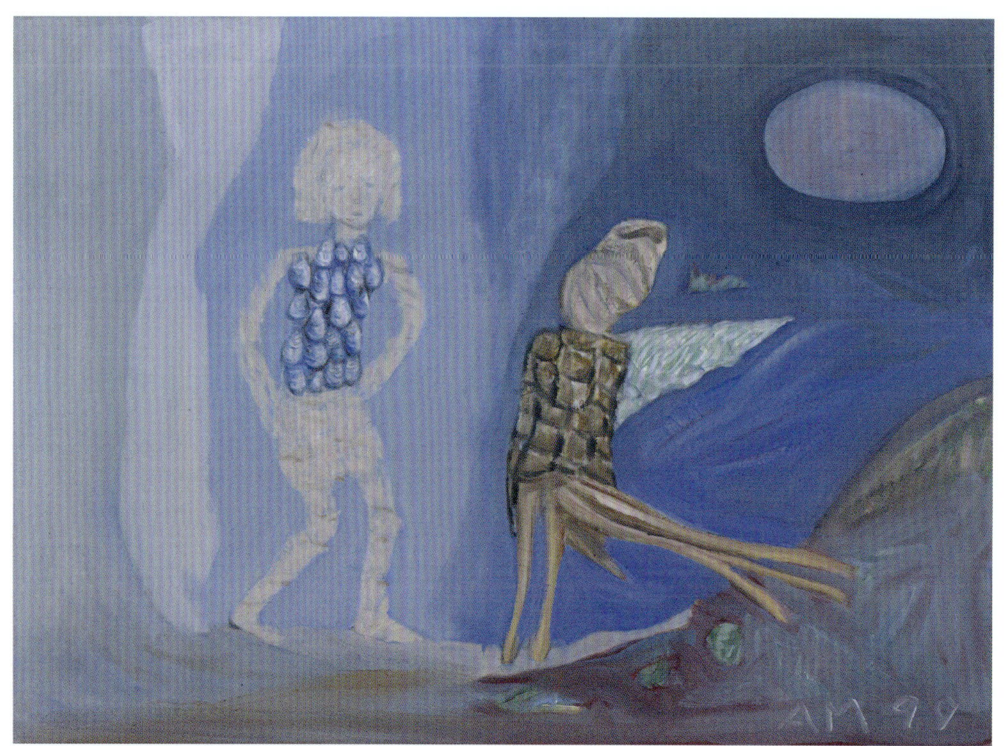

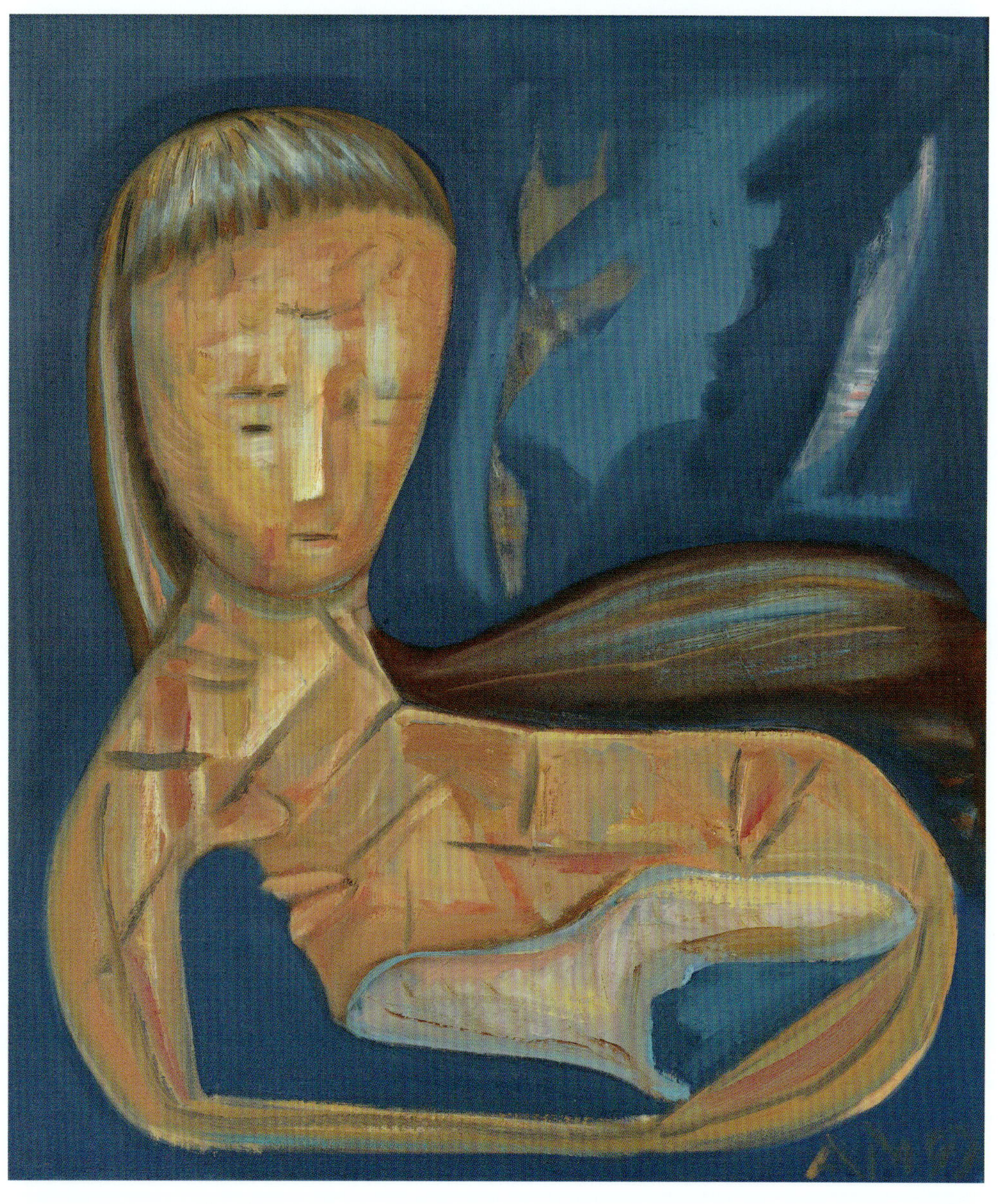

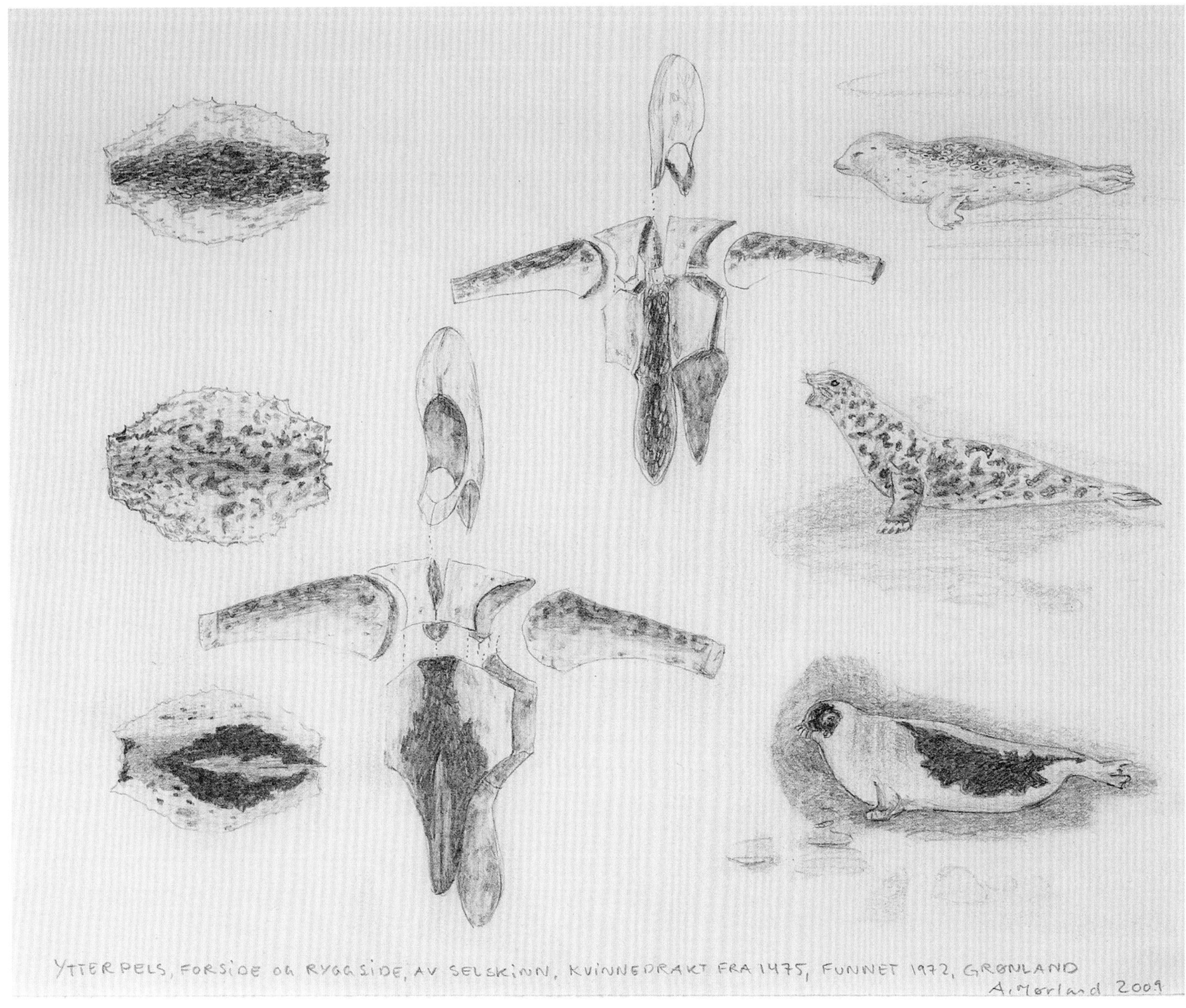

Plan Based on the Discovery of the Mummies, with Seal Fur for Clothes, 2009
Pencil on paper, 22 x 26 cm

of the Norwegian government are squabbling about where to draw the Arctic ice edge (which is not an edge at all, but an ocean area entirely or partially covered by ice throughout the year),[11] and the Svalbard Global Seed Vault must be cooled down because the permafrost protecting the vault is thawing.[12] What is more, our cultural heritage is melting away along with this permafrost.[13] There are many graves in Svalbard's meagre soil, of which several date back centuries, and as yet these graves have been well protected by the permafrost. Softer objects such as clothes and other textiles have therefore been well conserved until they were one day excavated. It is because of the cold permafrost that we can today see the felt hat worn by the Dutchman Willem Barents (who discovered Svalbard in 1596), which was found in his camp on Novaya Zemlya and is now displayed at Svalbard Museum in Longyearbyen.[14] But because of the worsening climate of our times, it will not be long until a significant proportion of the cultural heritage in the Arctic rot and decompose into nature. Like the permafrost, Mørland protects her swaddled mummy figures in her drawings. Each line in *What I Am* has been executed with care for and contemplation on the subject matter and its history. Perhaps these drawings reflect the artist's concern for how we ourselves are taking care of one another and

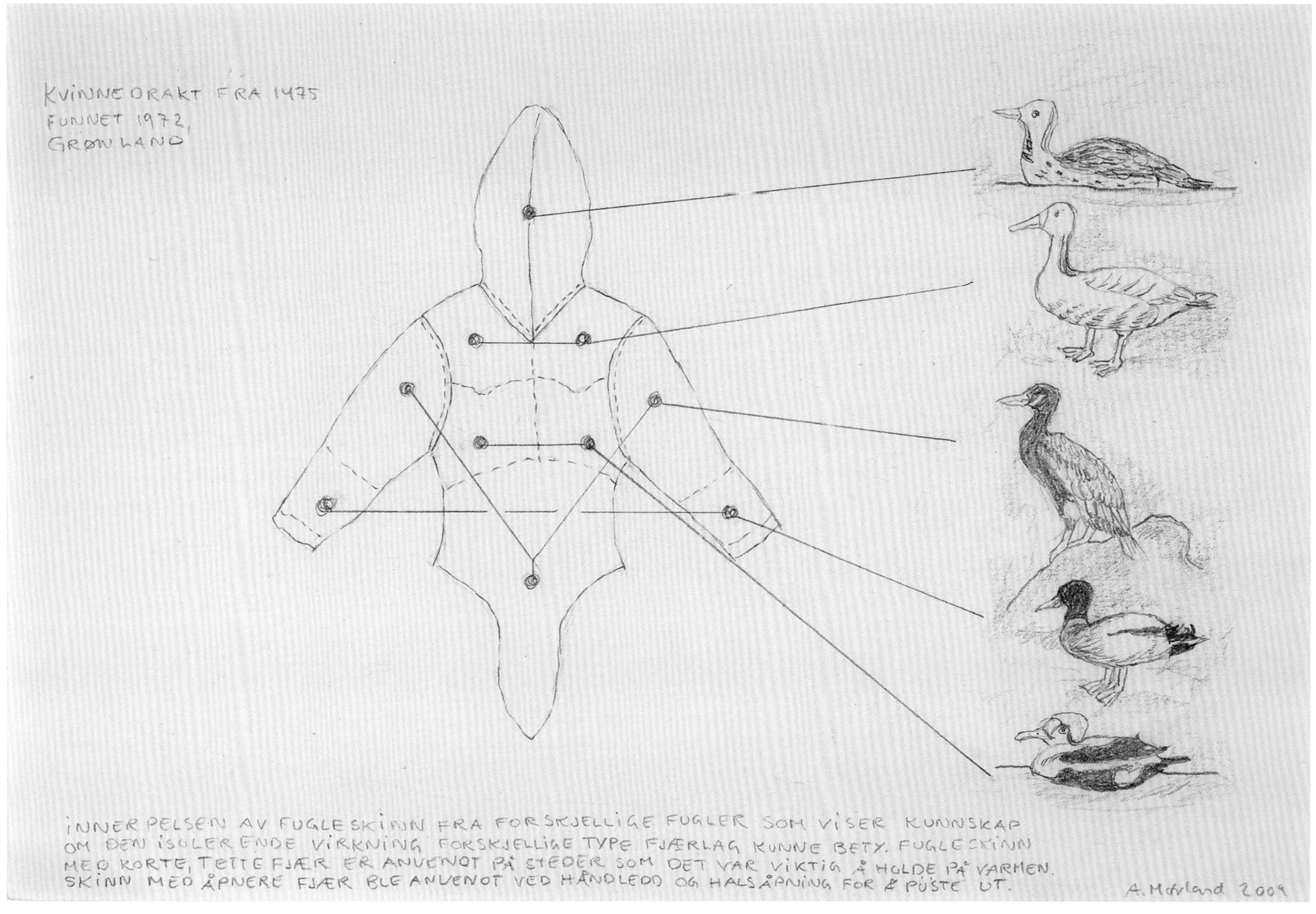

Plan Based on the Discovery of the Mummies, with Seabird Feathers inside the Clothes, 2009
Pencil on paper, 22 x 26 cm

everything surrounding us, for humanity is part of the cycle of nature, a theme that recurs in many of Mørland's works. For life is both fragile and fleeting.

During a filmed studio visit published on Haugar Art Museum's Facebook page, we see Mørland present paintings of bucks as well as dresses with embroideries of sparrows and insects.[15] We live in the era of mass extinction, during a profound ecological crisis. Species come into being and disappear all the time – that is the essence of evolution – and there are many species we are unaware of. But it is the species' degree of importance as part of an ecosystem we must focus on: when a keystone species disappears, the effects impact the well-being of the whole ecosystem. The loss of our global biodiversity is an issue that has preoccupied Mørland for quite some time, as part of the relationship between humankind and nature. The artist's commitment to fight insect extinction was reinforced when Maja Lunde's novel *Bienes historie* (*The History of Bees*) was published in 2015.

The exhibition *Insect Dresses and an Open Heart* at Galleberg gallery displayed several girl's dresses, delicate and gauzy, with dense, detailed, and beautiful

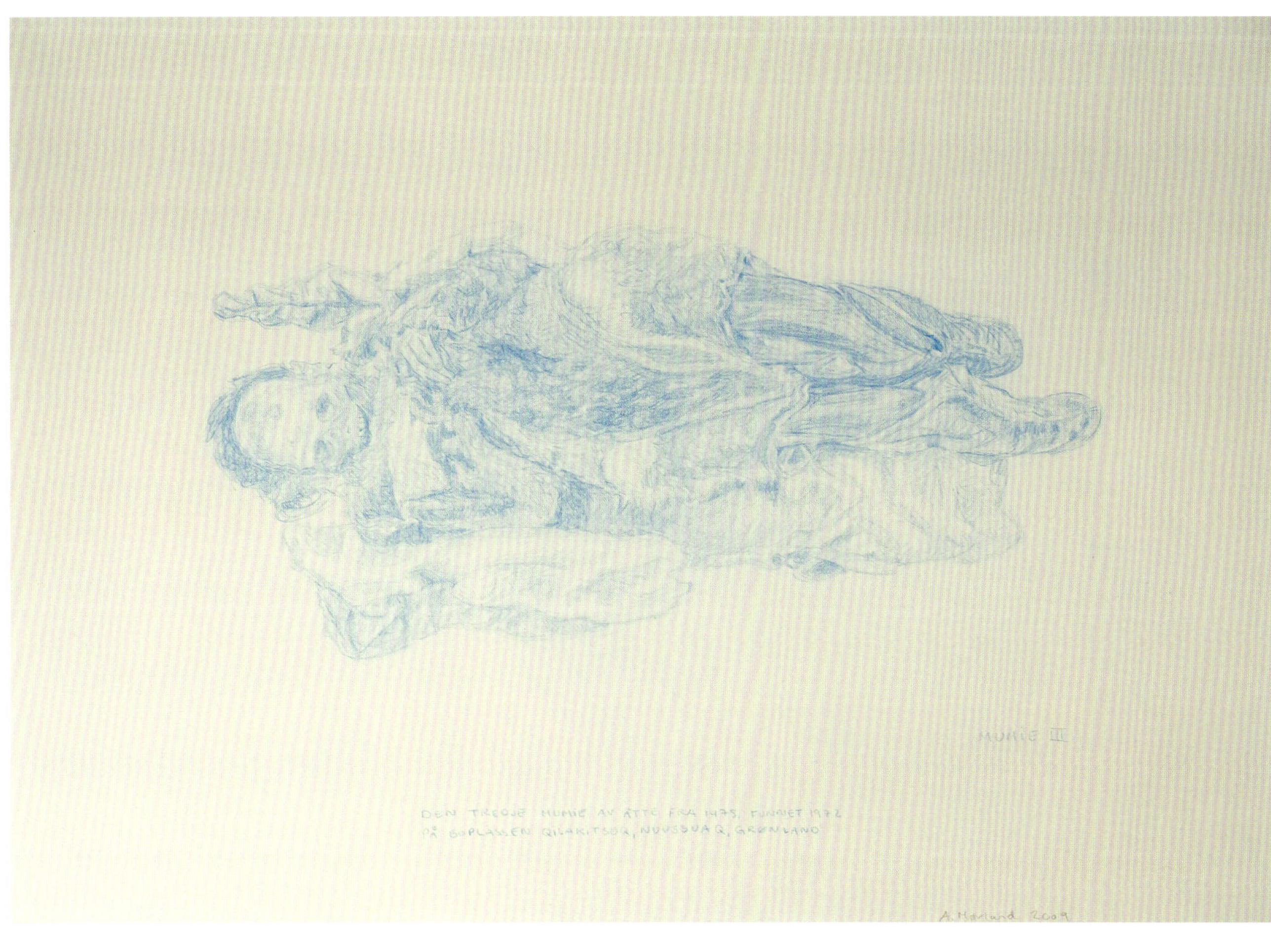

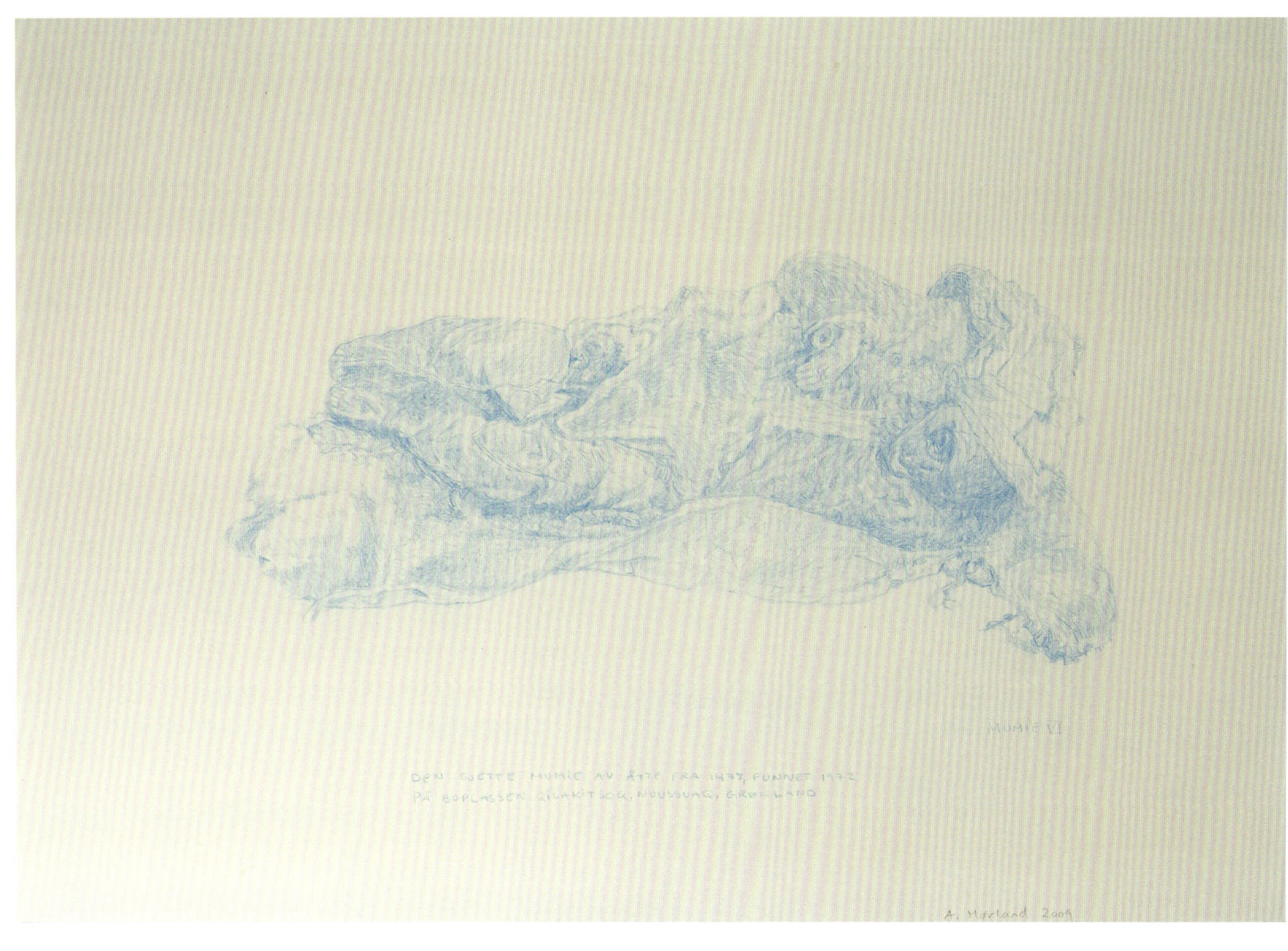

What I Am, Happy Mummies 1,
2009
Crayon on paper, 30 x 42 cm

What I Am, Happy Mummies 2,
2009
Crayon on paper, 30 x 42 cm

What I Am, Happy Mummies 3,
2009
Crayon on paper, 30 x 42 cm

Pages 110–11
*Extra Clothes on the Journey
to the Realm of Death 1*, 2009
Red ink on paper, 24 x 24 cm

*Extra Clothes on the Journey
to the Realm of Death 2*, 2009
Red ink on paper, 24 x 24 cm

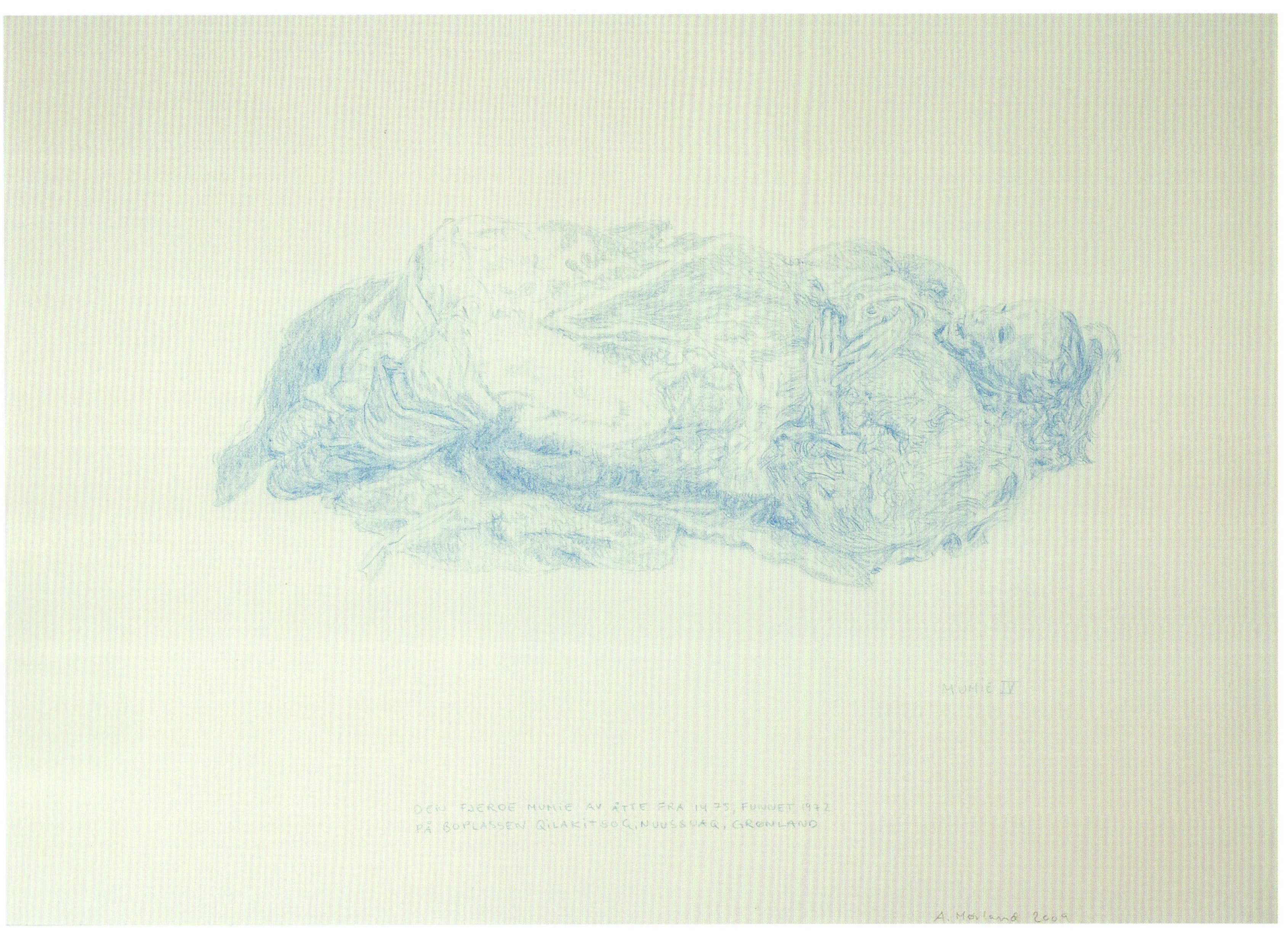

MUMIE IV
DEN FJERDE MUMIE AV ÅTTE FRA 1475, FUNNET 1972
PÅ BOPLASSEN QILAKITSOQ, NUUSSUAQ, GRØNLAND
A. Morland 2009

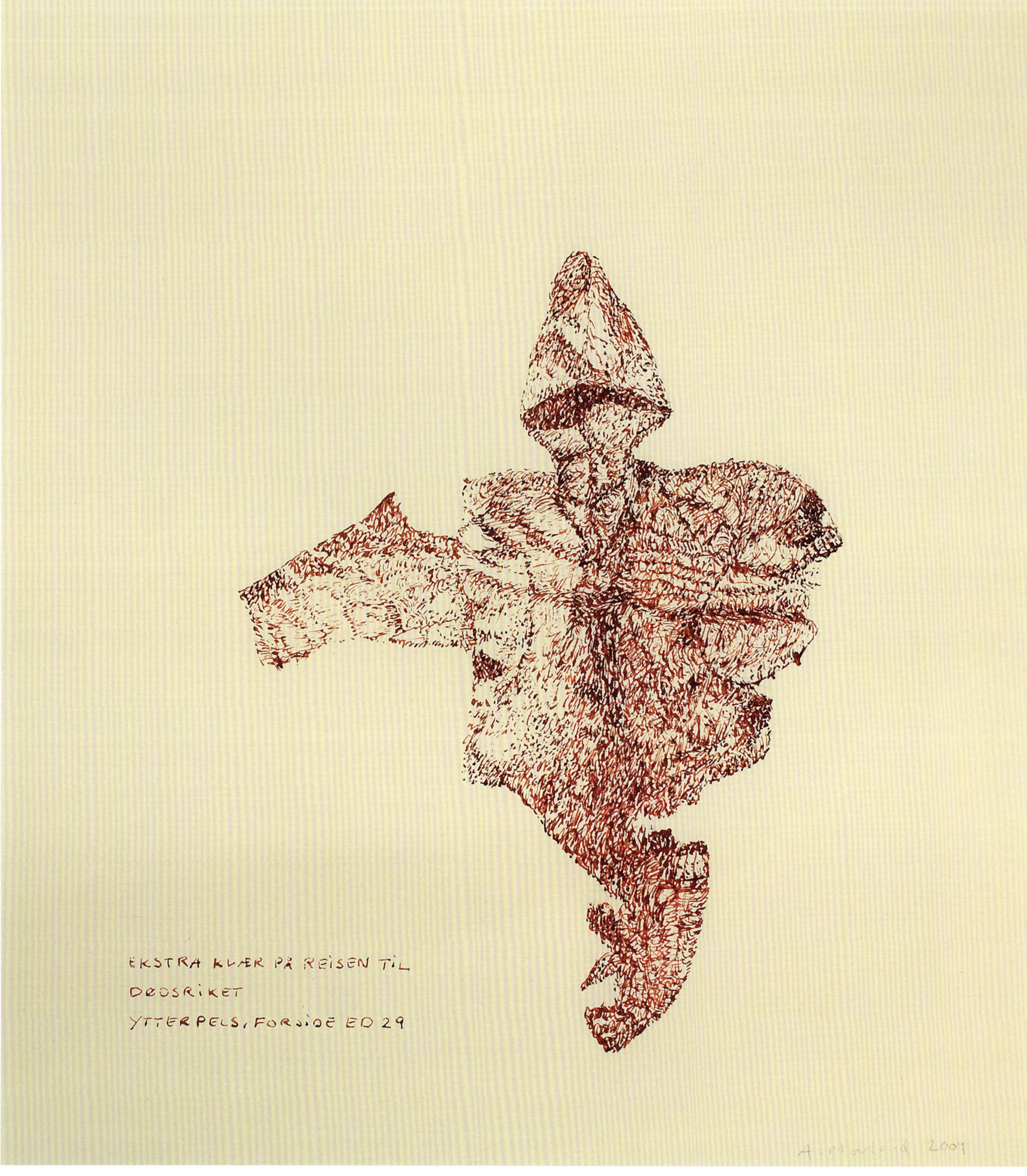
EKSTRA KLÆR PÅ REISEN TIL
DØDSRIKET
YTTERPELS, FORSIDE ED 29

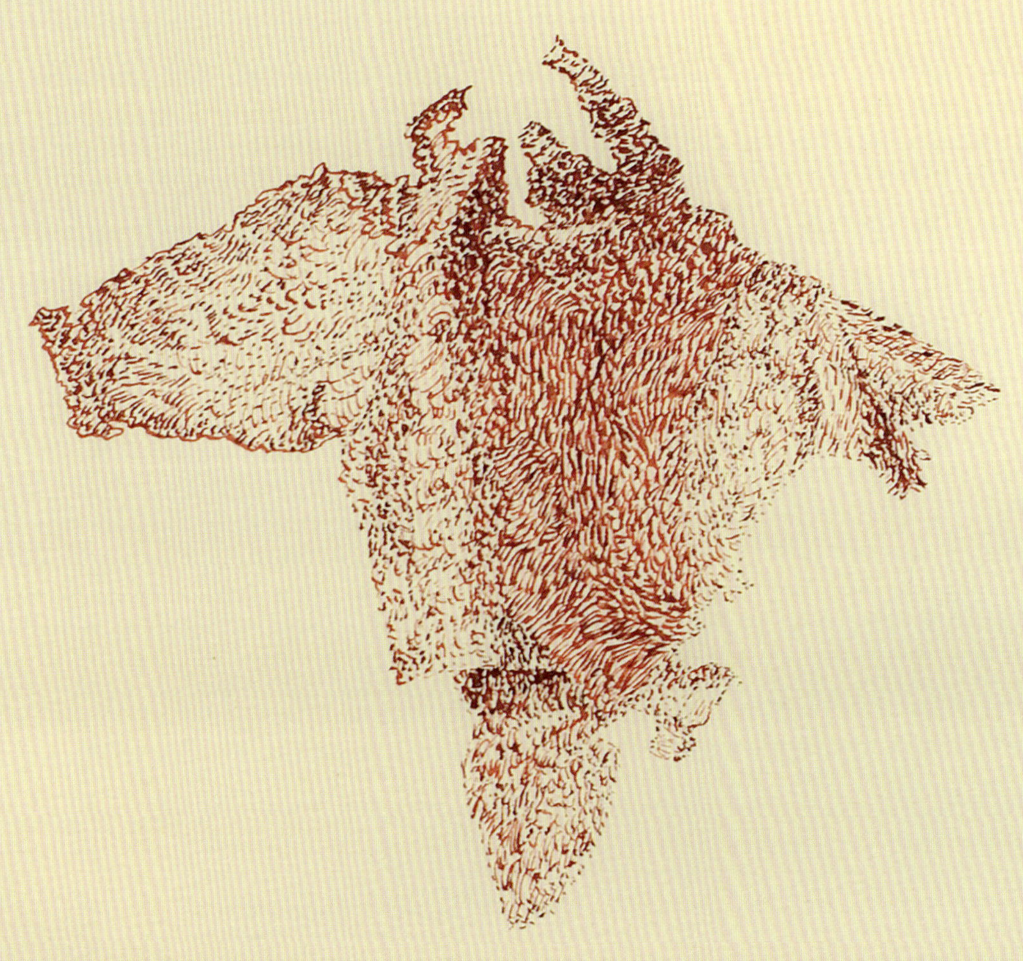

EKSTRA KLÆR PÅ REISEN TIL DØDSRIKET
YTTERPELS, FORSIDE ED 29

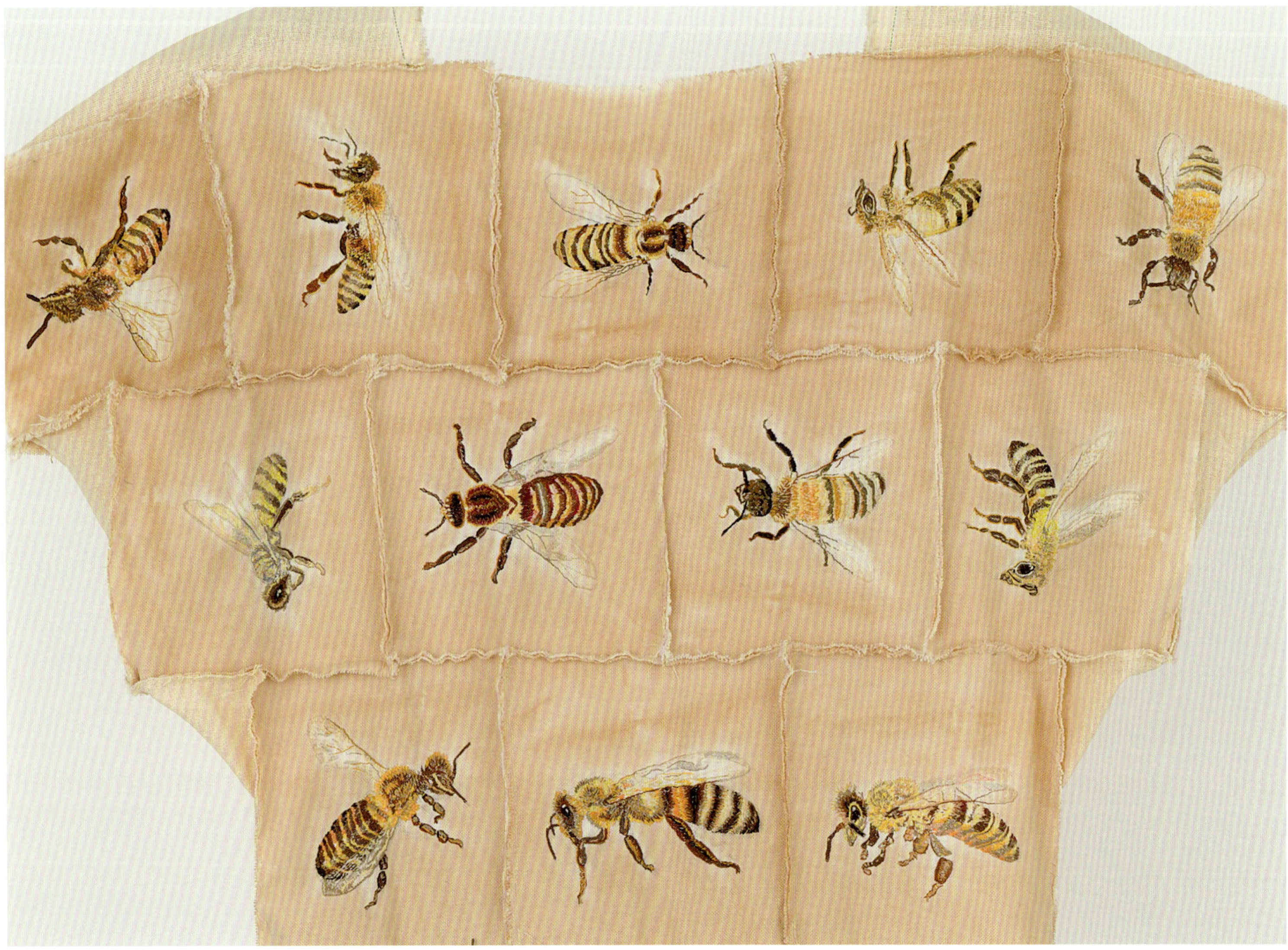

Bee Dress (detail), 2019
Mixed media object, 140 x 60 cm

Bee Dress, 2019
Mixed media object, 140 x 60 cm

embroideries of various insects.[16] The bees, flies, ants, and beetles seem more or less alive as they crawl up the dress's arms, back, or front. It is as though the viewer hears them buzzing and scuttling about in the gallery.

In 1962 the American zoologist and biologist Rachel Carson published her famous book *Silent Spring*, which investigates the detrimental effects of pesticides, that is the chemical agents used in the agricultural sector to kill insects. Such pesticides do not only kill their targets, however, but also become dispersed throughout the cycles of nature, wreaking massive damage. "The history of life on earth has been a history of interaction between living things and their surroundings", writes Carson, who has greatly influenced environmentalists the world over. "Only within the moment of time represented by the present century has one species – man – acquired significant power to alter the nature of his world", she continues.[17] In Norway, organisations such as the Bellona Foundation campaign against pollutants that are not biodegradable but instead circulate throughout our ecosystems, harming both animals and humans.[18]

In Mørland's series of paintings titled *Buck and Orchid*, we see how animal and human merge into one. Animals and torsos are recurring motifs in drawing and painting, and they are shown here with the feminine human represented by

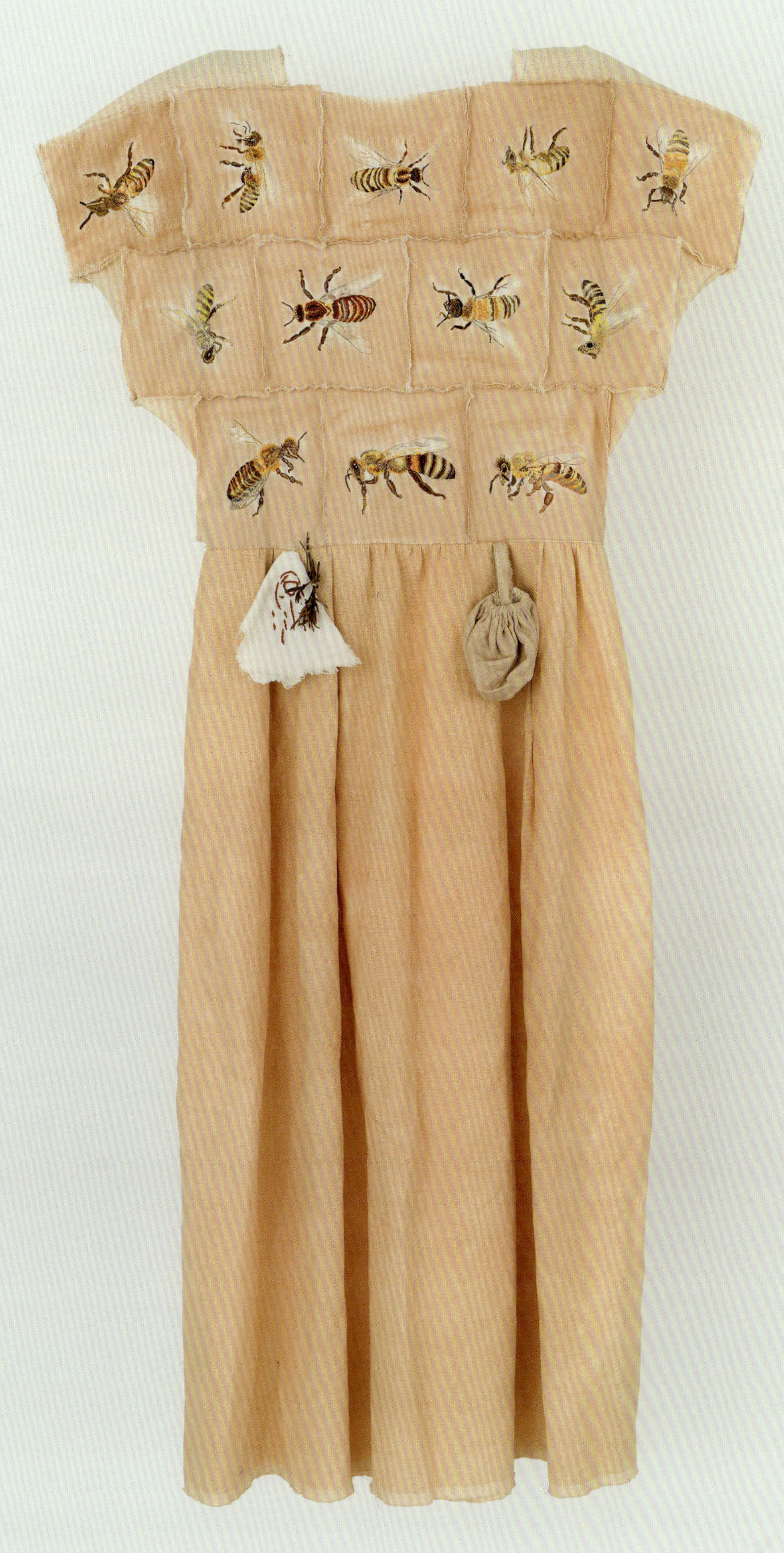

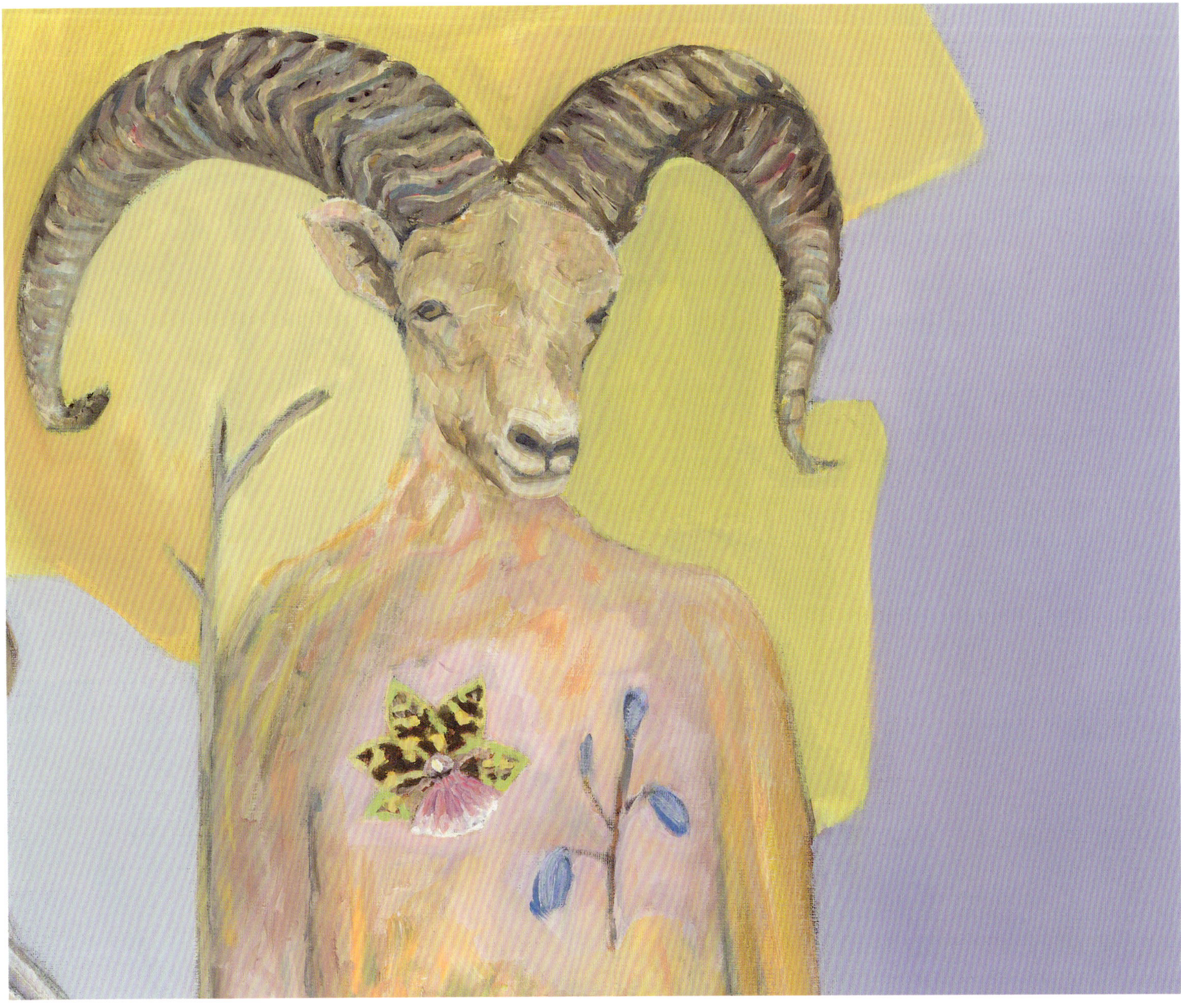

Buck and Orchid 1 (detail), 2019
Oil on canvas, 120 x 90 cm

the dress, combined with the head of a buck. Mørland frequently uses vibrant, striking colours and recognisable, surrealistic touches that add a dreamy veil to the imagery. The paintings often evince a strong connection between the inner and the outer, and several of the figures have been painted with a translucent exterior so that we can peer into them and see their organs. In other instances, the dress is used as a disguise to cover something up. According to the artist, the orchid symbolises a higher order, in this case an environmental whistle-blower. Like the series *What I Am*, *Buck and Orchid* is about caring and protecting. It is about a respect for the fragility of life, but also about what we as humans risk when we open ourselves to others.

In certain works we see how the figure, the human, *becomes* nature, as in *Blue Mussel Dress* and *Moss Dress*, installations in the guise of dresses made from the eponymous materials. There is no longer a divide between human and nature in these works: on the contrary, the human is nature. In his book-length essay *Down to Earth: Politics in the New Climate Regime*, the French

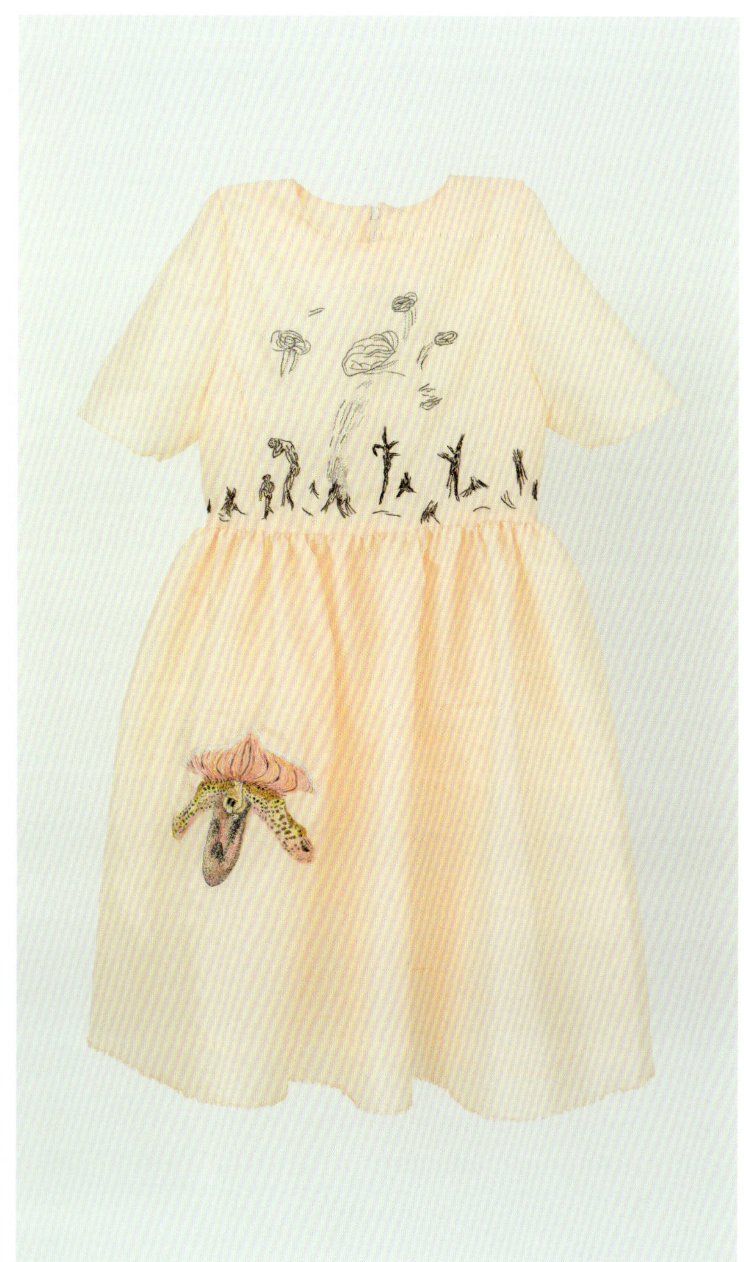

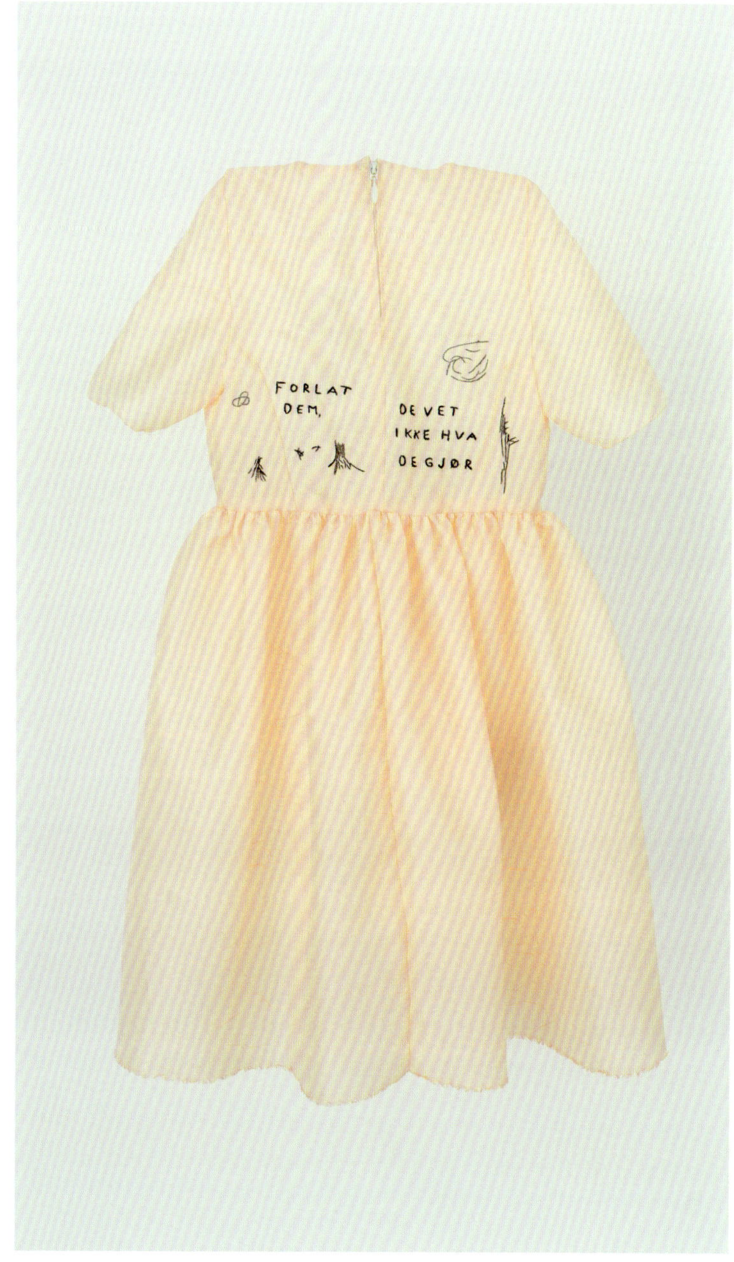

Orchid and Black Forest
(front and back), 2019
Mixed media object, 60 x 40 cm

philosopher Bruno Latour argues that we must understand that the climate issue lies at the heart of every geopolitical concern related to questions of global injustice and inequality. This again became evident when American President Donald Trump withdrew the United States from the Paris Agreement in 2017. According to Latour, the question of how to deal with the climate crisis divides us even more than our left- or right-leaning political positions. Like Thunberg, Latour makes it clear that in order to reach the goals of the Paris Agreement and make the planet inhabitable for future generations, we must completely change our way of life. No planet exists that could bear globalisation. In line with the message we can infer from Mørland's art, Latour contends that we must stop regarding humankind as separated from nature, but rather as part of it. As the very title of his essay states, we must once again get "down to earth" and reconnect with nature.[19]

We are living during an exciting time where we have set ambitious goals. It is important that we view today's reality not only through the prism of yesterday's

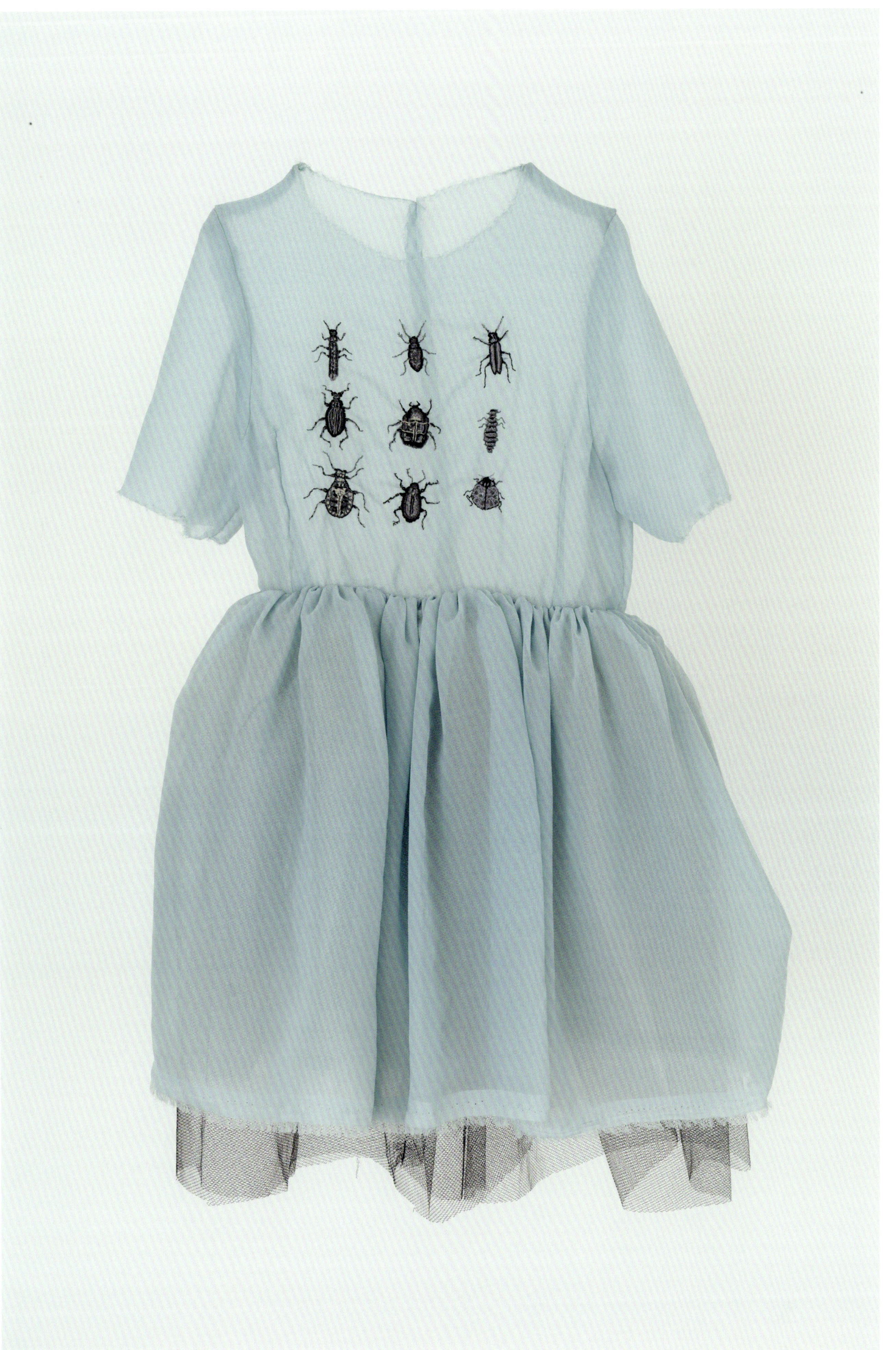

Beetle Dress, 2019
Mixed media object, 60 x 40 cm

Yellow Fly Dress, 2019
Mixed media object, 60 x 40 cm

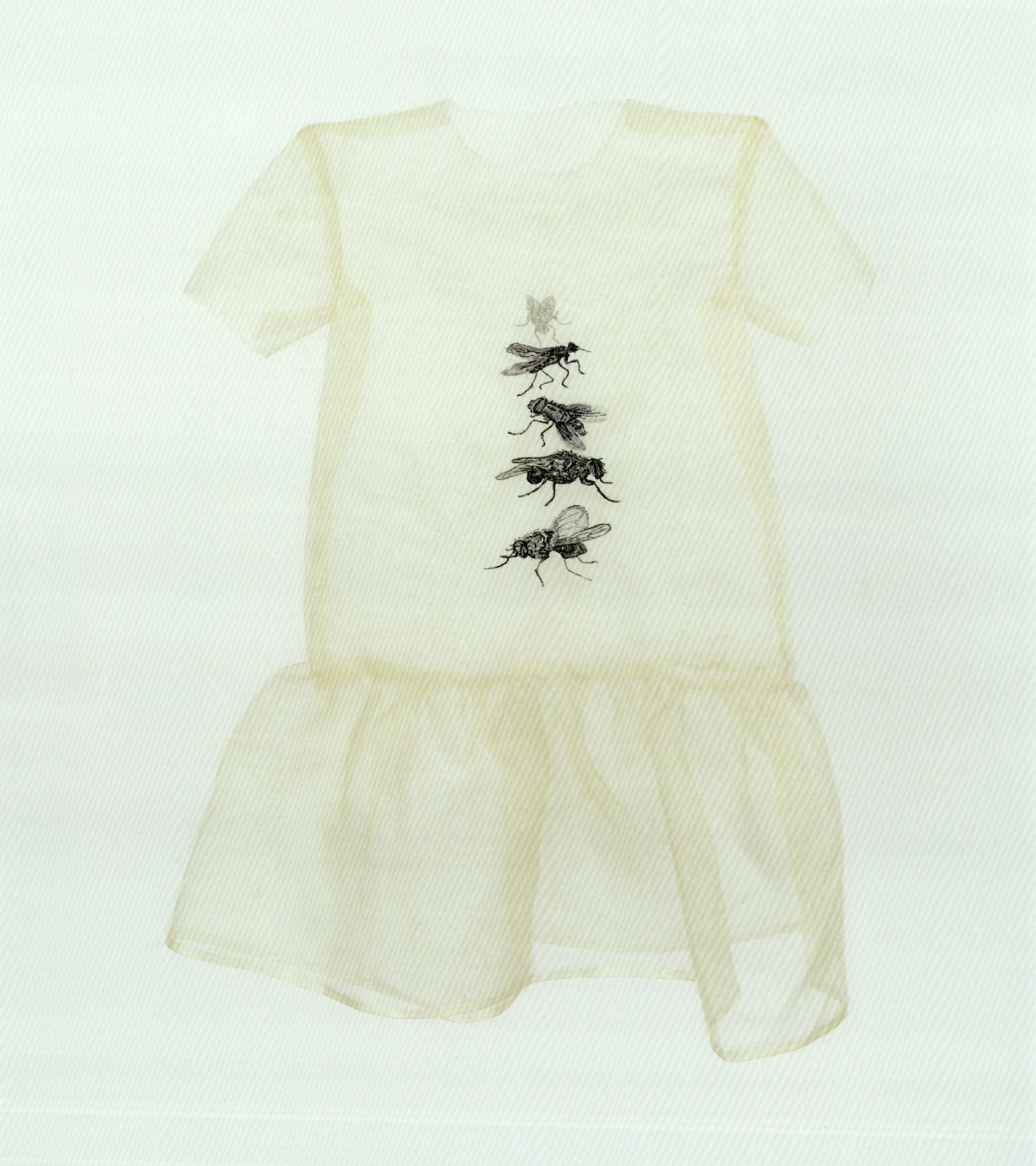

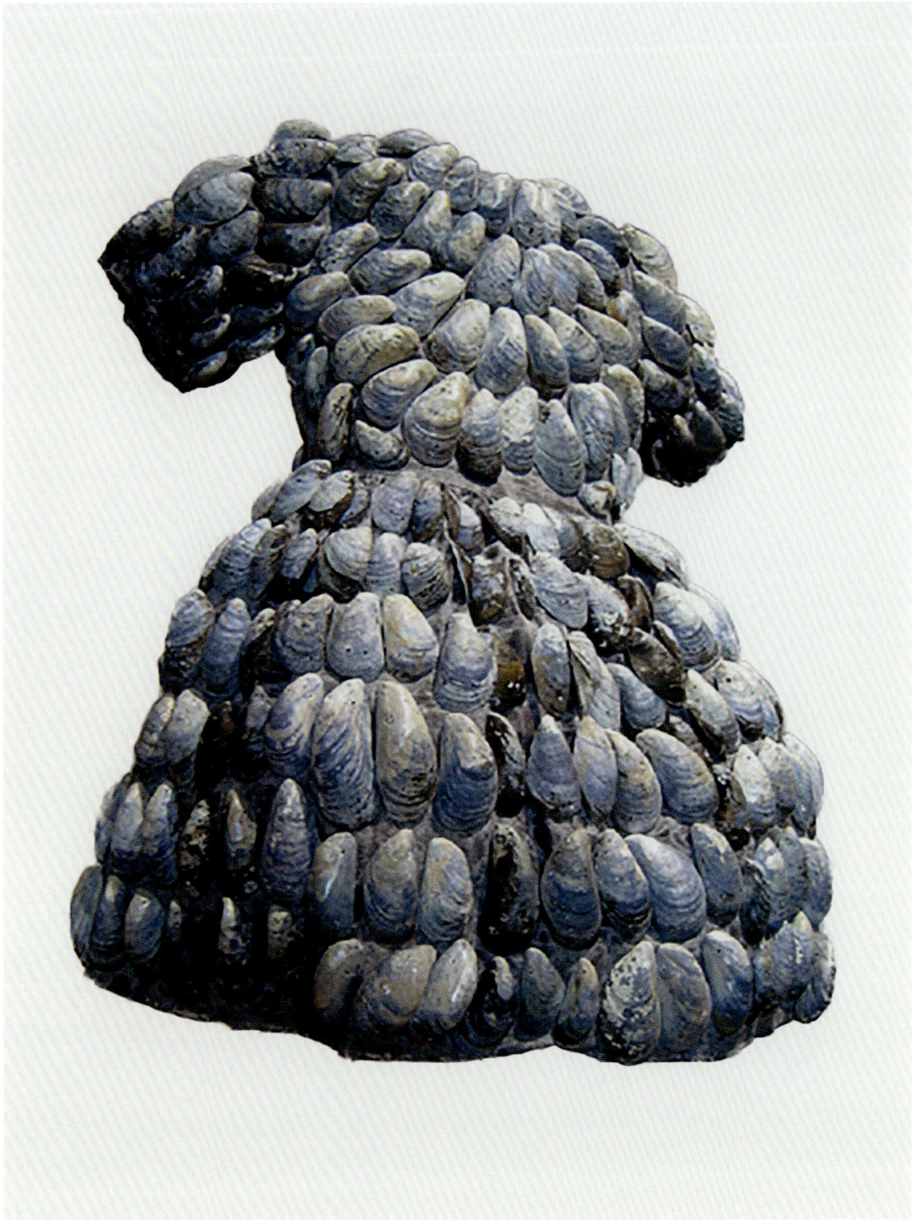

Blue Mussel Dress, 2004
Mixed media object, 65 x 50 cm

experiences, but also in the light of tomorrow's possibilities. None of us benefits from going backwards into the future. Art provides us with new perspectives on well-known issues in ways that no other discipline can. With art as her tool, Astrid Mørland turns a mirror towards contemporary society and addresses the vital issues of our day and age, twisting and turning them around, thinking about them in new ways, and inspiring us to find new solutions.

[1] Donella Meadows, Dennis Meadows, Jørgen Randers, and William Behrens III, *The Limits to Growth: A Report for the Club of Rome's Project on the Predicament of Mankind* (New York: Universe Books, 1972), http://www.donellameadows.org/wp-content/userfiles/Limits-to-Growth-digital-scan-version.pdf.

[2] Arild Hermstad, "Ny bok fra Erik Dammann", *Arilds blogg* (blog), 8 December 2014, https://www.framtiden.no/201412086626/blogg/arilds-blogg/ny-bok-fra-erik-dammann.html.

[3] *På tvers: Arne Næss 80 år*, "I den grønne bøl-gen", episode 2, NRK, accessed 19 August 2020, https://tv.nrk.no/serie/paa-tvers-arne-naess-80-aar/1992/FALM01002391/avspiller.

[4] *Mitt liv*, "Erik Dammann", season 3, episode 3, NRK, accessed 19 August 2020, https://tv.nrk.no/serie/mitt-liv/sesong/3/episode/3.

[5] Donella Meadows, Jørgen Randers, and Dennis Meadows, *Limits to Growth: The 30-Year Update* (White River Junction, VT: Chelsea Green Publishing, 2004).

[6] Charlotte Alter, Suyin Haynes, and Justin Worland, "TIME 2019 Person of the Year: Gre-

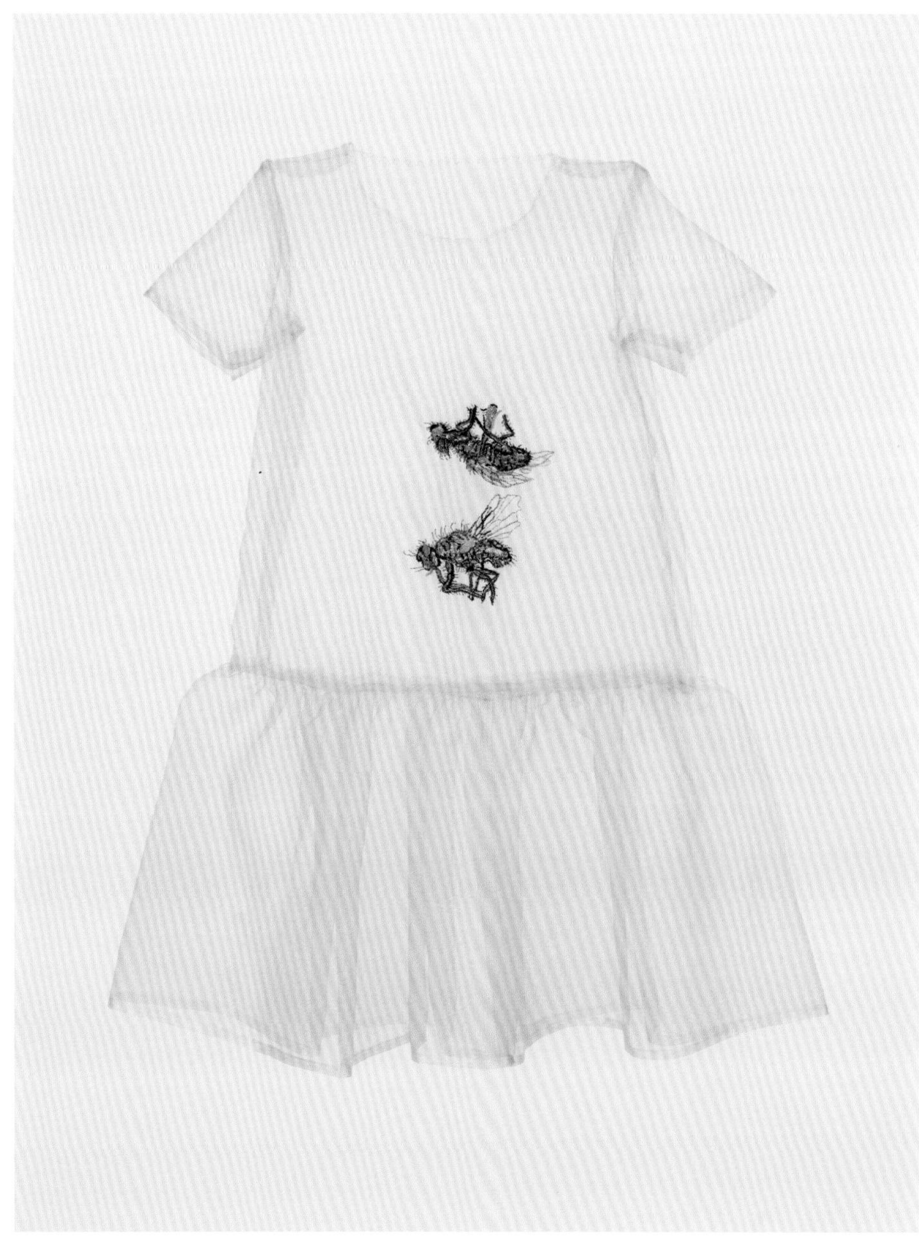

Grey Fly Dress, 2019
Mixed media object, 60 x 40 cm

ta Thunberg", *Time*, accessed 19 August 2020, https://time.com/person-of-the-year-2019-greta-thunberg/.

[7] Greta Thunberg, "Six Months on a Planet in Crisis: Greta Thunberg's Travel Diary from the U.S. to Davos", *Time*, 10 July 2020, https://time.com/5863684/greta-thunberg-diary-climate-crisis/.

[8] Fred Kleiner, Christin Mamiya, and Richard Tansey, *The Gardner's Art through the Ages* (San Diego: Harcourt College Publishers, 2001), 608.

[9] ItalianRenaissance.org, "Masaccio's Holy Trinity", accessed 19 August 2020, http://www.italianrenaissance.org/masaccios-holy-trinity/.

[10] Line Nagell Ylvisåker, *Verda mi smeltar: Å leve med klimaendringar på Svalbard* (Oslo: Samlaget, 2020), 28–29.

[11] WWF, *På kant med kunnskapen: Livet i Arktis trenger iskantsonen* (Oslo: WWF, 2019), https://www.wwf.no/assets/attachments/P%C3%A5-kant-med-kunnskapen-Final.pdf.

[12] Kjersti Nipen, "Nedsmelting", *A-magasinet*, 12 June 2020, p. 27.

[13] Leif Magne Helgesen, Kim Holmén, and Ole Arve Misund, *Isen smelter: Etikk i Arktis* (Bergen: Fagbokforlaget, 2015), 197–211.

[14] Svalbard Museum, "Hatt", accessed 19 August 2020, https://digitaltmuseum.no/011025165368/hatt.

[15] Haugar Art Museum, "Astrid Mørland – studiobesøk", 20 May 2020, https://www.facebook.com/haugarkunstmuseum/videos/917238972037511/.

[16] Galleri Galleberg, "Utstillinger og arrangementer", accessed 19 August 2020, https://gallerigalleberg.no/pages/utstillinger-og-arrangementer.

[17] Rachel Carson, *Silent Spring* (London: Penguin, 1962), 23.

[18] Bellona, "Miljøgifter", accessed 19 August 2020, https://bellona.no/fagomrader/miljogifter.

[19] Bruno Latour, *Down to Earth: Politics in the New Climate Regime*, trans. Catherine Porter (Cambridge: Polity Press, 2018), 3–7.

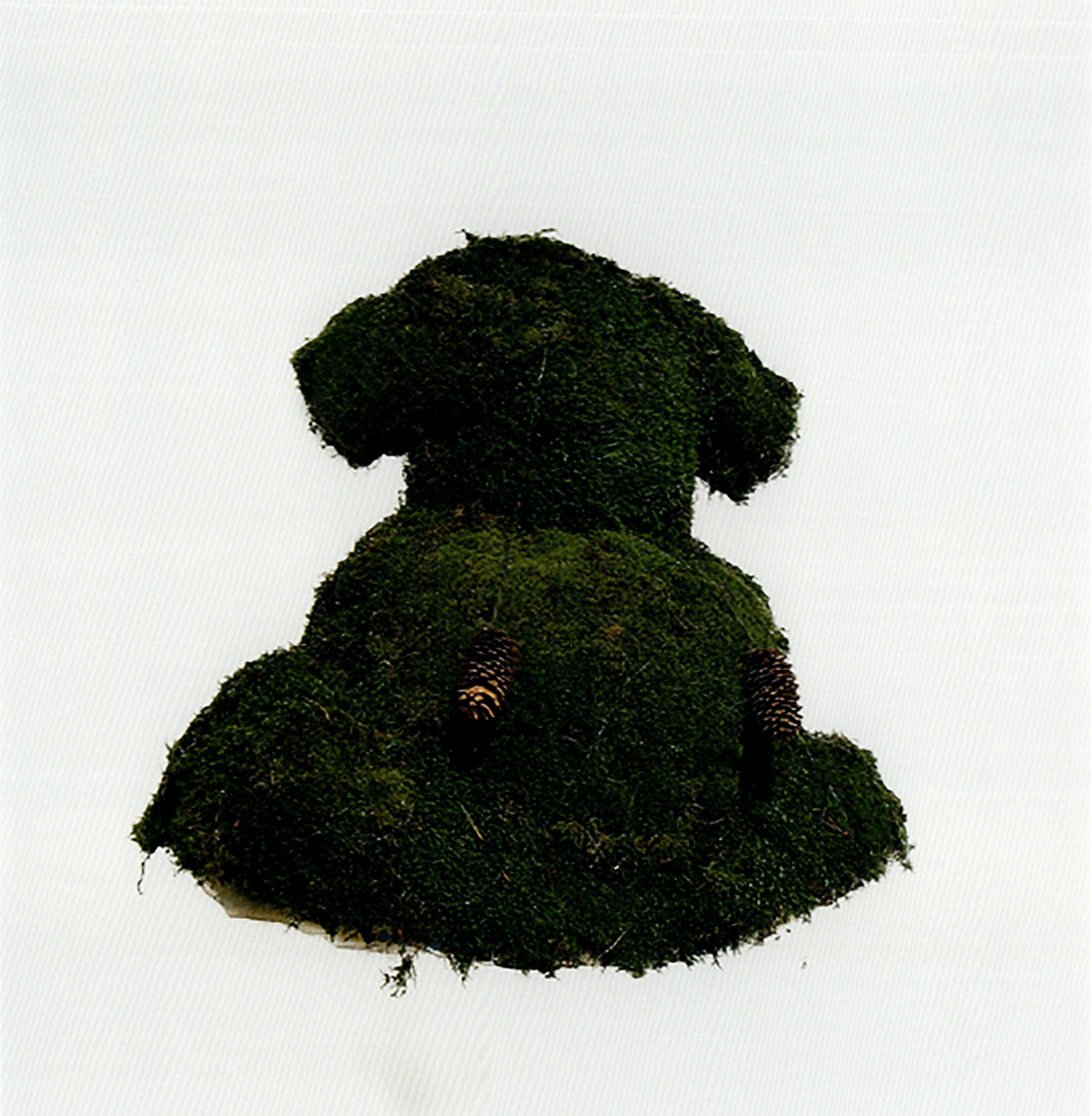

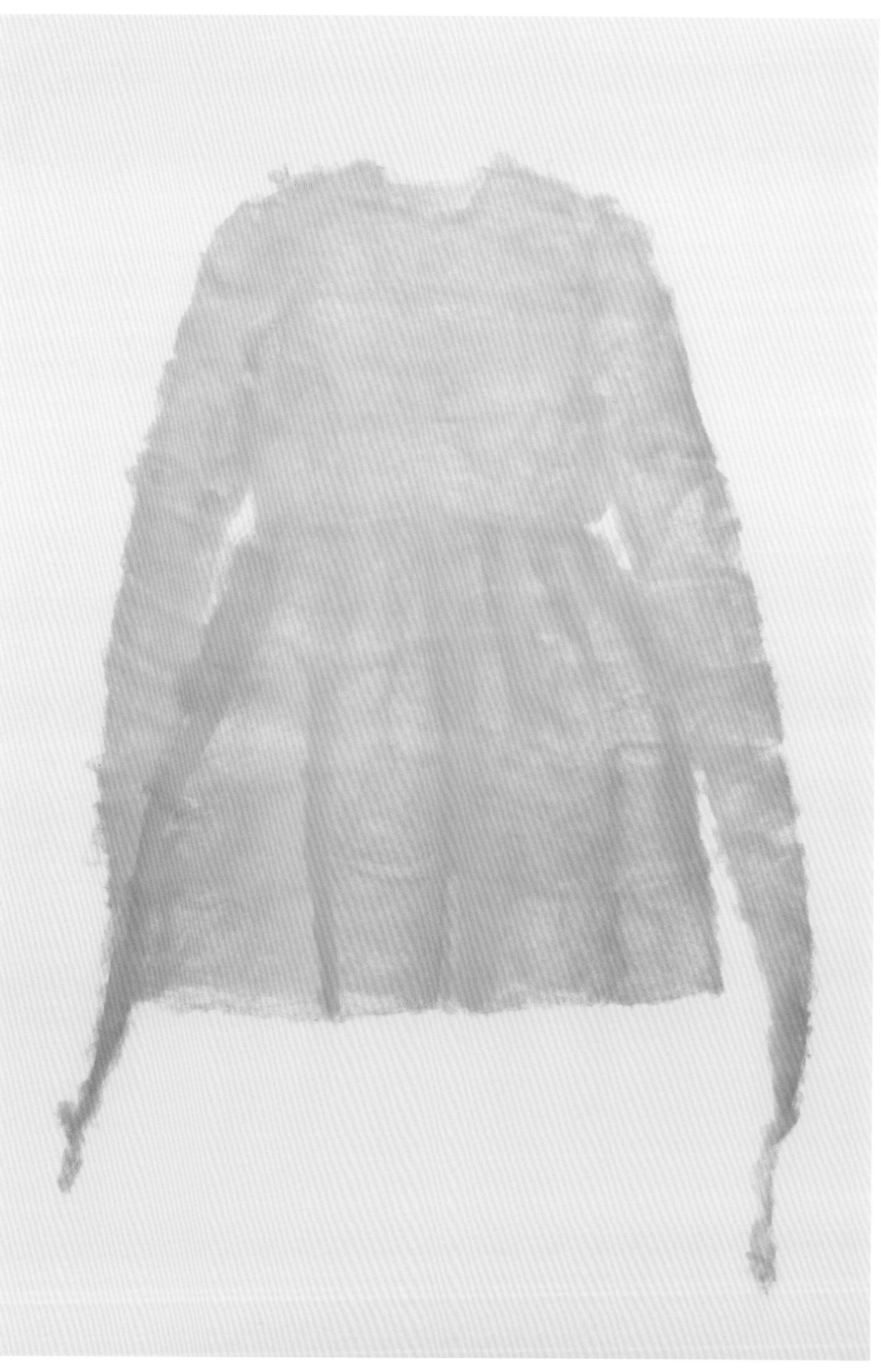

Moss Dress, 2004
Mixed media object, 70 x 50 cm

Amorphous, 2004
Mixed media object, 60 x 40 cm

Pages 122–23
Red and White Skirt, 1989
Oil on canvas, 120 x 80 cm

*Spring and Autumn, Mother
and Daughter*, 2002
Oil on canvas, 110 x 90 cm

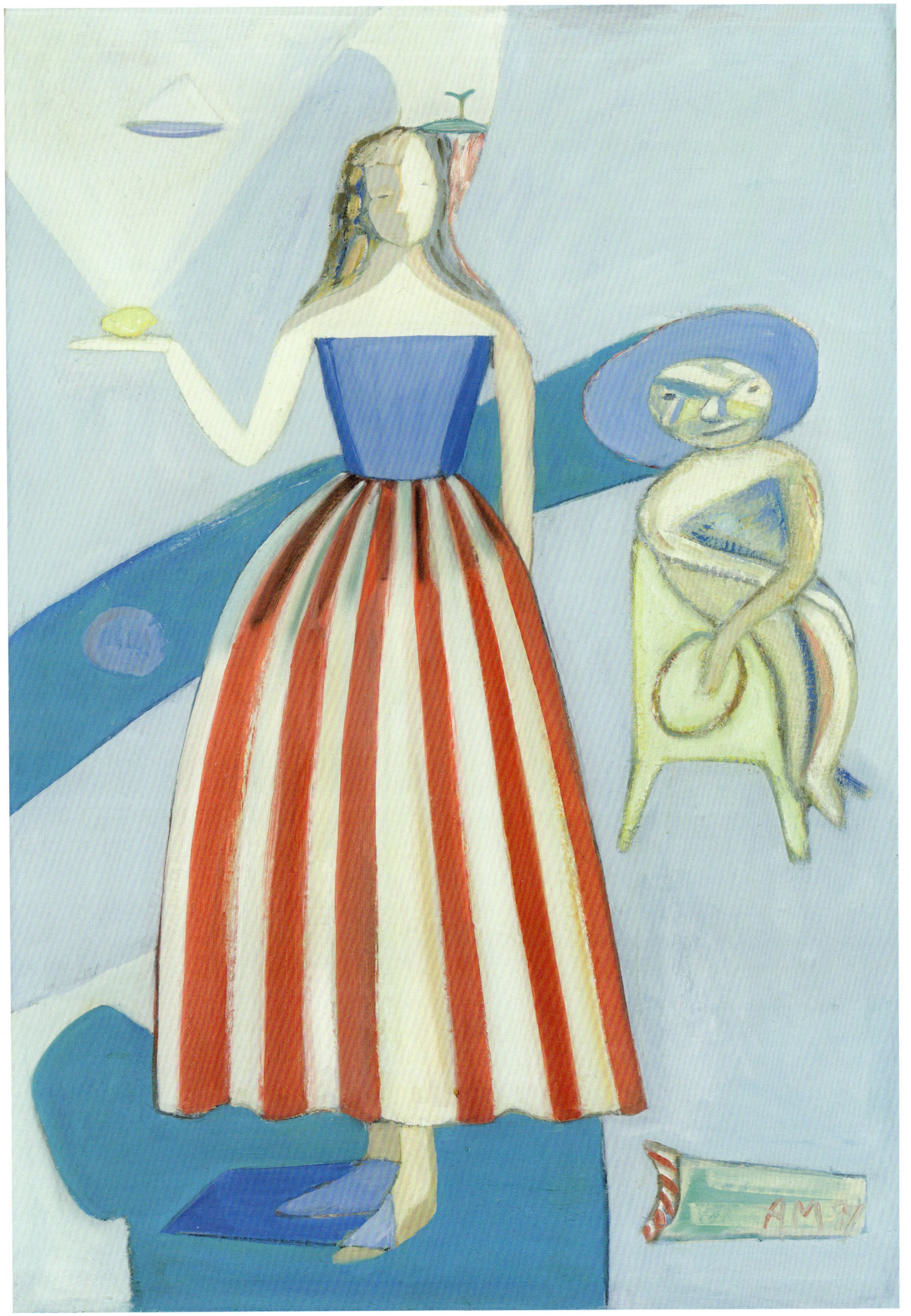

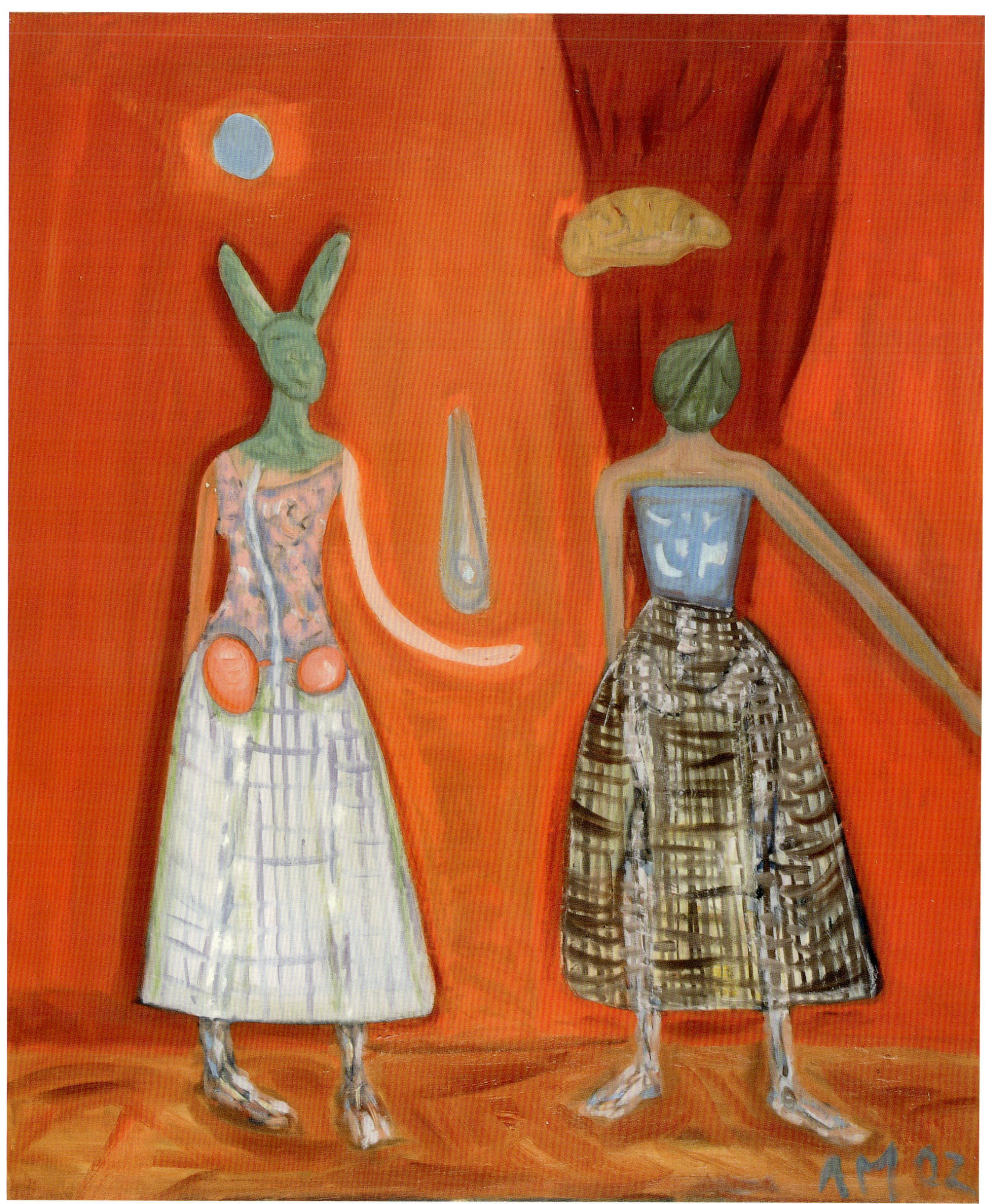

AM 02

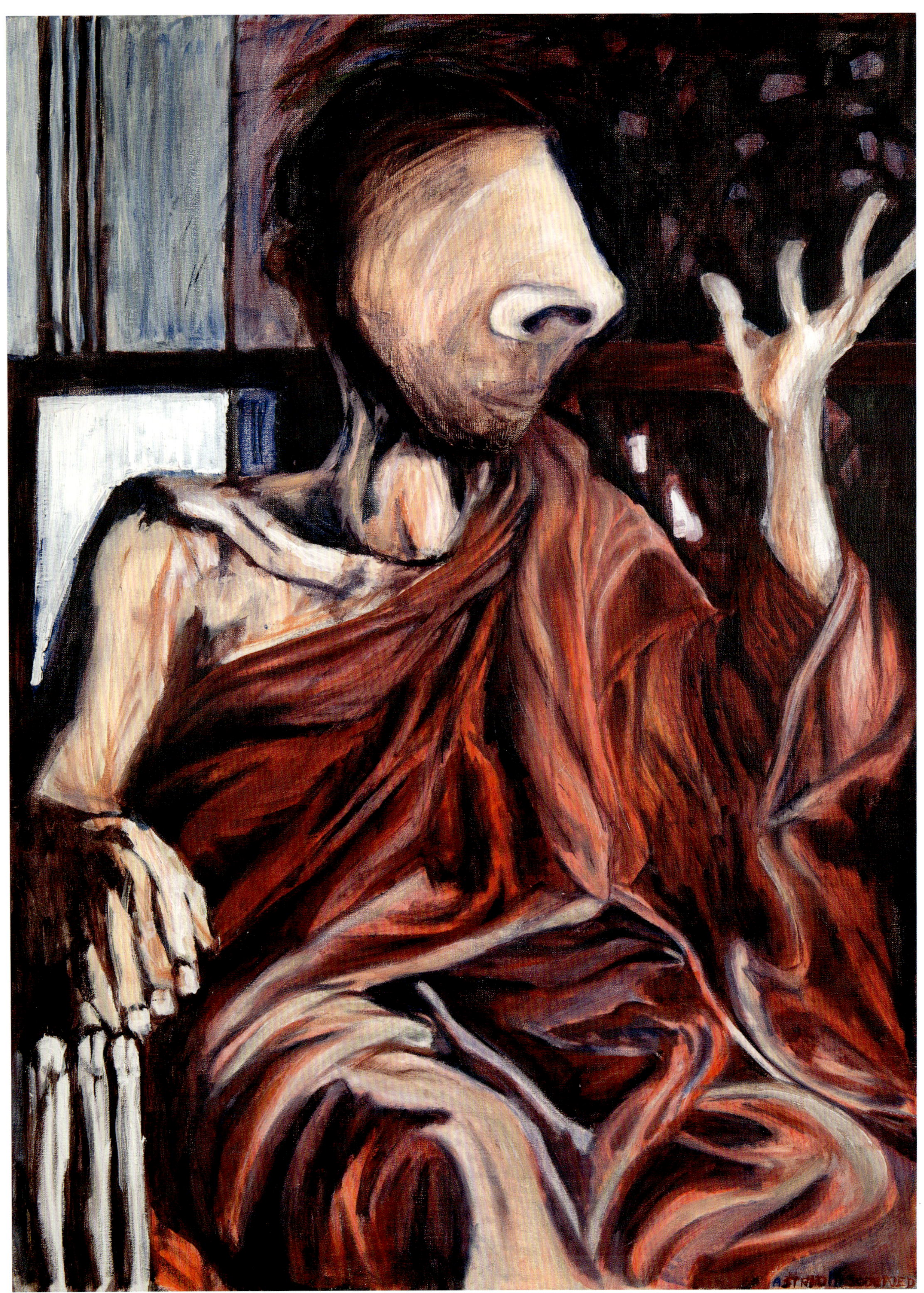
ASTRID GODFRED

Astrid Mørland in the 1970s and 1980s
Contrasts, Awakening, Surrealism, and Feminism

Frida Forsgren

Contrasts

A big, aristocratic nose with wide open nostrils. A face without eyes. One hand gesticulating theatrically in the air, the other hand resting on a radiator with a bony surface. A restless, slender, toga-clad figure painted in deep-red hues against a beige background – an ancient Roman emperor, perhaps, making a few incisively scornful comments on the state of society. This is the eccentric personage depicted in *The Nose Knows* (1973), the painting Astrid Mørland submitted when applying to the Norwegian National Academy of Fine Arts in 1974. The painting may perhaps evoke the wild, expressive, and intense painting of the Neo-Expressionists of the 1970s and 1980s, where painters such as Francis Bacon and Albert Oehlen used loud, garish colours and agitated shapes to capture the turbulence and frantic pulse of the time. In Norway, Mørland's painterly style set her apart from the main trends within painting in the early 1970s, whether the political and activist art of groups such as GRAS or GRUPPE 66, or feminist artists who addressed the lack of gender equality, or figure-oriented political painters such as Kjell Nupen, Odd Nerdrum, and Franz Widerberg. *The Nose Knows* clearly diverges from this overriding current and seems almost to originate from somewhere else. When Mørland today looks at the red-dressed man with his gargantuan nose and haughty appearance, she also wonders where he came from. "He looks so full of himself – what is he trying to tell us?" And what was she herself trying to say through him?

Hidden, 1973
Collage paper, 12 x 10 cm

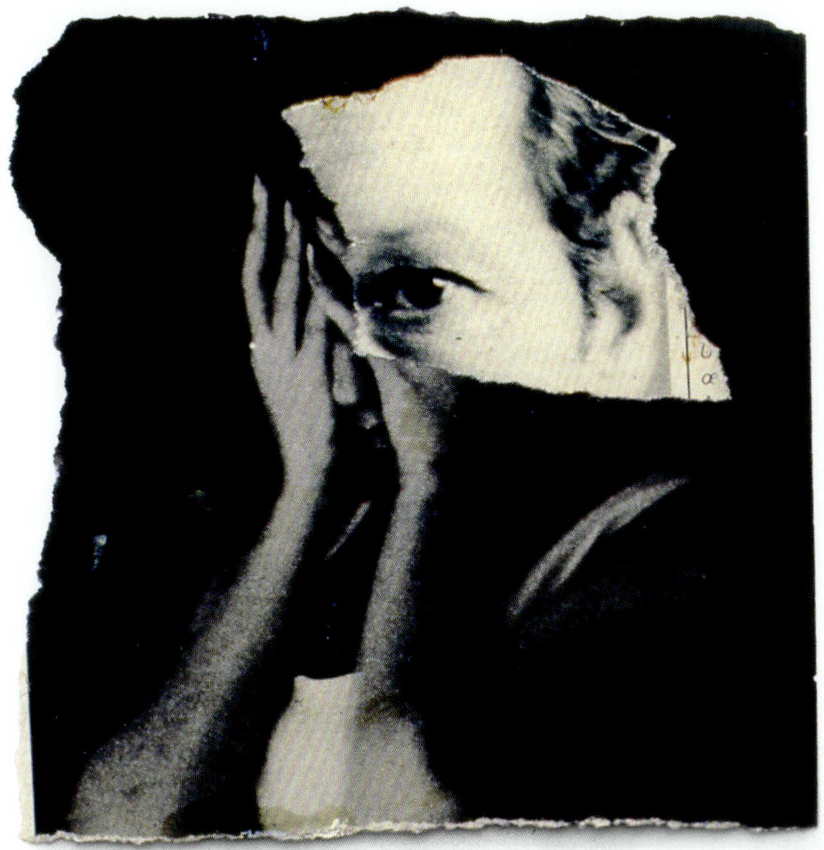

The Nose Knows, 1973
Oil on canvas, 95 x 76 cm

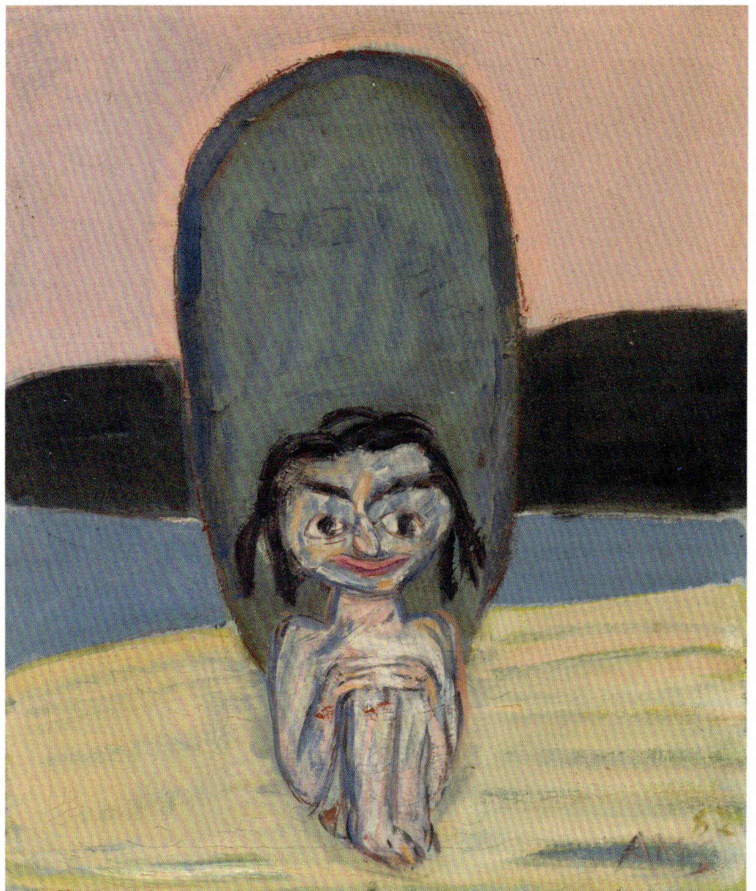

Wide-Eyed Girl, 1982
Oil on canvas, 57 x 48 cm

The Awakening

Mørland describes herself as being a cautious and shy young woman in the early 1970s. Her mother was a housewife, and the ideal for women was to ensure their home was clean, pleasant, and proper. When she was five years old, her family moved from Flekkefjord in Southern Norway to New York, replacing small, white, wooden houses with endlessly tall skyscrapers: the little girl's eyes lit up in wonder. Mørland recalls some strong impressions from her youth, as when she saw Roman Polanski's horror film *Rosemary's Baby*. The title itself promised something romantic, but Mia Farrow's beautiful innocence soon transformed into something unnerving, and under that innocence lurked evil. By conjuring up a sense of dread, the film provided food for thought about looking behind the seemingly idyllic – a perfect outer appearance did not always match the inner reality. It was like waking up. There were many new contrasts to deal with, and in her later oil painting *Wide-Eyed Girl* (1982) a young girl sits and gazes upon this strange new world. For Mørland, art would gradually become a way of interpreting and working through such impressions and impulses. Her first artistic apprenticeship was spent as an intern for the textile artist Synnøve Anker Aurdal (1971–73), with Aurdal's husband Ludvig Eikaas, himself an artist, also figuring as a vital source of inspiration. A man and a woman who made a living from creating and experimenting freely became yet another powerful eye-opener for her.

But the truly profound awakening occurred in 1973 – the year Mørland began attending the Kunstgewerbeschule in Basel, Switzerland. Following a brief spell taking courses in textile art, she transferred to the courses in painting taught by the Swiss artist Franz Fedier (1922–2005). Well acquainted with both the New York School and the Surrealists, Fedier had an outgoing, dynamic personality endowed with a surplus of energy and an international outlook. His educational philosophy resembled the open attitude of the performance artist Joseph Beuys, where every process was regarded as a possibility. There were no fixed routines in the classroom, which was instead a place where students could work freely. They were also taken seriously and listened to, exploring many genres as they were guided on the way to their own artistic expression. The students had to deliberately think through which direction they wanted to take, and the entire class would always discuss things together. Everyone presented their particular project and received feedback. Some of the students had attended the class for a couple of years and had already developed their own artistic expression. One student painted on a canvas in a photorealistic style using a slide as a model, another drew only hair structures; some made drawings of folded paper ornaments, while others made entirely abstract paintings. For her part, Mørland painted expressive portraits and abstracts, and she experimented by creating potato-shaped lumps of clay that she then used as a basis for drawing portraits. She assembled collages and used them as models for paintings, even as she sketched plants and insects. She would also frequently visit the ethnological Museum für Völkerkunde in Basel to make drawings of African and Indian sculptures.

Fedier was an acquaintance of Alberto Giacometti and Meret Oppenheim, and recounted his meetings with these and other international artists. In particular, Mørland remembers once when Fedier came back from New York and had gathered his students in his tiny cubbyhole of an office. He wanted to show them something from a certain artist in New York who had bought an entire factory. The artist's name was Andy Warhol. Warhol was not interested in signing his own works, and he let his workers make art along with him. He also experimented with film, training a camera on a single spot for hours on end, recording it all . . . maybe something would happen, maybe not. Mørland recalls the cramped atmosphere in the office and the attentive students. Fedier also took his students on field trips, for example to the Venice Biennale and to museums and galleries in Paris, Düsseldorf, and Basel. Mørland cites the experience of personally viewing Salvador Dalí's *Burning Giraffe* (1937), which she had previously only seen as a reproduction and which she now was surprised to discover was actually quite small; in the painting, a blue, wavering female figure is outfitted with drawers that open up to the inner rooms of the soul, and behind the woman stands a mysterious flaming giraffe in flames. Mørland also cites being enamoured of Max Ernst's painting of vibrant, green plants. As with Dalí, Ernst's work also included a surrealist component she found intriguing, namely a small, green figure in the bottom right that was a cross between a bush and a bunny. The figure was fascinating, and she still recalls it.

Fedier also displayed new and contemporarily relevant art, such as provocative performance videos from Austria. The class saw photographs by the Viennese Actionists, such as Otto Muehl's *Piss Aktion* (1969) and a photograph of a Christmas tree decked out in blood-soaked intestines. The sight of Muehl and Günter Brus urinating on one another, and of the Christmas tree full of blood and guts, made a lasting impression. This was far removed both from the middle-class Christmas tree decorations of her childhood and from what was permissible to do, whether in public or in art. In Basel, there were plenty of discussions about what art could be. For her part, Mørland experimented on making collages with imagery from *Time* magazine, mixing news photos from the Vietnam War with advertisement photos. In her painting *Vietnam Jigsaw Pieces* (1973) we see grey, translucent people hovering like ghosts on the canvas, as though profoundly disturbed. When she returned to Norway, she submitted her painting *The Nose Knows* to the Norwegian National Academy of Fine Arts to get admission. And perhaps the style of this picture can sum up, in essence, the art she experienced in Switzerland? The mysterious man without eyes; the oversized nose and agitated movements; the brushstrokes and colours that evoke sinews and blood . . .

Regarding her studies in Switzerland, Mørland says they stirred something entirely new in her and thereby in her art. She became fascinated by the unnatural, the surprising, and the different and peculiar: "I felt that period was incredibly inspiring – it was an awakening to all the possibilities inherent in the discipline of art. We were able to experience a good deal that was new, provocative, experimental, crazy, playful, fantastical. Everything was possible. And you weren't following the conventional path."[1]

Surrealism as impulse

If we look at the paintings Mørland made after her admission to the academy in 1974 and until her debut exhibition at the artist-run UKS gallery in 1977, they are greatly influenced by the impulses she received in Basel, perhaps above all by her encounter with Surrealist art. As Mørland recollects, the experimental art she had seen and experienced in Switzerland, such as performance, laser art, installation, and experimental teaching, had not yet reached the academy in Oslo, where students still painted nudes and attended their particular professor's painting class. Mørland studied at the academy during two separate periods: first painting and graphic art under Ludvig Eikaas, Knut Rose, Arne Malmedal, and Guttorm Guttormsgård (1974–80), and then graphic art under Zdenka Rusova (1985–86). While studying in Oslo, however, her experiences from Basel continued to have a lasting impact, and her budding fascination with the abnormal, the unusual, the surprising, began to manifest itself in her art. She painted imaginative portraits where the classical model underwent a full makeover. *Portrait of a Woman* (1976) features a female figure with black hair, white skin, and an intensely red dress against a blue background. Classical beauty has been supplanted here by a confused Janus face: a sensual profile with soft lips merges with an empty mask that stares unnervingly ahead. Such self-contradictory and incongruous elements are also apparent in *Female Portrait. Inspired by the Renaissance 1*: a portrait of a wealthy, beautiful Renaissance woman has been blinded, and she has entangled

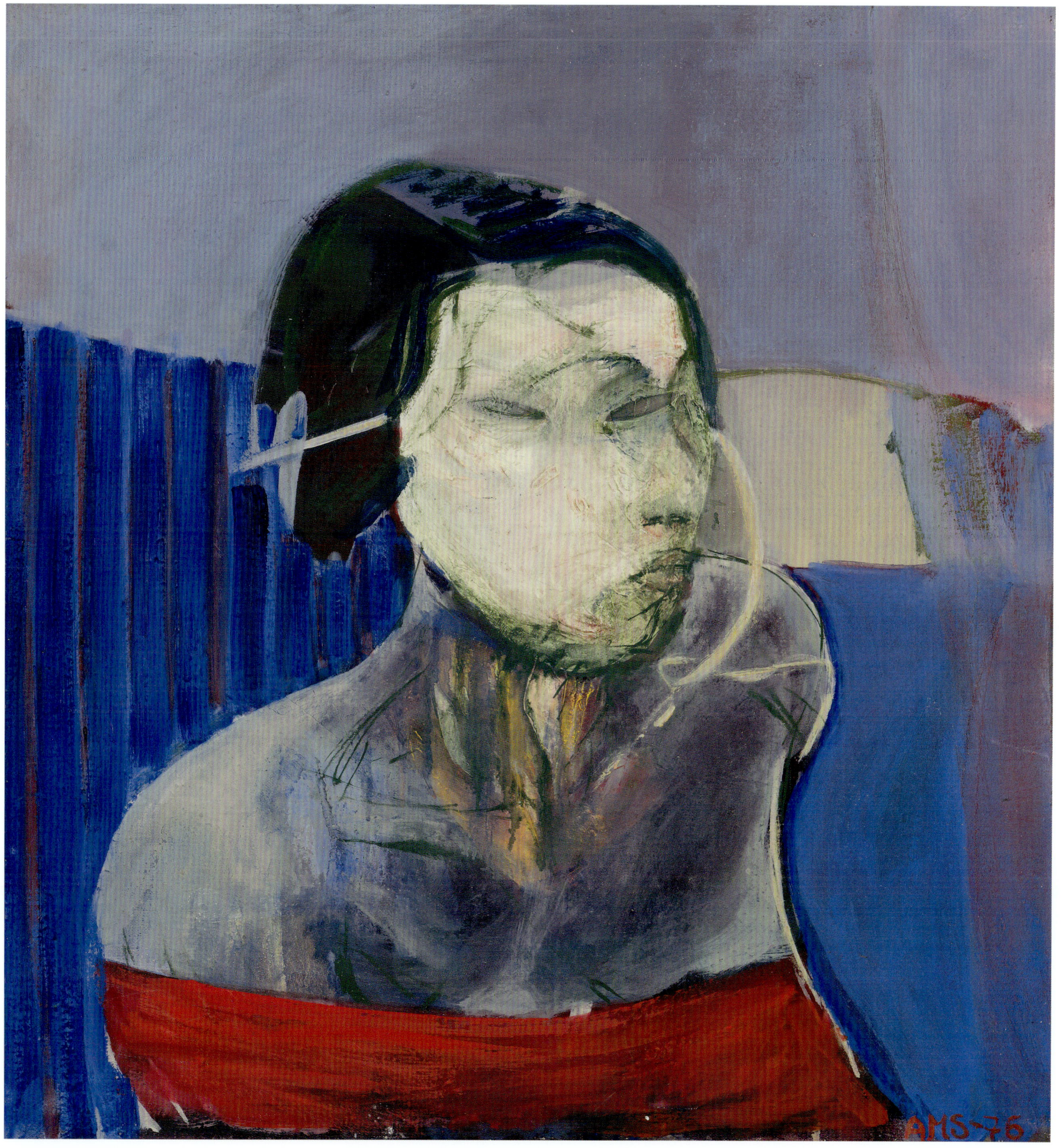
AMS-76

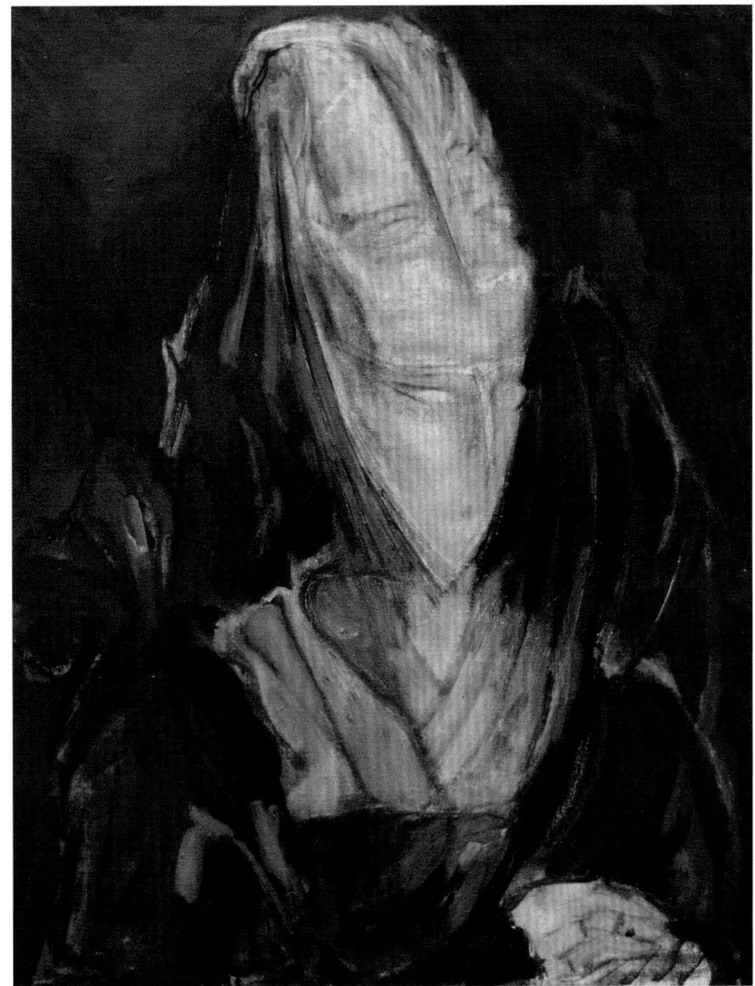

Female Portrait. Inspired by the Renaissance 1, 1977
Oil on canvas, 80 x 65 cm

herself completely in her copious strands of hair. Her high forehead and the aristocratic back of her head seem macabre and frightening rather than good-looking and graceful. *Three Portraits in Movement* features up-close portrayals of three Renaissance women in various degrees of contortion and dissolution. Their faces seem embalmed, while their heads look like they have become entangled in the confusion of their own thoughts. The portraits are mask-like, exuding a raw, primeval force that expresses ambiguity and complexity. They are far from the pure, harmonious, and seemingly uncomplicated Renaissance women they are playing on. This way of combing elements so as to create a third element is a strategy that Mørland has fetched directly from Surrealism. The Surrealist idiom, with its fascination with dreams, ambiguities, paradoxes, chance events, ruptures, and dislocation, had opened a way to the subconscious and to a world that was more profound than what was superficially obvious.

Paintings in the same year also include a male portrait, trapped in a chessboard room, and a similar large painting, *Room in Movement*, with three heads placed on a chessboard floor. Mørland's chessboards have little in common with the rigid, mathematical structures of real-life chessboards, but instead sway and fluctuate. This is a chaotic world where the portrait seeks to find its permanent form. We commonly use a number of metaphors from the world of chess, for example the notion of being checkmated, which does not mean to be as dead as a conquered king in chess, but to be in a hopeless situation. Conversely, the person who keeps someone or something else in check is definitely the one in control. Life itself can be seen as a game where we are allocated different roles,

*Portrait. Inspired by
the Renaissance 1*, 1977
Oil on canvas, 80 x 72 cm

*Portrait. Inspired by
the Renaissance 2*, 1977
Oil on canvas, 83 x 109 cm

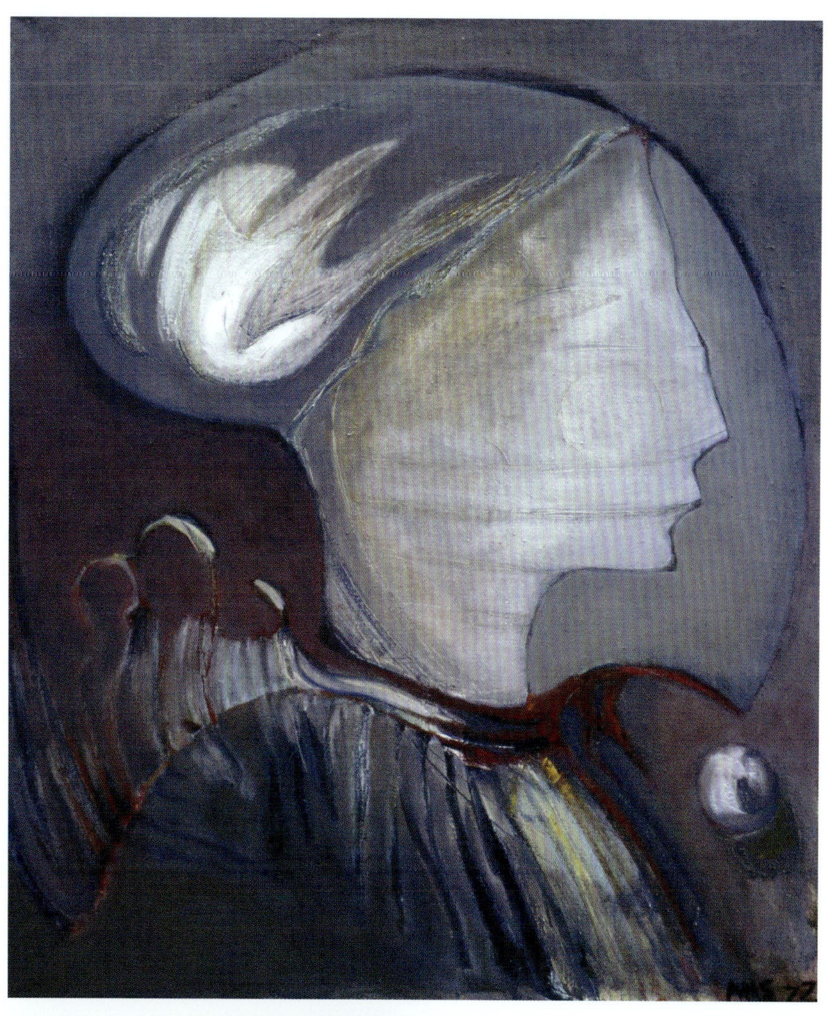

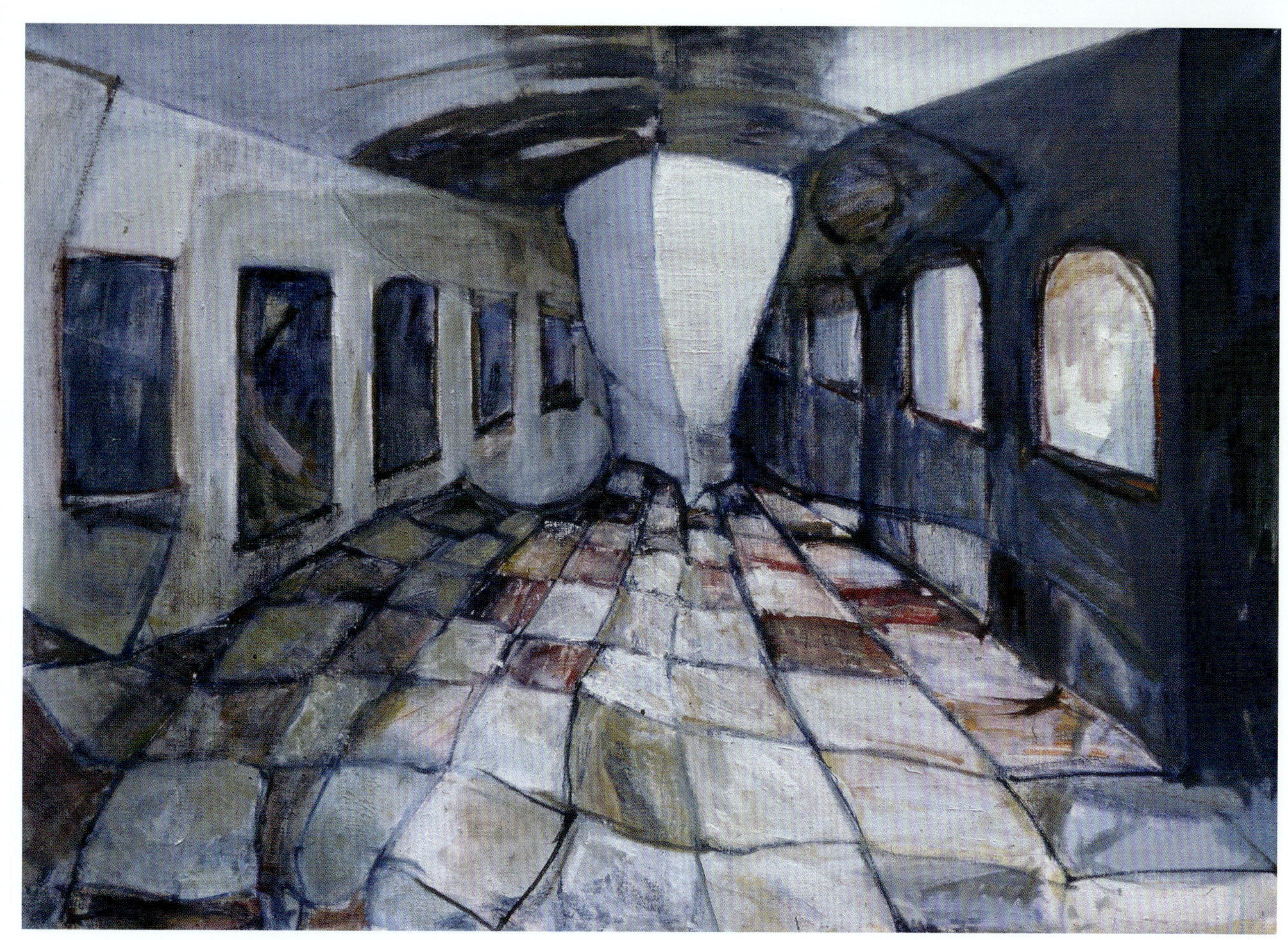

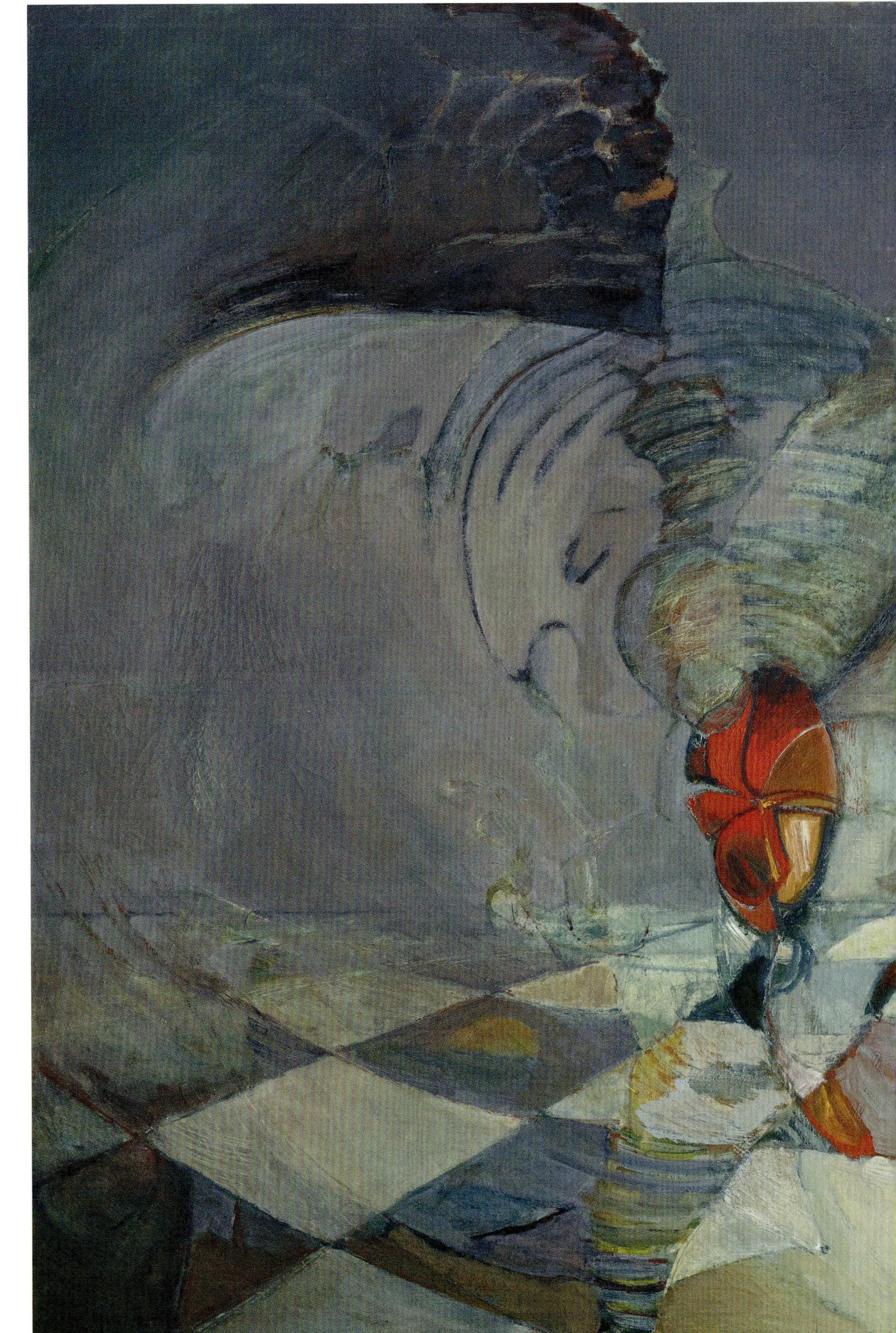

Room in Movement, 1977
Oil on canvas, 151 x 200 cm

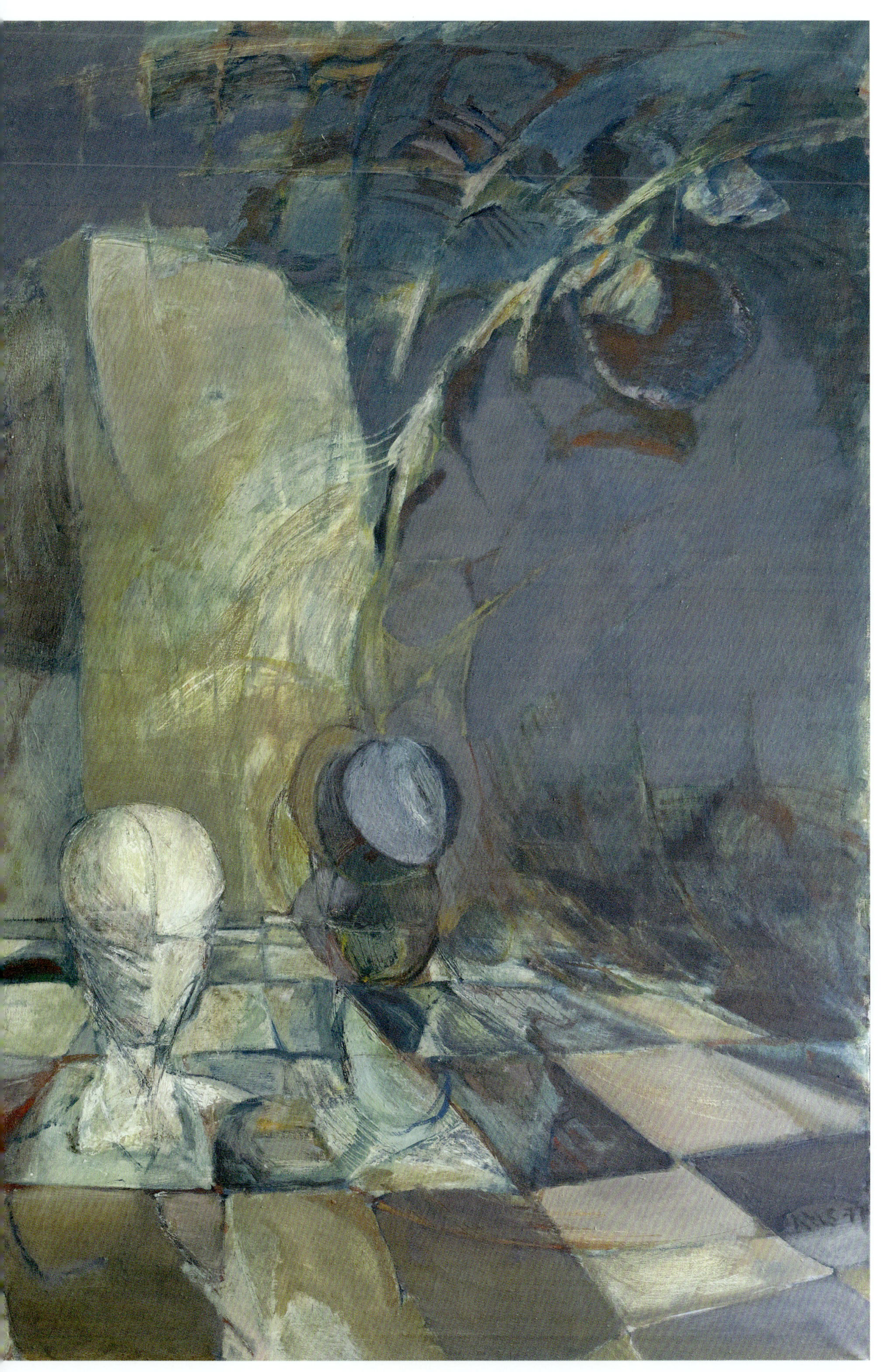

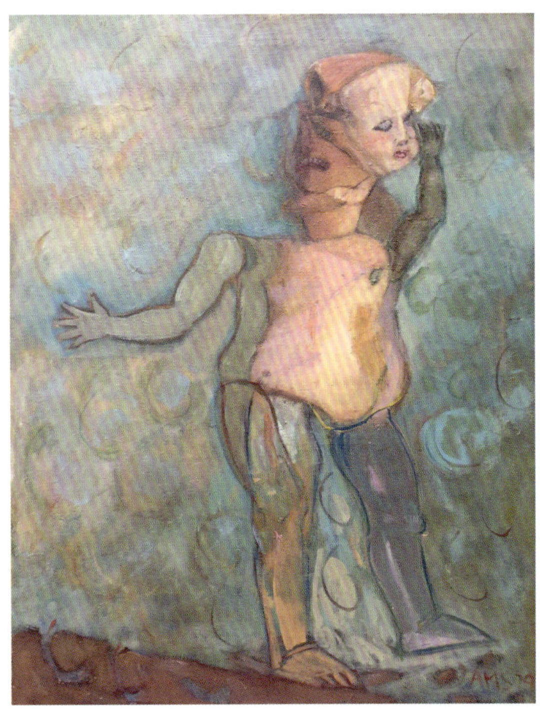

Fragmented Doll, 1979
Oil on canvas, 92 x 64 cm

Doll, 1979
Oil on canvas, 130 x 92 cm

such as pawn or queen, and where we often fall victim to the vagaries of chance. Mørland plays around with such connotations between the chessboard and life, creating a wealth of different fates for the women she portrays.[2]

This method of creating multivalent interpretations may bring to mind the type of playful visual juxtapositions the Swiss Surrealist Meret Oppenheim developed. Oppenheim is most famous for her sculpture *Le Déjeuner en fourrure* (*The Luncheon in Fur*, 1936), where she covered an entirely ordinary teacup, saucer, and teaspoon in gazelle fur. It is a work that creates associations between the known and the unknown, and that conjures a certain physical and corporeal sensation of getting hair in your mouth. For Mørland, this enigmatic and complex artist would be an enduring inspiration and a feminist icon. Mørland was introduced to Oppenheim's art on her first trip to Switzerland, when she studied at Therese Oppliger's studio outside Bern in 1970. Opplinger told her of an artist living nearby, a lady who had enjoyed a successful career in Paris in her younger years, but who had now withdrawn from the field. Oppliger showed her pictures of drawings and of the fur-lined cup from her days in Paris. Mørland would subsequently see works by Oppenheim in Swiss art museums. In addition to the fur cup, other highlights mentioned by Mørland include the painting *War and Peace* (1943), an ominous landscape featuring a lamb gazing across a battlefield, and *The Secret of Vegetation* (1972), which she saw later on at the Kunstmuseum Bern and which depicts nature evolving organically from a trunk. When I ask why exactly Oppenheim is such a lodestar for her, Mørland replies that it is the Swiss surrealist's mix of lightness and complexity that intrigues her: "What fascinates me about Meret Oppenheim's art is that she varied her expression and medium so freely. And her works seem so light, so playful and fantastical – even as they, upon a second or third glance, contain a more profound content that reveals itself in layers."[3]

A doll from Cape Town

An imaginative playfulness used to convey deeper truths can also characterise the works Mørland exhibited at Prosess gallery in 1979 along with Liv Clementz (Pettersen), whom she had met at the academy in Oslo. Their joint exhibition focused on a certain toy doll that belonged to Clementz, whose father had bought her in Cape Town when he was a sailor in the 1950s. Old and worn out, the doll had an unnervingly threadbare appearance: one arm was missing, and its hair was sooty and dishevelled. Mørland and Clementz produced a series of drawings and paintings based on this symbol of childhood, innocence, and play, morphing it into something grotesque, confusing, and scary.

The pair worked together in Clementz's studio, where they painted, experimented, and talked through their various solutions. Like the Surrealists, they would take a familiar object and "distort it" so as to create other connotations. The resulting works were exhibited at Prosess gallery, an artist-run gallery at Sandakerveien 26 in Oslo. Founded by Synnøve Ellingsen in 1978 as an alterna-

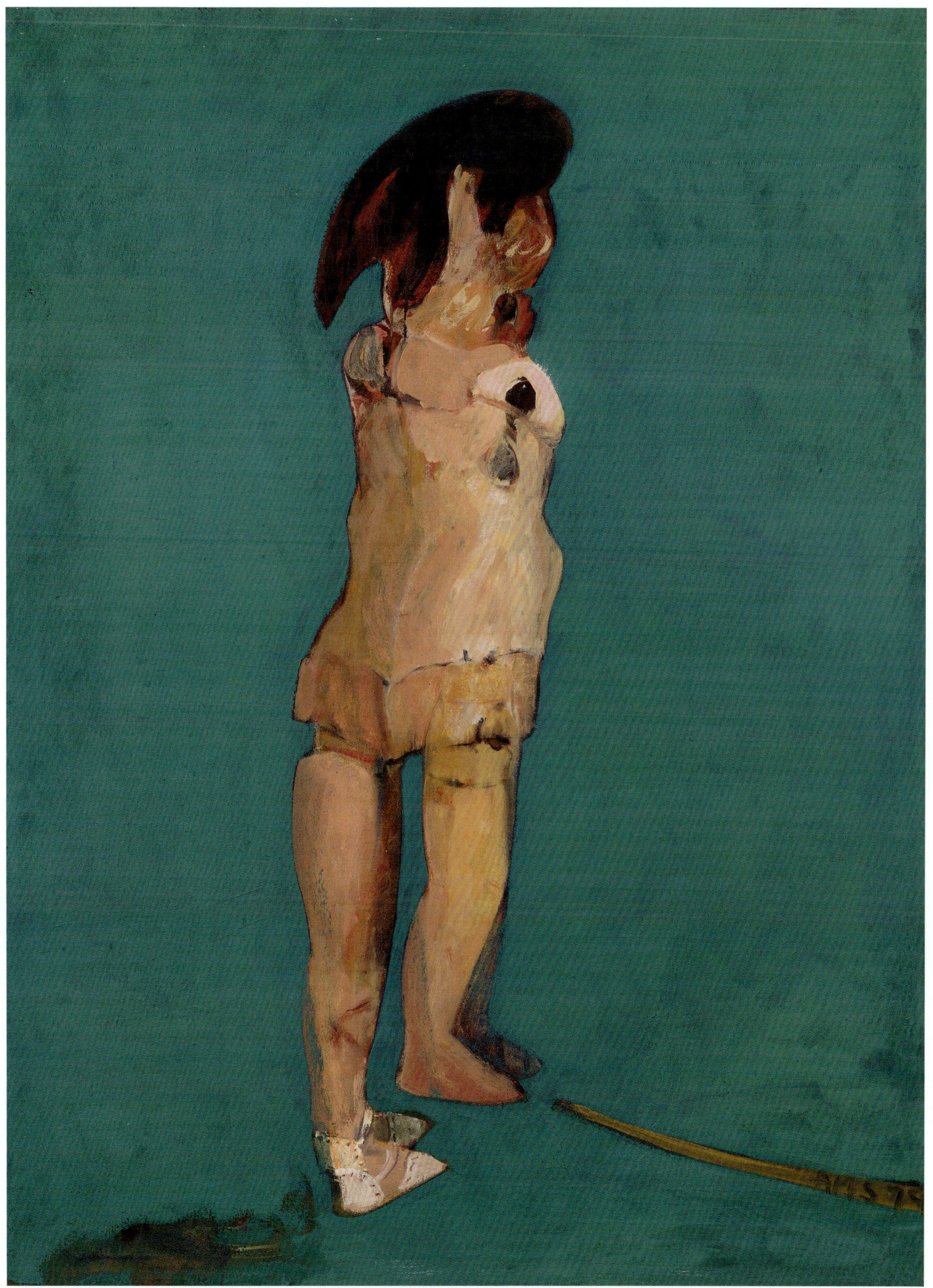

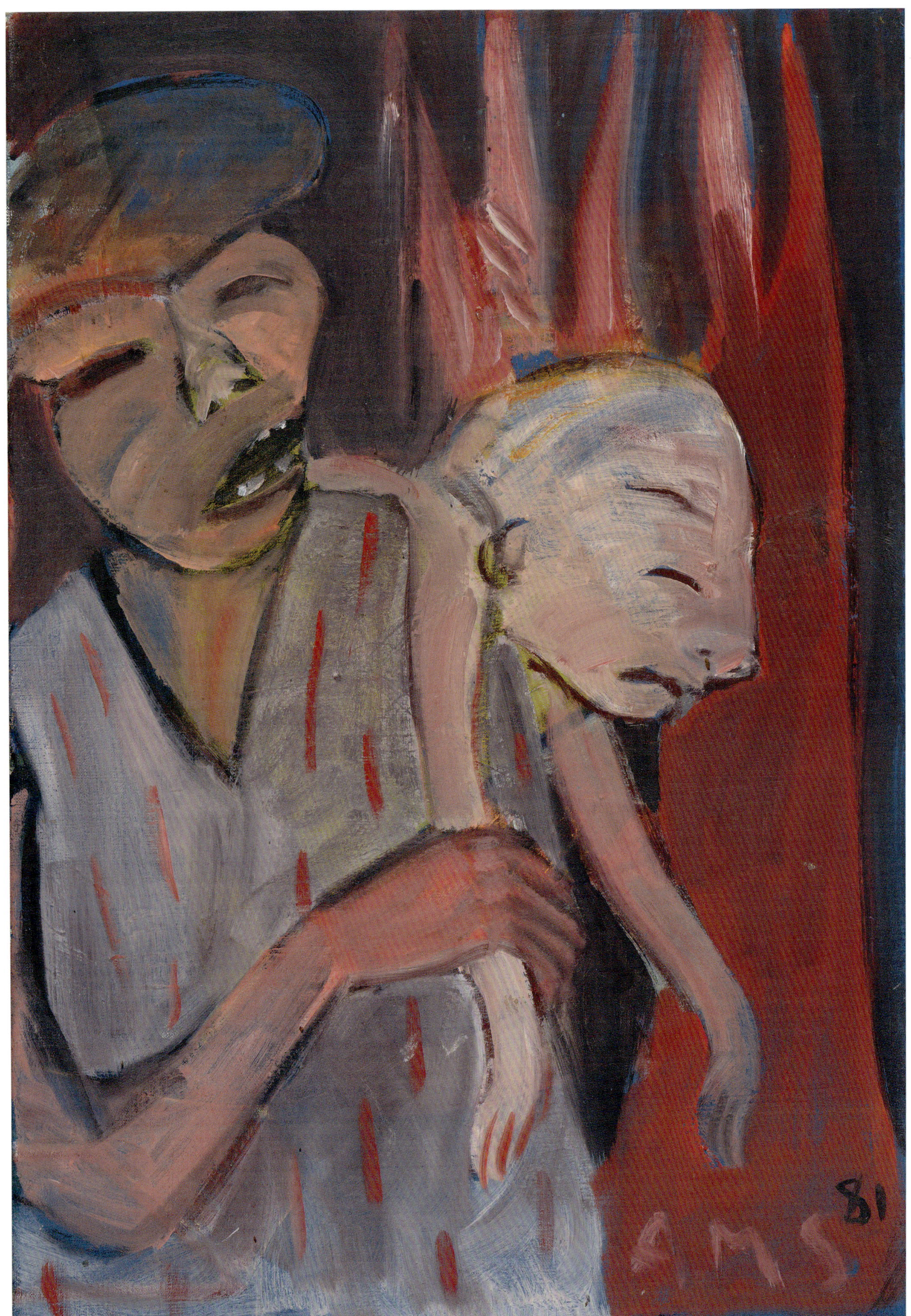

A Hundred Years of Solitude, 1981
Oil on canvas, 80 x 65 cm

tive to the commercial galleries of western Oslo, Prosess was known for its open, relaxed style. The gallery wanted to reach out to "regular people", and admission cost a mere three kroner. It was run by artists who volunteered their time and effort, and it was mainly students from the academy who showed their works there. As implied by its very name, the Norwegian word for "process", the gallery sought to display works that "were still in a state of development", as noted by one reviewer.[4]

One of Mørland's paintings from the exhibition at Prosess gallery is the oil painting *Doll* (1979), which shows a doll's body levitating against a turquoise background. The doll's arms have been chopped off and its facial features are blurred, giving it a macabre look. As in her earlier Renaissance-inspired portraits, *Doll* manifests Mørland's willingness to dissolve form and create uncertainty. The doll is here no longer a symbol of motherhood and femininity but is more complex and open to interpretation. The way in which it hovers in the room, in addition to the marked displacement that adds movement and life to its body, may bring to mind Francis Bacon's hovering, isolated figures. *Fragmented Doll* (1979) shows a doll unveiling its empty face and screaming; its body is disfigured, and the background is restless. This "assault" on the doll can perhaps be seen as an attack against middle-class values, something that would be in line with the rebellious, anti-bourgeoisie attitude of Surrealism. But while the Surrealists themselves reserved their barbs for traditional Western ideals such as church, state, and family (as distinct from the patriarchy), Mørland's works also manifest an overtly feminist outlook. In her doll and Renaissance portraits alike, she shows us portrayals of women that contain something "more" than society's patriarchal expectations. These women are complex, multi-faceted, and determined figures with strong, individual personalities. And the one depicted in *Doll*, turning as it does away from the viewer, sends a strong signal that it does not want to be subject to the male gaze, choosing instead to go its own way.

Feminism in practice

The 1970s were the decade when women's liberation truly became an issue both in Norwegian art and in public life in general. Until the 1960s, art was not regarded as a real profession but rather as a hobby, on the same level as stamp collecting and the like, and artists who were not wealthy or provided for found themselves in a dire financial situation. Female artists were more or less always reliant on being supported by their husband or family, and the roles of artist and woman seemed an incompatible combination. In a report written for the fiftieth anniversary of the UKS (Unge Kunstneres Samfund – Young Artists' Society) in 1971, the sociologist Aina Helgesen addressed this very dimension, concluding that "a female artist is thrice oppressed: as a woman, as an artist, and as a female artist".[5] Elisabeth Haarr once recalled how, when she was beginning her studies at the National College of Art and Design in Oslo, the school's rector noted that only 2 per cent of the students would succeed as artists, but that the others

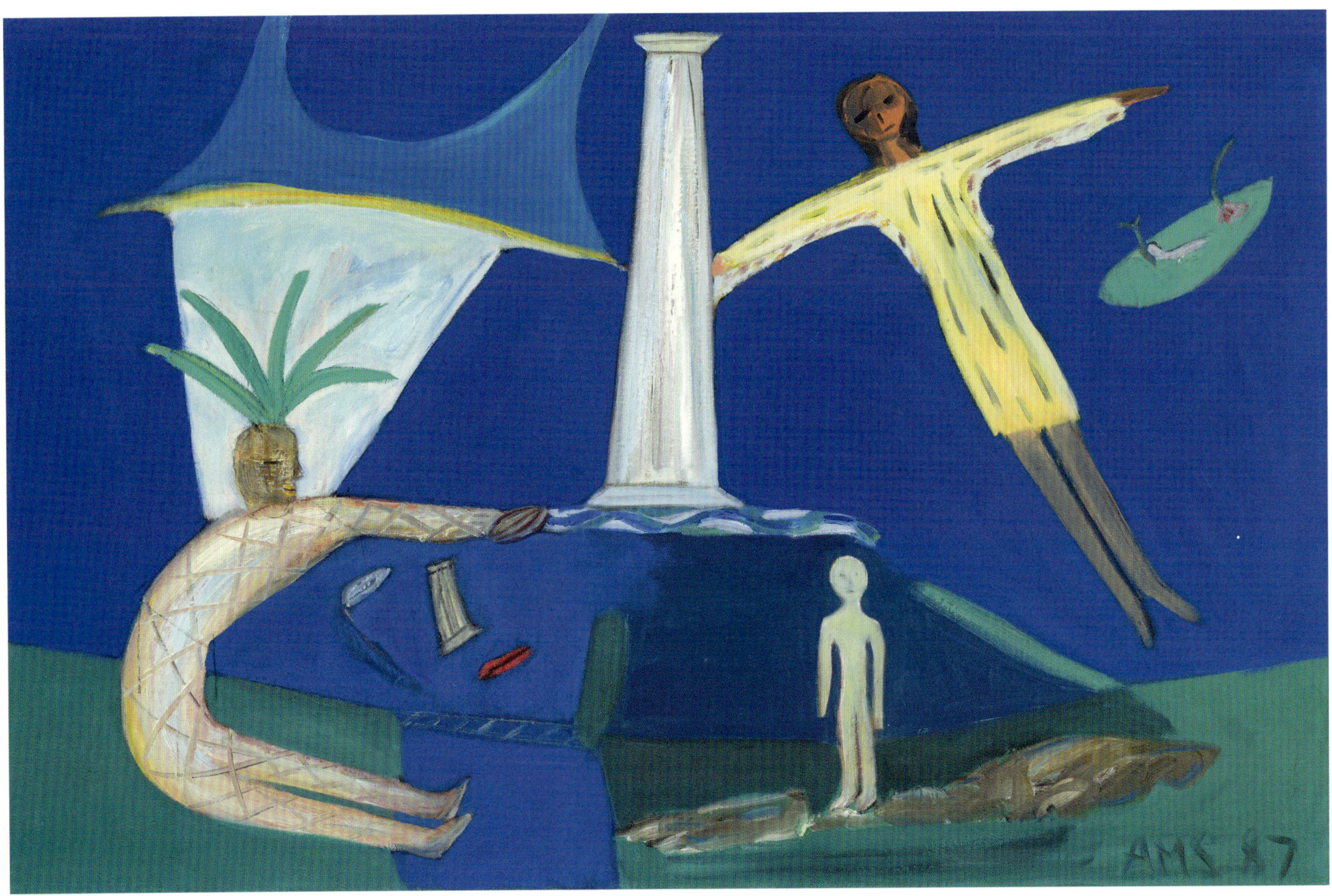

White Column, 1987
Oil on canvas, 90 x 115 cm

The House Falls, 1986
Oil on canvas, 93 x 80 cm
Sandefjord Municipality Art
Collection

would at least create "many beautiful homes".[6] And when Astrid Mørland herself became pregnant, she was advised that she might as well just "hand over her brushes" to her little daughter, the professor said. When she later returned from maternity leave, a male professor sternly informed her that she "had lost all her creative force".[7]

Mørland did not join the activist artists, but she did become involved in the women's rights movement. She participated in the annual International Women's Day demonstrations on 8 March, read the feminist monthly *Sirene*, and engaged in what could be called "practical feminism". At home, she and her husband practised gender equality – this part of the living room is mine, this part is yours. And he actively supported her in her work. When Mørland received an artist grant and travelled to Basel and Paris in 1985, it was natural for her husband to stay at home and look after the house and their daughter. Her own mother had been a housewife, but for Mørland it was important to work independently and to create. She lived according to the ideal that "if I am happy, my children will also be happy". Once again, we may draw a parallel to Astrid Mørland's artistic idol Meret Oppenheim. In a famous speech where Oppenheim reflected on how it was to be a female artist in a highly male-dominated field, she noted, "Nobody will give you freedom. You have to take it."[8] And this way of actively finding your own place, of carving out your own creative niche, also typifies Mørland's attitude towards feminism. Feminism is inherent in the art she creates and in the continuous endeavour of studying at the academy, working in the studio, travelling abroad to seek inspiration, and holding exhibitions.

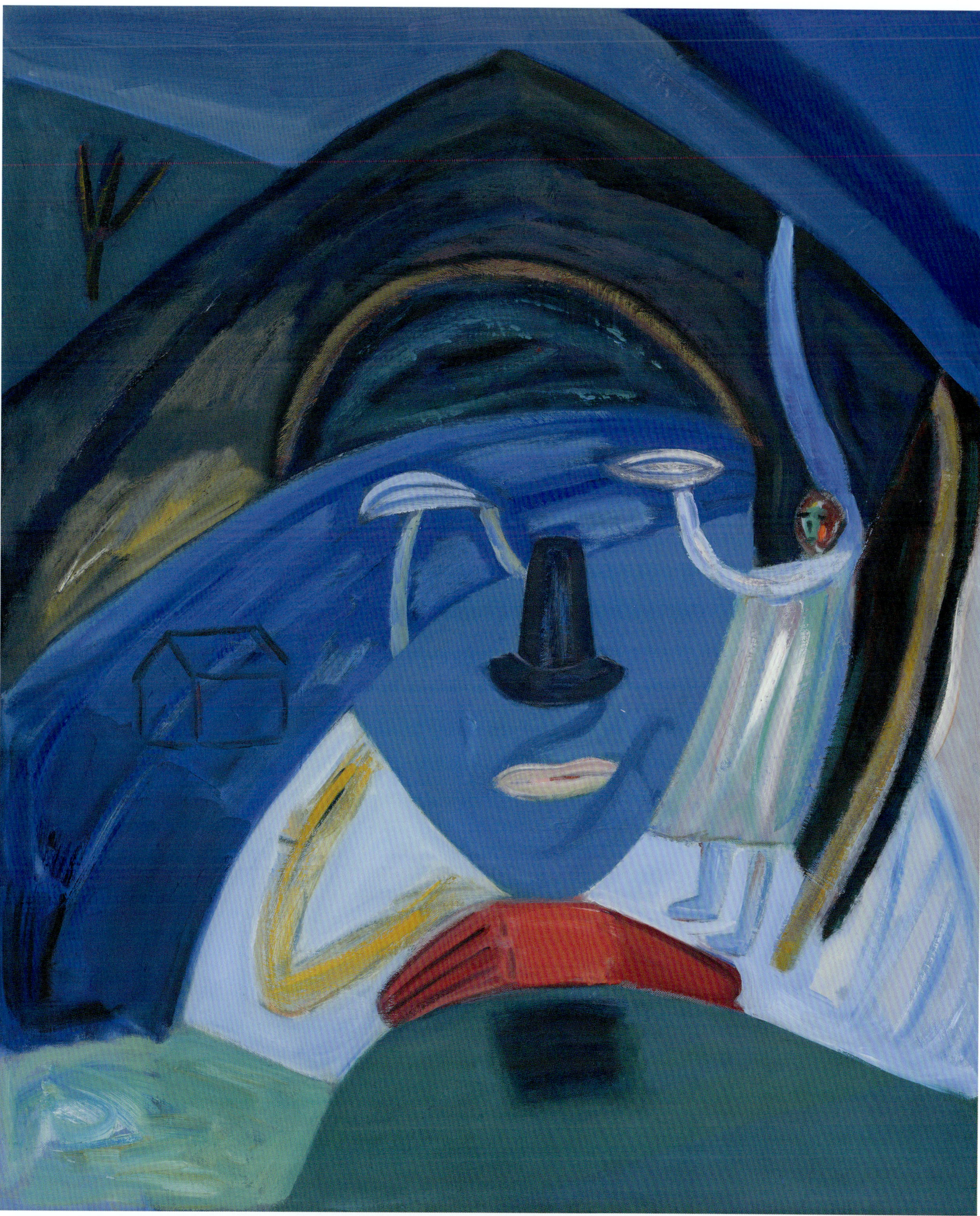

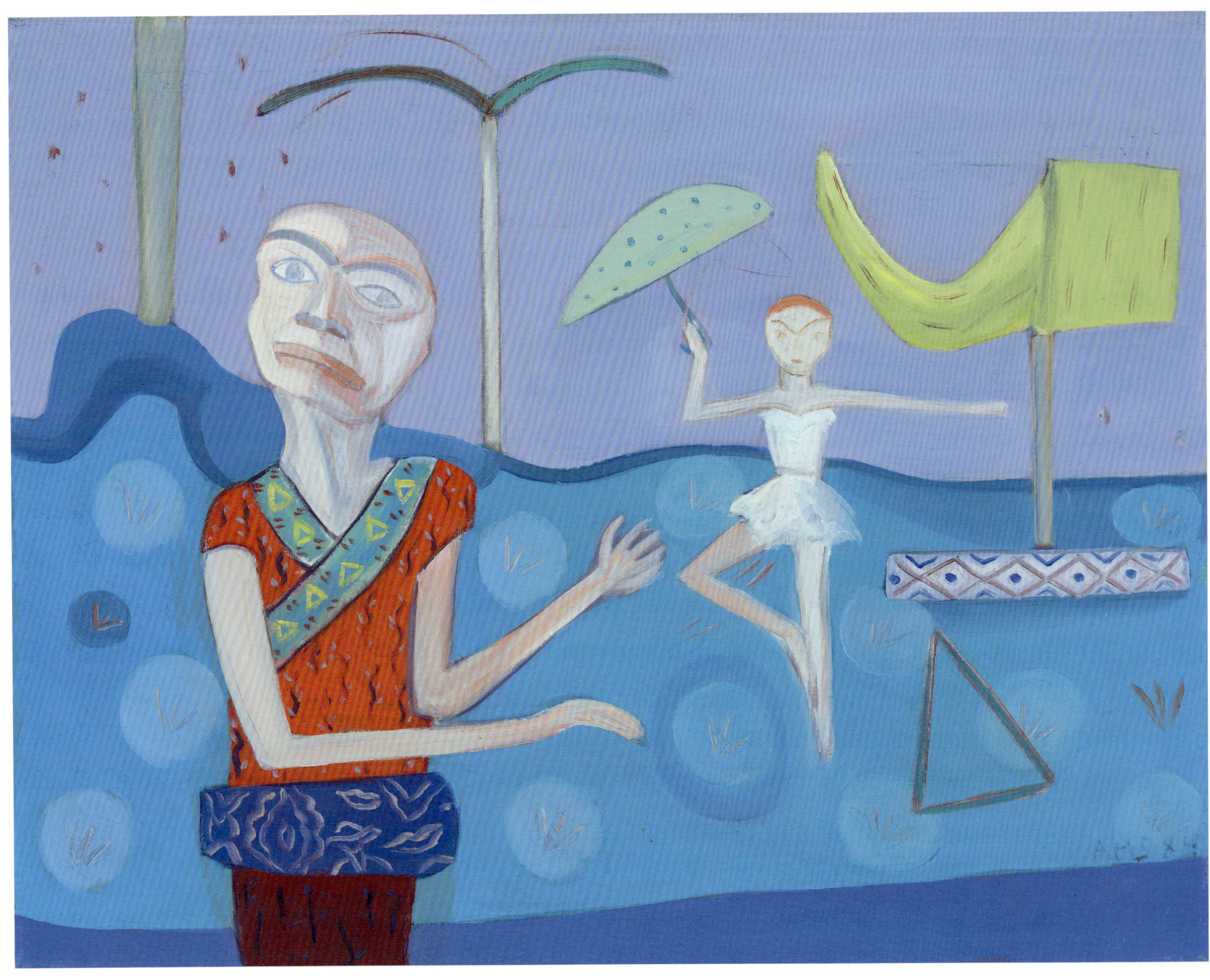

The Screening, 1984
Oil on canvas, 85 x 100 cm

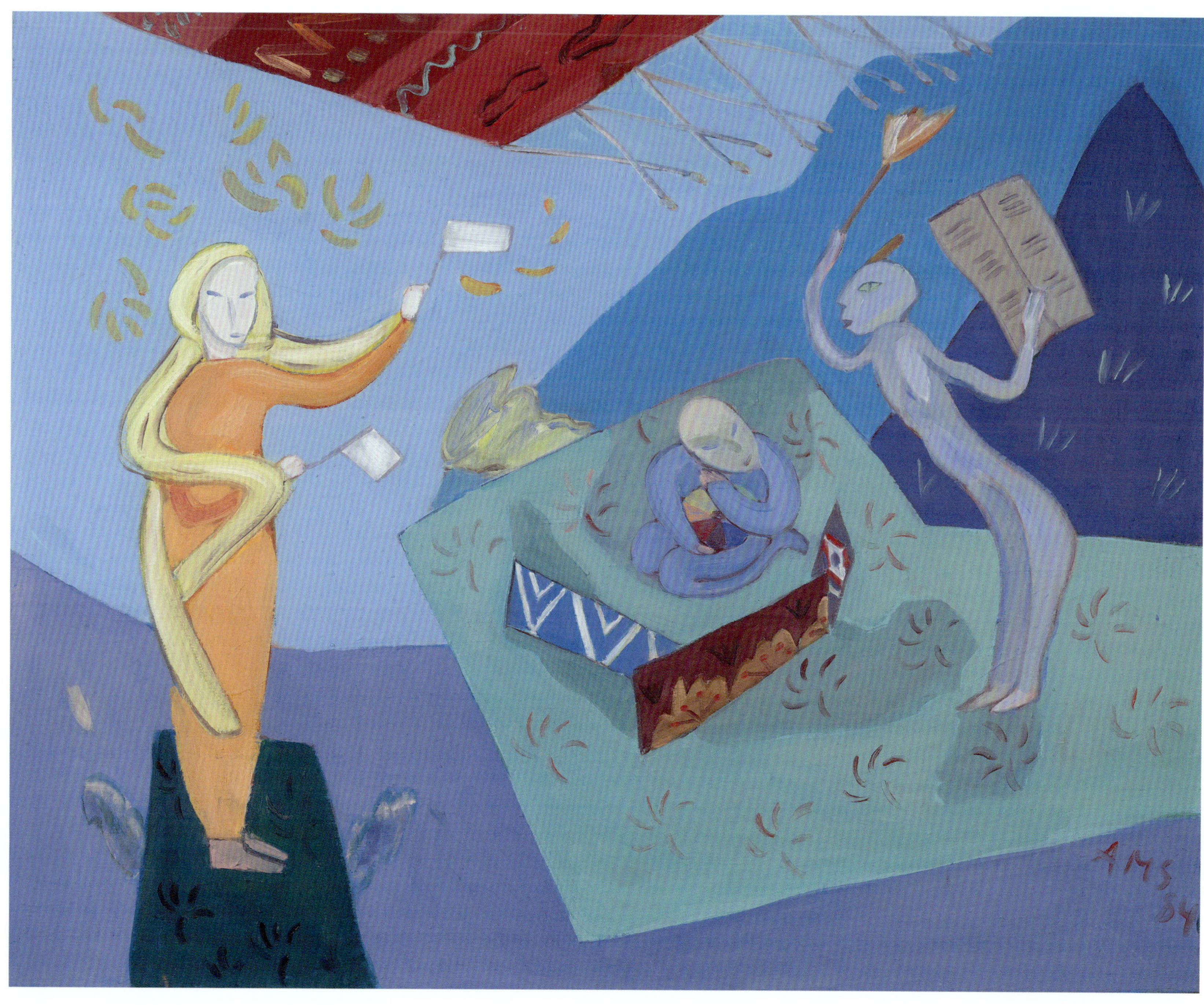

Three Truths 1, 1984
Oil on canvas, 80 x 100 cm

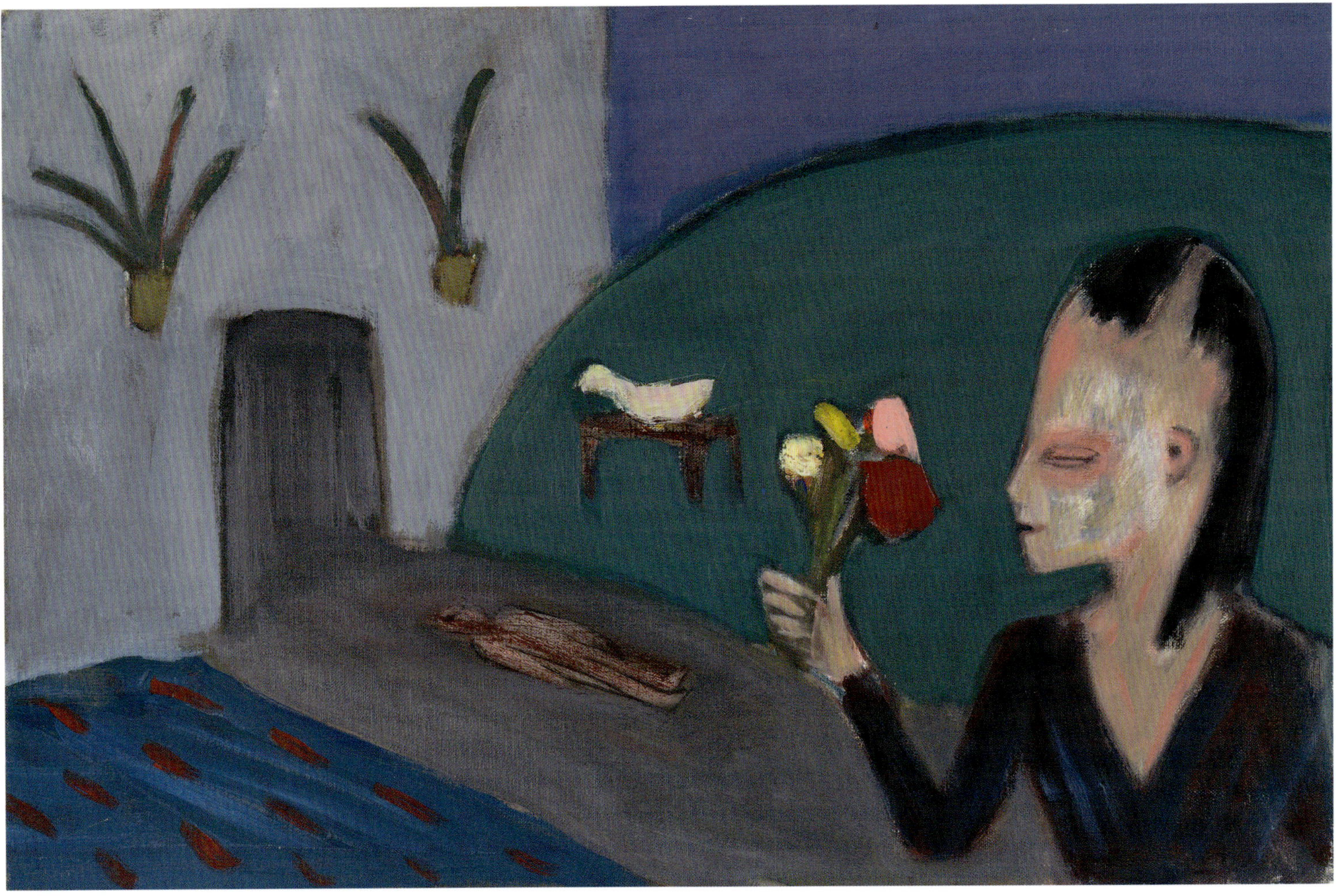

Farewell, 1984
Oil on canvas, 25 x 55 cm

The 1980s: towards a personal mythology

The 1980s witnessed a renewed interest in the discipline of painting, as heralded by the slogan "Back to painting!" and designations such as New Image Painting, Heftige Malerei, and Die Neue Wilden. For Astrid Mørland herself, the 1980s were largely a continuation of the themes and trends of the decade before – after chiefly working on painting in the 1970s, she continued to do so in the new decade. One difference, however, is that her new works tended to explore themes that allude more clearly to her own personal experiences as well as to myths and fantasy. Her paintings from the early 1980s, for example, depict imagery that addresses the relationship between women and men, and between mothers and children. The figures move about in dreamy, mythological landscapes and often wear masks that give them an ambiguous, inscrutable, and sometimes frightening appearance. The paintings dwell on the tense relationship between a man and a woman and the traditional role expectations both in society and internally in the home. On the whole, there is a sharp divide between her works in the 1980s, with the period prior to 1985 characterised by the breakup of her marriage and her sorrow over her daughter's tragic death, something that manifests itself in dark, restless colours and images that portray dislocation and a lack of communication. In the painting *Three Truths 1* (1984) there is a battle for the truth, as a strict lady wielding white flags mediates between a figure squeezing a painting palette and another holding an open book in one hand and a torch in the other. In *Woman on a Carpet outside the Cave* (1984), the woman has lain down naked with her handful of symbolic

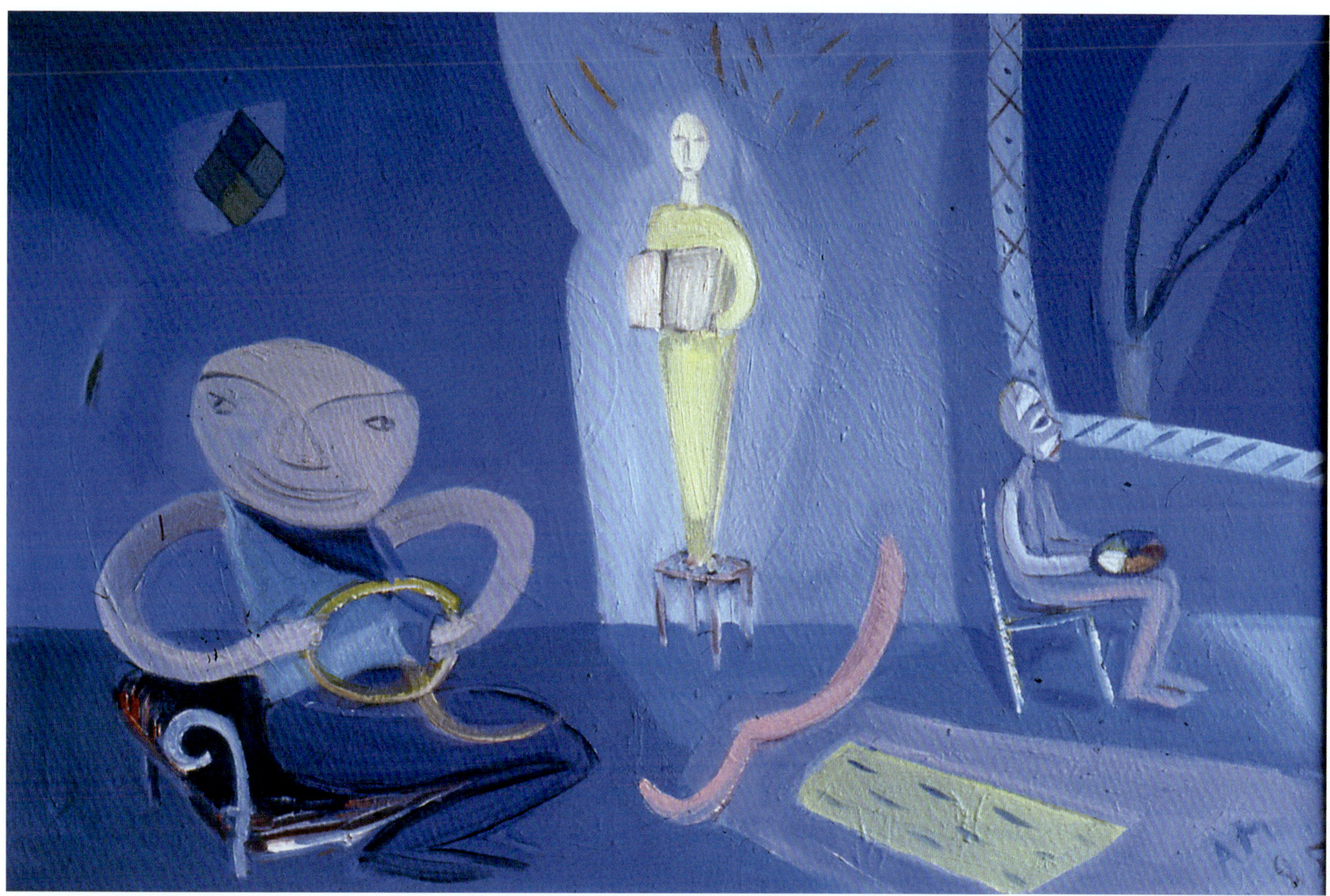

Three Truths 2, 1985
Oil on canvas, 90 x 100 cm

items, while the man tries to coax her back in the cave. And in *Guardian* (1984), a woman prostrates herself humbly before a masked ruler.

Titles such as *Sick Woman Carrying an Even Sicker Man*, *A Hundred Years of Solitude*, *Ballerina in the Sunset*, *Death Carries*, and *Farewell* attest to a rough patch in her life. But things would eventually improve in 1985, when Mørland once again began studying at the academy in Oslo, this time under Zdenka Rusova, a highly inspiring professor of graphic art who taught her to trust her own linework. Mørland also received a travel grant that allowed her to return to the Kunstgewerbeschule in Basel. For a few months she once again studied in the painting class taught by her "old teacher" Franz Fedier, and slowly but surely she regained her footing both artistically and personally. Her stay in Basel allowed her to catch inspiring exhibitions, go to the theatre, see happenings and performances – to somehow be back where it all began. And this is almost discernible in the colours and the themes she explored after 1985. *In a Red Chair 1* (1985), for instance, evinces a completely different self-confidence and *attitude* in the woman sitting in the red chair. The patronising, forward-leaning masked man to the left is unable to exert power over the woman; her body, curving gently, turns away from him, and she has determinedly crossed her arms and legs. The bright, pastel colours are feminine, and the ceiling is high and airy. The same kind of joy is on display in the uplifting *Portrait with Coloured Stripes* (1986). A meditation on what it means to be an artist and creator, the painting shows a small, vivid woman in a dress standing on her head, symbolising bright ideas that are shooting out.

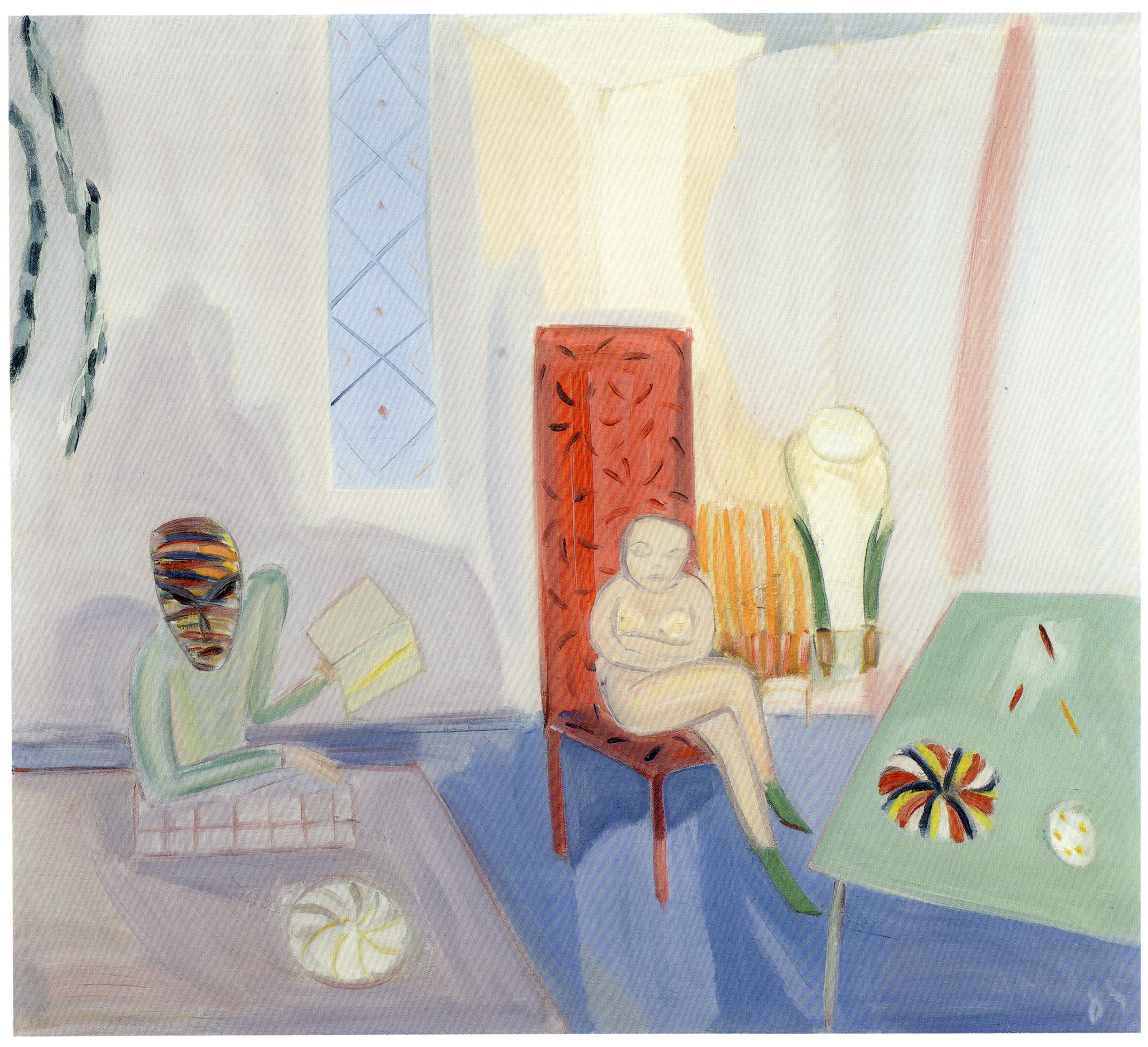

In a Red Chair 1, 1985
Oil on canvas, 80 x 100 cm

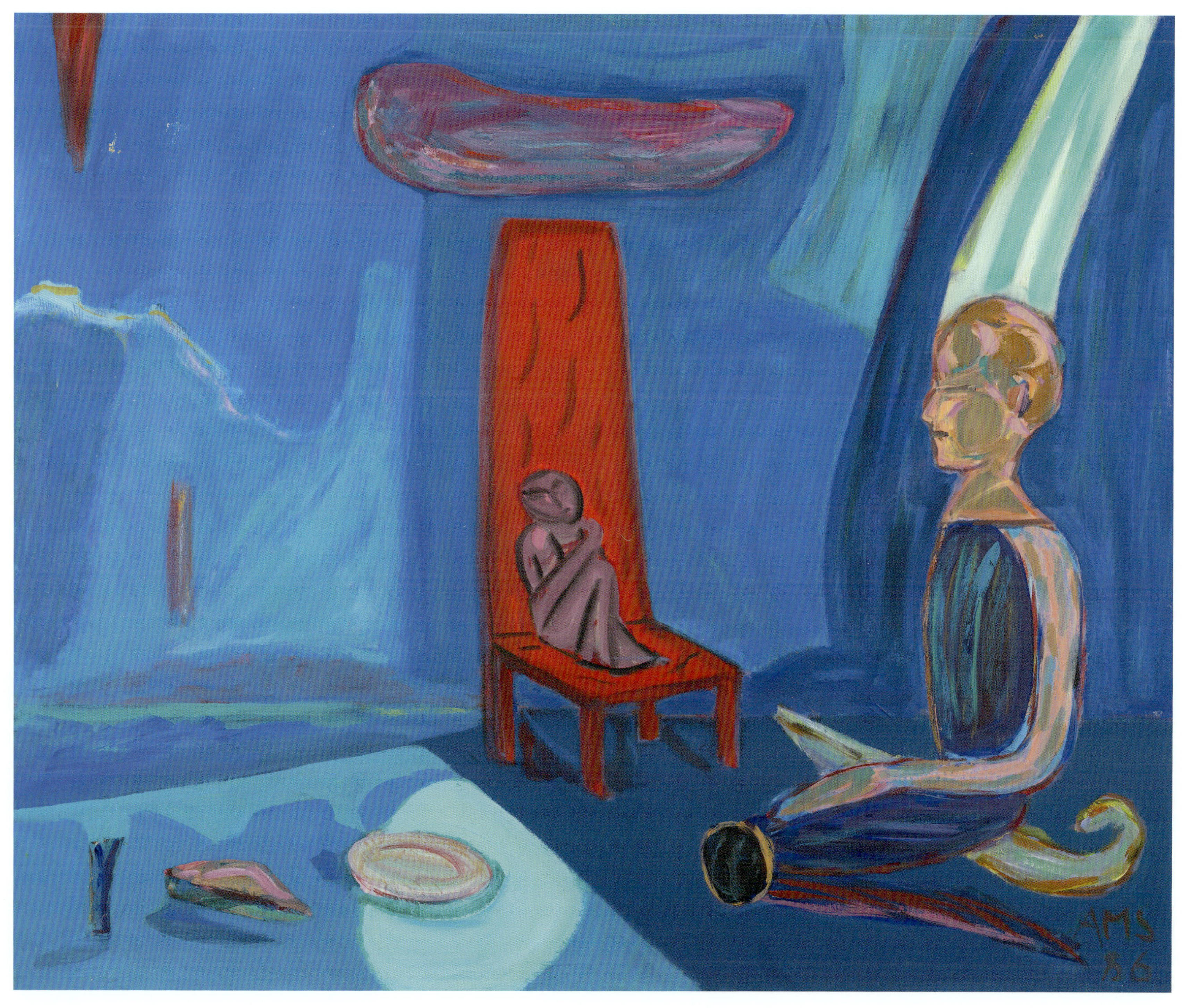

In a Red Chair 2, 1986
Oil on canvas, 90 x 100 cm

Portrait with Coloured Stripes, 1986
Oil on canvas, 90 x 80 cm

Restoration / Reinstatement

Anyone looking for Astrid Mørland's name in reference works of Norwegian art from the 1970s and 1980s will search in vain. A 1980 publication on Norwegian painting in the 1970s, for example, almost exclusively highlights male artists, and the focus there is squarely on artists who were political activists and engaged in the artists' movement.[9] Nor was Mørland included in a 2009 exhibition catalogue that presents the Norwegian art of the 1980s, even though her symbolic, "inner" painting was very much in sync with the trends of the time.[10] Moreover, the rewriting of art history that has taken place in the 2010s has primarily concentrated on crafts and on female artists' struggle for gender equality in the 1970s. An artist such as Mørland, who worked more quietly and kept more in the background, is rarely featured as an exponent of this era. Nevertheless, she definitely does capture the zeitgeist: the enigmatic, ambiguous figures that recall the Heftige Malerei of continental Europe; the markedly Surrealist impulse that is also evident in works by Knut Rose, Bjørn Ransve, and Marianne Heske, among others; and perhaps above all, a feminist impulse and outlook that comes clearly to the fore in her portrayals of women and her explorations of themes such as liberation and release. The present exhibition and catalogue therefore represent an important effort to fill in the gaps that have accumulated in the male-dominated canon of Norwegian art from the 1970s and 1980s.

[1] Astrid Mørland, conversation with the author, Astrid Mørland's studio, 22 June 2020.

[2] At her debut exhibition, the largest painting garnered the most press attention: "Astrid Mørland Sodefjed paints in an expressionist, figurative style, which does seem to have its forerunners – *Portrait of a Woman* is for example inspired by Bacon . . . *Room in Movement* follows up its title, displaying a firmness in its character and conjuring spatiality in the colour itself. Second only to the women's portrait, it seems to be the exhibition's best picture." See Even Hebbe Johnsrud, "Uvant gjest i UKS", *Aftenposten*, 26 April 1977. Arne Durban as well cites the largest painting in his review, noting that "her largest picture was by far the best and most interesting one"; see Arne Durban, "Mest malerier og grafikk", *Handel og Sjøfartstidene*, 20 April 1977.

[3] Mørland, conversation with the author, 22 June 2020.

[4] Wan Soong-Kai, "Kunst-prosess på Østkanten", *Morgenbladet*, 20 June 1978.

[5] See Aina Helgesen, "Kvinnelige kunstnere: En sosiologisk tilnærming", in *Engasjert kunst: Hannah Ryggen, Elisabeth Haarr*, exhibition catalogue (Trondheim: Nordenfjeldske Kunstmuseum, 2008), 6–7.

[6] Kunsthall Stavanger, "Textiles, Women's Liberation, Ugly and Nice: An Interview with Elisabeth Haarr", 21 May 2014, https://kunsthall-stavanger.no/en/news/on-textiles-womens-liberation-ugly-and-nice-an-interview-with-elisabeth-haarr.

[7] Mørland, conversation with the author, 22 June 2020.

[8] Bice Curiger, *Meret Oppenheim: Defiance in the Face of Freedom* (Zurich: Parkett, 1989), 130–31. In her "Acceptance Speech for the 1974 Art Award of the City of Basel, January 16, 1975", Oppenheim declared, "Men, as artists, can live as they please without provoking censure, but people look disdainfully at a woman who claims the same privilege. This and much more is a woman's lot. I think it is the duty of a woman to lead a life that expresses her disbelief in the validity of the taboos that have been imposed upon her kind for thousands of years. Nobody will give you freedom, you have to take it."

[9] Even Hebbe Johnsrud, Gunnar Sørensen, and Bjørn Melbye Gulliksen, *Norsk maleri: 70-tallet* (Oslo: Tanum-Norli, 1980).

[10] Eli Okkenhaug, *Blodig alvor: Norsk kunst på 80-tallet* (Bergen: Bergen Kunstmuseum, 2009).

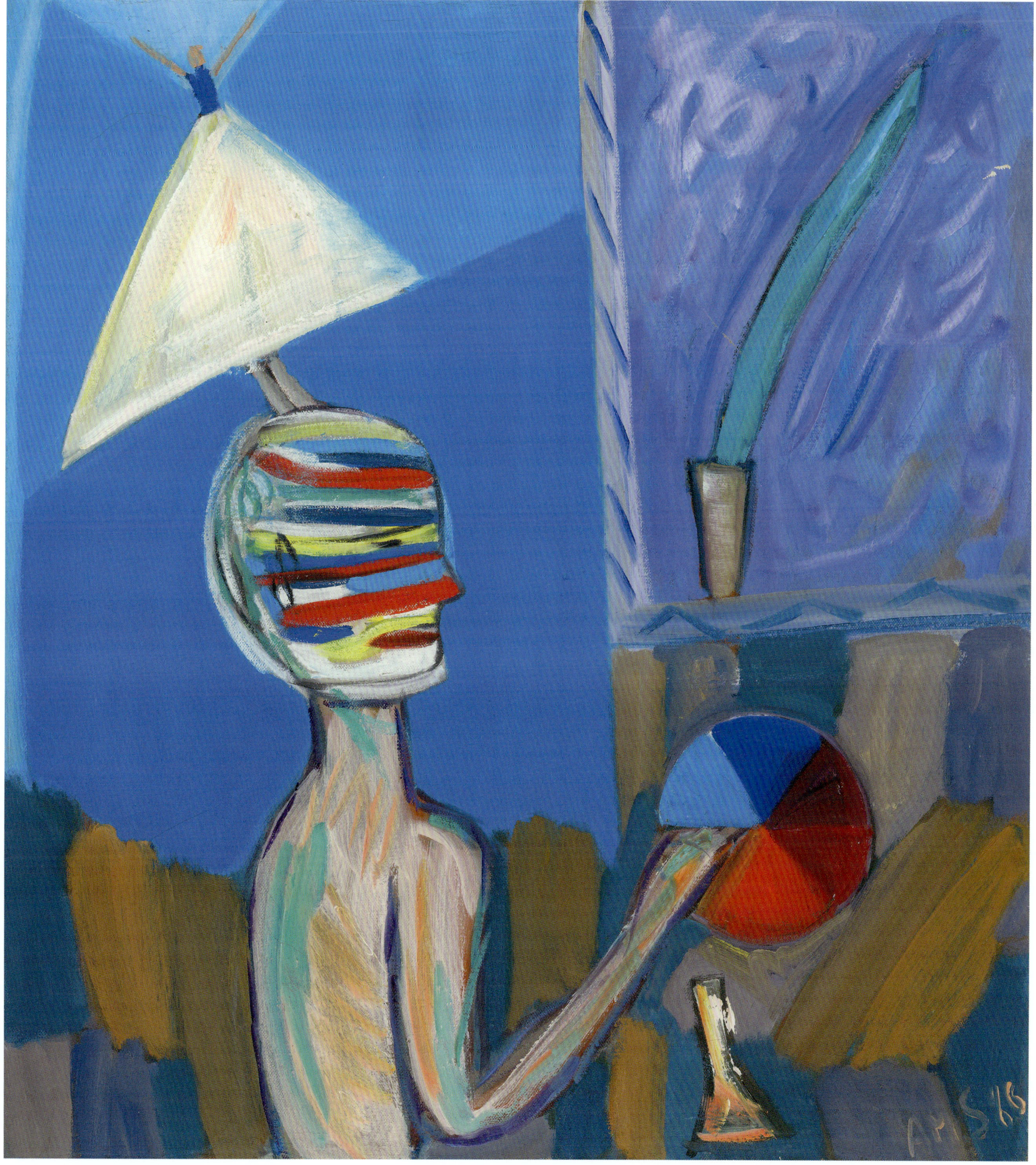

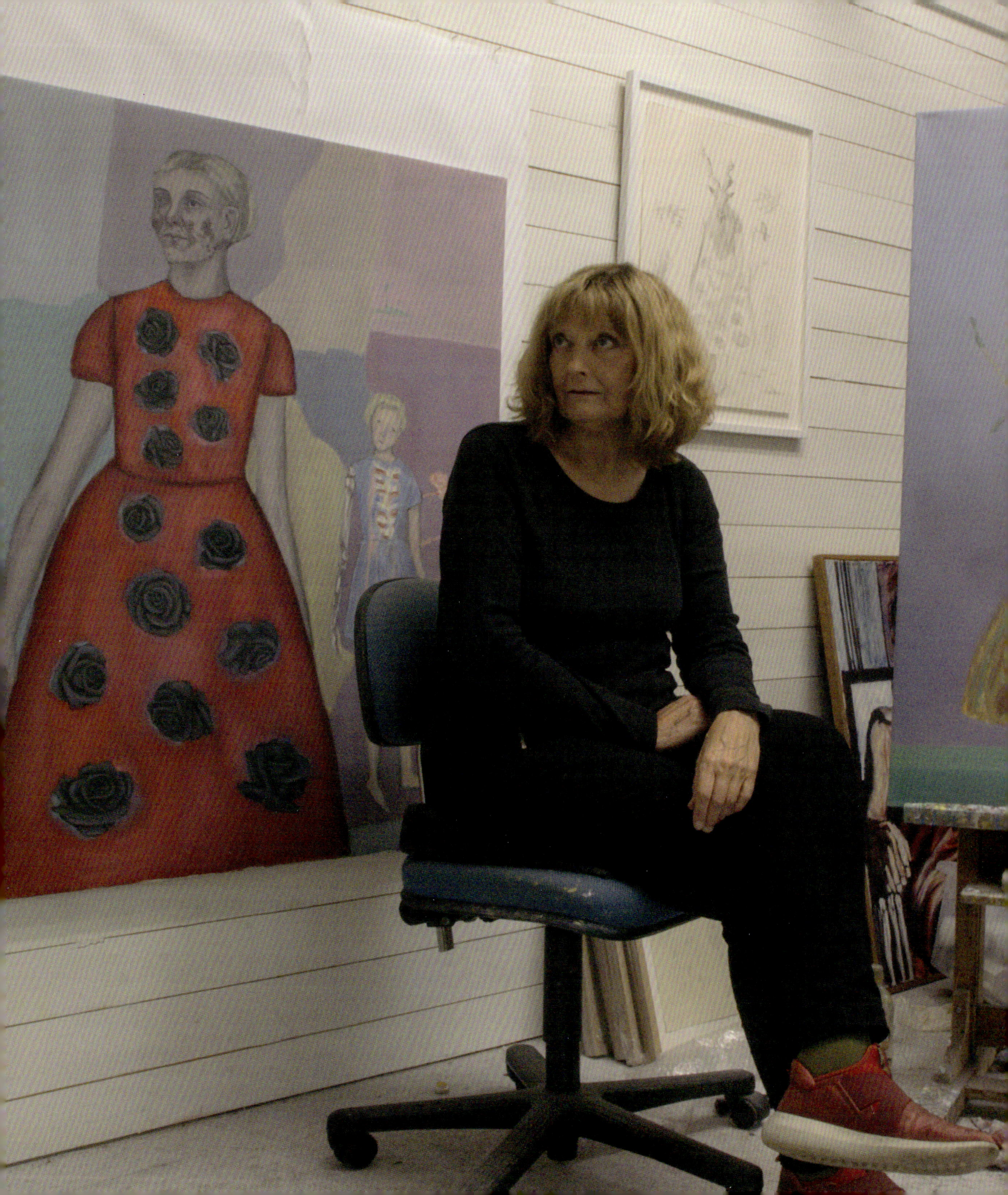

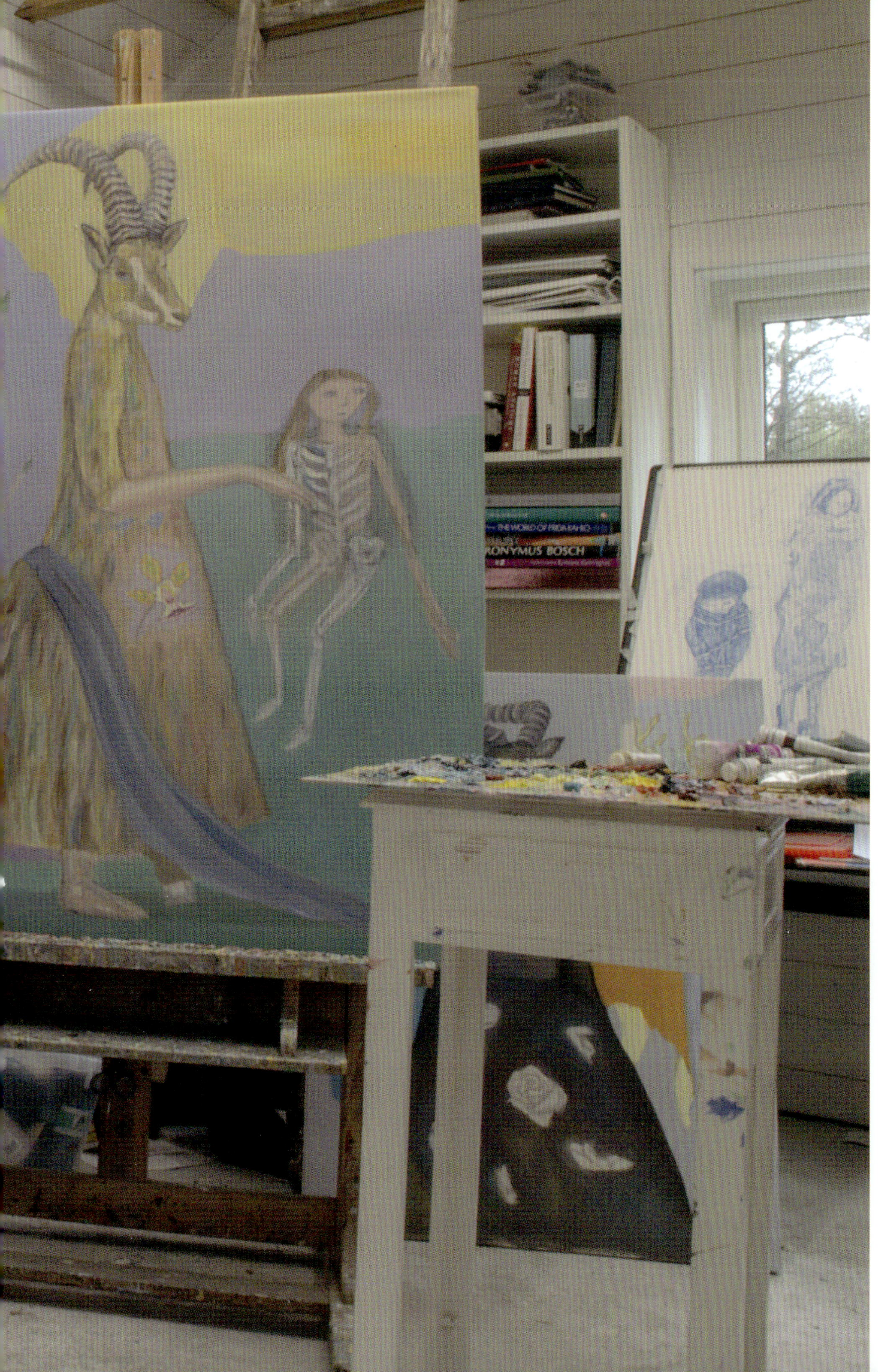

Appendix

Exhibitions / Collections

Astrid Mørland was born in Kragerø and works in Lillesand
www.astridmorland.net

Education
1973–74
• Kunstgewerbeschule Basel
1974–80
• National Academy of Fine Arts, Oslo
1985–86
• National Academy of Fine Arts, Oslo
1991–95
• University of Oslo

Solo exhibitions
2021
• Haugar Art Museum, Tønsberg
• Art Association, Arendal
2019
• Gallery Galleberg, Horten
2017
• Gallery Galleberg, Horten
• Art Center, Tønsberg
2015
• Gallery Ask, Horten
2014
• Gallery S, Östersund, Sweden
2013
• Gallery Smalgangen, Horten
• Art Association, Larvik
2009
• Gallery Smalgangen, Horten
• Art Association, Risør
2008
• Art Association, Lørenskog
2007
• Art Association, Sandefjord
2006
• Visual Artists' Art Center, Gallery Boa, Oslo
• Gallery Hå Gamle Prestegård, Jæren
2005
• Art Association, Trondheim
2004
• Art Association, Lillesand
• Art Center, Tønsberg

2002
• Gallery S, Östersund, Sweden
2001
• Lysekil Konsthall, Bohuslän, Sweden
2000
• Gallery Ask, Åsgårdstrand
1999
• Munch's Studio, Åsgårdstrand
1989
• Kunstnerforbundet, Oslo
1984
• Art Association, Sandefjord
• Art Association, Skien
1982
• Visual Artists' Art Center, Larvik
• Art Association, Sandefjord
1977
• Gallery UKS, Oslo

Group exhibitions
2018
• Eastern Region Exhibition, Gallery Vestfossen, Vestfossen
2014
• 12th International Festival of Arts, Monastir, Tunisia
2013
• 4th Kin Biennale, Kjerringøy
• Haugar Art Museum, Tønsberg
Munch by Others
2012
• Norwegian Drawing Biennial, Drawing Art Center, Oslo
2011
• Gallery Galleberg, Horten
Life and Death Plus Everything Else
2010
• Haugar Art Museum, Tønsberg
Border District
• Stenersen Art Museum, Oslo
Good Right Then You! Surrealism in Norwegian art 1930–2010
2008
• Akershus Art Center
9 Rooms
• Art Association, Kongsberg

2003
• Eastern Region Exhibition II
Young Silence and Trauma
2002
• Spring Exhibition, Tegnerforbundet, Drawing Art Center, Oslo
• Jølstra Art Museum Eikaas Students
2000
• Telemark County Gallery, Notodden
1992
• Gallery Brandstrup, Moss
1991
• Art Association, Students of Ludvig Eikaas, Oslo
1989
• Visual Artists' Art Center, Larvik
1987
• Visual Artists' Art Center, Larvik
• Galerie Vorstadt, Basel, Switzerland
1986
• Kunstnerforbundet, Oslo
1985
• Art Association, Skien
• Gallery LNM, Oslo
1981
• Art Association, Sandefjord
1980
• Gallery UKS, Oslo
1979
• Gallery Prosess, Oslo
• Gallery No. I, Bergen
• Gallery UKS, Oslo
1978
• Gallery UKS, Oslo
1977
• Gallery UKS, Oslo

Collections
Hå Municipality, Stavanger, Jæren
Haugar Art Museum, Tønsberg
Jämtland County Council, Östersund, Sweden
National Academy of Fine Arts Collection, Oslo
Norwegian Culture Council
Sandefjord Municipality Art Collection, Sandefjord

Authors' Biographies

Frida Forsgren (Oslo, 1974) is an art historian, writer and critic. She has a Ph.D. from the University of Oslo in Renaissance Studies, and now works with American and Nordic modernism. She has authored *San Francisco Beat Art in Norway* (2008), *Beat Lives* (2013), *Out of the Shadows* (2015), *Beatgenerasjonen og kjønnsroller* (2017), and several articles on historic and contemporary art. She is a regular contributor to *Billedkunst*, *Fædrelandsvennen*, *Tidsskriftet Kunsthåndverk* and *Kunstavisen*.

Anna Lange Malmanger (Oslo, 1969) received her education as an art historian at the University of Oslo. For many years she has been living in Florence, where she works as a freelancer in addition to managing a wine estate with her husband. Malmanger has done extensive research on Florentine sixteenth-century sculpture and art theory. She has written several essays on art, in particular on the Italian Renaissance. Her latest contribution is the introductory chapter to the forthcoming publication in Norwegian of Giorgio Vasari's biographies of artists (publishing house is Thorleif Dahls Kulturbibliotek).

Synne Lea (1974, Oslo) is an author of fiction for both adults and children. She has written poetry, novels, and picturebooks. Her books have been nominated to several awards, among them the Deutcher Jugendliteraturpreis, Brageprisen, Kritikerprisen, and Kulturdepartementets Priser. They are translated into a number of languages and are to be found in Germany, Bulgaria, USA, Denmark, Belgium, Czech Republic, Holland, South Korea, and Taiwan. Her writings have also been published in magazines, newspapers, textbooks, and anthologies. She has been working for the Norwegian Institute for Children's Literature for several years. Her published books: *Alt er noe annet* (2003), *Du har et sted å løpe inn* (2010), *Leo og Mei* (2012), *Night Guard* (2013), *Å, Flamme Forlag* (2014), *Du og jeg* (2018).

Tone Lyngstad Nyaas (Levanger, Norway, 1962) is an art historian and writer. She is the director of Bomuldsfabriken Kunsthall in Arendal. She has won an award for her outstanding research in the field of gender studies at the University of Oslo and published a number of catalogues and books covering a broad spectrum of themes, from contemporary to historic art. She has curated several exhibitions, among them *Munch by Others* (2013) and Rose Wylie's first solo exhibition in Scandinavia, also in 2013.

Eli Skatvedt (Horten, Norway, 1980) is a curator and writer, currently based in Horten, Vestfold. For the past two years, she has worked as director and curator for Artica Svalbard, an international artist residency and public programme based in Longyearbyen, the High Arctic. Before her time in Svalbard, Skatvedt was based in Berlin for ten years where she ran her own gallery, Salon Mutlu, and curated public art and exhibitions, working with institutions such as Museum Berggruen – Staatliche Museen zu Berlin, Kunstraum Kreuzberg/Bethanien, and The Drawing Hub. In Norway, she has been working with Haugar Vestfold Kunstmuseum, Gallery F15, LIAF, Tromsø Kunstforening, Kunstforum, Kunstpluss, and Numer.

Irene Haslund (Rjukan, Nroway, 1969) has a Ph.D. in Pedagogical Philosophy from NTNU, Norwegian University of Science and Technology. Currently she works as an associate professor at the Department of Teacher Education at NTNU (since 2011). In her Ph.D. degree she wrote about perspectives on knowledge in educational policy on the basis of Hannah Arendt's philosophy. From 1998 to 2011 she taught Examen Philosophicum at NTNU. She is author of an article about liberal education / *Bildung* in Wolfgang Klafki's philosophy and of an essay about power and being in Foucault and Heidegger.